Lecture Notes in Computer Science   3917

Commenced Publication in 1973
Founding and Former Series Editors:
Gerhard Goos, Juris Hartmanis, and Jan van Leeuwen

Hsinchun Chen   Fei Yue Wang
Christopher C. Yang   Daniel Zeng
Michael Chau   Kuiyu Chang (Eds.)

Intelligence and Security Informatics

International Workshop, WISI 2006
Singapore, April 9, 2006
Proceedings

 Springer

Volume Editors

Hsinchun Chen
Daniel Zeng
University of Arizona, College of BPA
Department of MIS, Tucson, AZ 85721, USA
E-mail: {hchen, zeng}@eller.arizona.edu

Fei Yue Wang
Chinese Academy of Sciences
P.O.Box 2728, Beijing 100080, China
E-mail: feiyue.wang@ia.ac.cn

Christopher C. Yang
The Chinese University of Hong Kong
Department of Systems Engineering and Engineering Management
Shatin, New Territories, Hong Kong, China
E-mail: yang@se.cuhk.edu.hk

Michael Chau
The University of Hong Kong, School of Business
Faculty of Business and Economics, Pokfulam Road, Hong Kong, China
E-mail: mchau@business.hku.hk

Kuiyu Chang
Nanyang Technological University, School of Computer Engineering
Singapore 639798, Singapore
E-mail: kuiyu.chang@pmail.ntu.edu.sg

Library of Congress Control Number: 2006922999

CR Subject Classification (1998): H.4, H.3, C.2, H.2, D.4.6, K.4.1, K.5, K.6

LNCS Sublibrary: SL 3 – Information Systems and Application, incl. Internet/Web
and HCI

ISSN   0302-9743
ISBN-10   3-540-33361-4 Springer Berlin Heidelberg New York
ISBN-13   978-3-540-33361-6 Springer Berlin Heidelberg New York

Springer is a part of Springer Science+Business Media

springer.com

© Springer-Verlag Berlin Heidelberg 2006
Printed in Germany

Typesetting: Camera-ready by author, data conversion by Scientific Publishing Services, Chennai, India
Printed on acid-free paper   SPIN: 11734628   06/3142   5 4 3 2 1 0

Preface

Intelligence and security informatics (ISI) can be broadly defined as the study of the development and use of advanced information technologies and systems for national and international security-related applications. The First and Second Symposiums on ISI were held in Tucson, Arizona, in 2003 and 2004, respectively. In 2005, the IEEE International Conference on ISI was held in Atlanta, Georgia. These ISI conferences brought together academic researchers, law enforcement and intelligence experts, information technology consultants and practitioners to discuss their research and practice related to various ISI topics including ISI data management, data and text mining for ISI applications, terrorism informatics, deception detection, terrorist and criminal social network analysis, crime analysis, monitoring and surveillance, policy studies and evaluation, and information assurance, among others. We continued these stream of ISI conferences by organizing the Workshop on Intelligence and Security Informatics (WISI 2006) in conjunction with the Pacific Asia Conference on Knowledge Discovery and Data Mining (PAKDD 2006). WISI 2006 provided a stimulating forum for ISI researchers in Pacific Asia and other regions of the world to exchange ideas and report research progress.

WISI 2006 was hosted by the Chinese University of Hong Kong, the University of Arizona, the Nanyang Technological University, and the Chinese Academy of Sciences. The one-day program included one keynote speech, four refereed paper sessions, two invited sessions and a poster reception. The keynote speech was delivered by Professor Bhavani Thuraisingham, who is the director of Cyber Security Research Center at the University of Texas at Dallas. There were seven long papers and eight short papers presented in the refereed paper sessions and 17th poster presentations in the poster reception. We had four invited speakers presenting on the topic of terrorism research tools in the two invited sessions. The workshop was co-sponsored by the Chinese University of Hong Kong, the University of Arizona, and other funding agencies.

We wish to express our gratitude to all workshop Program Committee members and additional reviewers, who provided high-quality, valuable and constructive review comments. Special thanks go to Ee Peng Lim and Ah Hwee Tan, who supported the local arrangement.

April 2006

Hsinchun Chen
Feiyue Wang
Christopher C. Yang
Daniel Zeng
Michael Chau
Kuiyu Chang

Organization

WISI 2006 was hosted by the Chinese University of Hong Kong, the University of Arizona, the Nanyang Technological University, and the Chinese Academy of Sciences. The one-day program included one keynote speech, four refereed paper sessions, two invited sessions and a poster reception. The workshop was co-sponsored by the Chinese University of Hong Kong, the University of Arizona, and other funding agencies.

Organizing Committee

Honorary Co-chairs	Hsinchun Chen, The University of Arizona
	Feiyue Wang, Chinese Academy of Sciences
Honorary Co-chairs	Christopher C. Yang, The University of Hong Kong
	Daniel Zeng, The University of Arizona
Program Co-chairs	Michael Chau, The University of Hong Kong
	Kuiyu Chang, Nanyang Technological University

Program Committee

Andy Chen, National Taiwan University, Taiwan
David Cheung, University of Hong Kong, Hong Kong, China
Lee-Feng Chien, Academia Sinica, Taiwan
Ruwei Dai, Chinese Academy of Sciences, China
Jason Geng, Chinese Academy of Sciences, China
Rohan Gunaratna, Institute for Defense & Strategic Studies, Singapore
Eul Guy Im, Hanyang University, Korea
Moshe Koppel, Bar-Ilan University, Israel
Kai Pui Lam, Chinese University of Hong Kong, Hong Kong, China
Wai Lam, Chinese University of Hong Kong, Hong Kong, China
Ee-peng Lim, Nanyang Technological University, Singapore
Ruqian Lu, Chinese Academy of Sciences and Fudan University, China
Anirban Majumdar, University of Auckland, New Zealand
Edna Reid, University of Arizona, USA
Dmitri Roussinov, Arizona State University, USA
Gheorghe Muresan, Rutgers University, USA
Marc Sageman, University of Pennsylvania, USA
Raj Sharman, State University of New York, Buffalo, USA

Andrew Silke, University of East London, UK
David Skillicorn, Queen's University, Canada
Aixin Sun, University of New South Wales, Australia
Fu Lee Wang, City University of Hong Kong, Hong Kong, China
Jau-Hwang Wang, National Central Police University, Taiwan
Jue Wang, Chinese Academy of Sciences, China
Jun Wang, Peking University, China
Ke Wang, Simon Fraser University, Canada
Chih-Ping Wei, National Tsinghua University, Taiwan
Zhaohui Wu, Zhejiang University, China
Yiyu Yao, University of Regina, Canada
Jerome Yen, Chinese University of Hong Kong, Hong Kong, China
Jeffrey Yu, Chinese University of Hong Kong, Hong Kong, China
William Zhu, University of Auckland, New Zealand

Additional Reviewers

Ahmed Abbasi, The University of Arizona
Wei Chang, The University of Arizona
Reynold Cheng, Hong Kong Polytechnic University
Yiuming Cheung, Hong Kong Baptist University
Siddharth Kaza, The University of Arizona
James Kwok, California State University, Long Beach
Jiexun Li, The University of Arizona
Kar Wing Jaffe Li, City University of Hong Kong
Xin Li, The University of Arizona
Byron Marshall, Oregon State University
Jialun Qin, The University of Arizona
Robert Schumaker, The University of Arizona
Chik How Tan, Gjøvik University College
Gang Wang, The University of Arizona
Haotian Wu, Hong Kong Baptist University
Jennifer Xu, Bentley College
Yilu Zhou, The University of Arizona

Table of Contents

Crime Data Mining

Posters

Data Mining for Security Applications

Bhavani M. Thuraisingham[1,2]

[1] Eric Jonsson School of Engineering and Computer Science,
University of Texas at Dallas,
Richardson, Texas 75083-0688, USA
bhavani.thuraisingham@utdallas.edu
http://www.cs.utdallas.edu/people/thuraisingham.html
[2] Bhavani Security Consulting, LLC,
Dallas, Texas, USA
http://www.dr-bhavani.org

Abstract. Dr. Bhavani M. Thuraisingham is the invited keynote speaker for WISI 2006. She is a Professor at the Eric Jonsson School of Engineering and Computer Science, University of Texas at Dallas. She is also director of the Cyber Security Research Center and President of Bhavani Security Consulting.

1 Keynote Summary

Data mining is the process of posing queries and extracting patterns, often previously unknown from large quantities of data using pattern matching or other reasoning techniques. Data mining has many applications in security including for national security as well as for cyber security. The threats to national security include attacking buildings, destroying critical infrastructures such as power grids and telecommunication systems. Data mining techniques are being investigated to find out who the suspicious people are and who is capable of carrying out terrorist activities. Cyber security is involved with protecting the computer and network systems against corruption due to Trojan horses and viruses. Data mining is also being applied to provide solutions such as intrusion detection and auditing.

This presentation will first discuss the various types of threats to national security and describe data mining techniques for handling such threats. Threats include non real-time threats and real-time threats. We need to understand the types of threats and also gather good data to carry out mining and obtain useful results. We also need to reason with incomplete data. Once the data is collected, the data has to be formatted and organized. Essentially one may need to build a warehouse to analyze the data. Data may be structured or unstructured. Once the data is gathered and organized, the next step is to carry out mining. The question is what mining tools to use and what outcomes to find? Do we want to find associations, links or clusters? Finally, how do we know that the mining results are useful? There could be false positives and false negatives. We will also explore techniques such as association rule mining and link analysis for national security.

The second part of the presentation will discuss data mining for cyber security applications For example, anomaly detection techniques could be used to detect unusual

H. Chen et al. (Eds.): WISI 2006, LNCS 3917, pp. 1–3, 2006.

patterns and behaviors. Link analysis may be used to trace the viruses to the perpetrators. Classification may be used to group various cyber attacks and then use the profiles to detect an attack when it occurs. Prediction may be used to determine potential future attacks depending in a way on information learnt about terrorists through email and phone conversations. Data mining is also being applied for intrusion detection and auditing.

The third part of the presentation will discuss some of the research challenges. There is a critical need to analyze the data in real-time and give the results to the war fighter to carry out actions. There is also a need to analyze the data about a passenger from the time he or she checks in at the ticket counter until he or she boards the plane. That is, while we need some form of real-time data mining, that is, the results have to be generated in real-time, we also need to build models in real-time for real-time intrusion detection. Data mining is also being applied for credit card fraud detection and biometrics related applications. Other challenges include mining unstructured data types. While some progress has been made on topics such as stream data mining, there is still a lot of work to be done here. Another challenge is to mine multi-media data including surveillance video. Finally, we need to maintain the privacy of individuals. Much research has been carried out on privacy preserving data mining. The presentation will analyze the developments made in the areas and determine the research directions.

In summary, the presentation will provide an overview of data mining, the various types of threats and then discuss the applications of data mining for national security and cyber security. Then we will discuss the consequences to privacy. That is, data mining enables one to put pieces of public data and infer data that is highly sensitive or private. We will discuss threats to privacy and discuss the developments in privacy preserving data mining. Other challenges such as real-time data mining as well as mining surveillance data will also be discussed.

2 Biography

Dr. Bhavani Thuraisingham joined The University of Texas at Dallas in October 2004 as a Professor of Computer Science and Director of the Cyber Security Research Center in the Erik Jonsson School of Engineering and Computer Science. She is an elected Fellow of three professional organizations: the IEEE (Institute for Electrical and Electronics Engineers), the AAAS (American Association for the Advancement of Science) and the BCS (British Computer Society) for her work in data security. She received the IEEE Computer Society's prestigious 1997 Technical Achievement Award for "outstanding and innovative contributions to secure data management."

Dr Thuraisingham's work in information security and information management has resulted in over 70 journal articles, over 200 refereed conference papers and workshops, and three US patents. She is the author of seven books in data management, data mining and data security including one on data mining for counter-terrorism and another on Database and Applications Security and is completing her eighth book on Trustworthy Semantic Web. She has given over 30 keynote presentations at various technical conferences and has also given invited talks at the White House Office of Science and Technology Policy and at the United Nations on Data Mining for counter-terrorism. She serves (or has served) on editorial boards of leading research and industry journals and currently serves as the Editor in Chief of Computer Standards and Interfaces Journal. She is also an Instructor at AFCEA's (Armed Forces Communications and Electronics Association) Professional Development Center and has served on panels for the Air Force Scientific Advisory Board and the National Academy of Sciences.

Dr Thuraisingham is the Founding President of "Bhavani Security Consulting" - a company providing services in consulting and training in Cyber Security and Information Technology.

Prior to joining UTD, Thuraisingham was an IPA (Intergovernmental Personnel Act) at the National Science Foundation from the MITRE Corporation. At NSF she established the Data and Applications Security Program and co-founded the Cyber Trust theme and was involved in inter-agency activities in data mining for counter-terrorism. She has been at MITRE since January 1989 and has worked in MITRE's Informa-tion Security Center and was later a department head in Data and Information Management as well as Chief Scientist in Data Management. She has served as an expert consultant in information security and data management to the Department of Defense, the Department of Treasury and the Intelligence Community for over 10 years. Thuraisingham's industry experience includes six years of research and development at Control Data Corporation and Honeywell Inc. Thuraisingham was educated in the United Kingdom both at the University of Bristol and at the University of Wales.

Unraveling International Terrorist Groups' Exploitation of the Web: Technical Sophistication, Media Richness, and Web Interactivity

Jialun Qin[1], Yilu Zhou[1], Edna Reid[1], Guanpi Lai[2], and Hsinchun Chen[1]

[1] Department of Management Information Systems, The University of Arizona,
Tucson, AZ 85721, USA
{qin, ednareid, yiluz, hchen}@bpa.arizona.edu
[2] Department of Systems and Industry Engineering, The University of Arizona,
Tucson, AZ 85721, USA
guanpi@email.arizona.edu

Abstract. Terrorists and extremists have become mainstream exploiters of the Internet beyond routine communication operations and dramatically increased their own ability to influence the outside world. Although this alternate side of the Internet, referred to as the "Dark Web," has recently received extensive government and media attention, the terrorists/extremists' Internet usage is still under-researched because of the lack of systematic Dark Web content collection and analysis methodologies. To address this research gap, we explore an integrated approach for identifying and collecting terrorist/extremist Web contents. We also propose a framework called the Dark Web Attribute System (DWAS) to enable quantitative Dark Web content analysis from three perspectives: technical sophistication, media richness, and Web interactivity. Using the proposed methodology, we collected and examined more than 200,000 multimedia Web documents created by 86 Middle Eastern multi-lingual terrorist/extremist organizations. In our comparison of terrorist/extremist Web sites to U.S. government Web sites, we found that terrorists/extremist groups exhibited similar levels of Web knowledge as U.S. government agencies. We also found that the terrorists/extremist groups are as effective as the U.S. government agencies in terms of supporting communications and interaction using Web technologies. Based on our case study results, we believe that the DWAS is an effective framework to analyze the technical sophistication of terrorist/extremist groups' Internet usage and our Dark Web analysis methodology could contribute to an evidence-based understanding of the applications of Web technologies in the global terrorism phenomena.

1 Introduction

International terrorist/extremist groups' use of the Internet has expanded beyond routine communication and propaganda operations to training, organizing logistics for their campaign, exploring collaborative networks, and developing their strategic intelligence and virtual communities. Their Web sites and online forums have increased in number, technical sophistication, content, and media richness. These dynamic Web

H. Chen et al. (Eds.): WISI 2006, LNCS 3917, pp. 4–15, 2006.
© Springer-Verlag Berlin Heidelberg 2006

sites and forums provide snapshots of terrorist/extremist activities, communications, ideologies, relationships, and evolutionary developments. Because of their politically controversial nature and depiction of gory details in some video clips, some are hacked or shut down by their Internet Service Providers.

The Internet is a potent and rich environment for analyzing terrorist/extremist organizations' behaviors since website features, contents, and online discussion forums are examples of cultural artifacts that mirror the organization's activities. Although the alternate side of the Internet which is used by terrorists and extremists, referred to as the Dark Web, has recently received extensive government and media attention [6, 14, 17], the problem is that there is a dearth in efforts expended for the quantitative analysis of the evanescent, multilingual resources to evaluate the groups' scale of investment in the Web to achieve their organizational goals. Therefore, some basic questions about terrorist/extremist organizations' Internet activities remain unanswered. For example, what are the major Internet technologies that they have used on their Web sites? How sophisticated and effective are the technologies in terms of supporting communications and propaganda activities?

In this study, we explore an integrated approach for monitoring terrorist-created Web contents and propose a systematic framework to enable quantitative assessment of the technical sophistication of terrorist/extremist organizations' Web usages. The rest of this paper is organized as follows. In Section 2, we briefly review previous works on terrorists' use of the Web. In Section 3, we present our research questions and collection building and analytical methodology. In Section 4, we describe the findings obtained from a case study of the analysis of technical sophistication, media richness, and Web interactivity features of major Middle Eastern terrorist/extremist organizations' Web sites. In the last section, we provide conclusions and discuss the future directions of this research.

2 Literature Review

2.1 Terrorism and the Internet

Previous research provides an abundance of illustrations of how the Internet supports terrorist/extremist organizations to enhance their information operations surrounding propaganda and psychological warfare [5, 14, 17]. To achieve their goals, terrorists/extremists often need to maintain a certain level of publicity for their causes and activities to attract more supporters. Prior to the Internet era, terrorists/extremists maintained publicity mainly by catching the attention of traditional media such television, radio, or print media. This was difficult for the terrorists/extremists because they often could not meet the editorial selection criteria of those public media [17]. With the Internet, terrorists/extremists can bypass the requirements by traditional media and directly reach hundreds of millions of people, globally – 24/7. They have full control over the contents they want published through the Internet.

Supporters and sympathizers are not the only ones that terrorists/extremists can reach through the Internet. Terrorists/extremists also deliver threats through the Internet to arouse fear and helplessness among the public, a tactic commonly referred to as psychological warfare. For example, the video clip of the American journalist Daniel Pearl's final hours was web-cast through several terrorist/extremist Web sites. Moreover, terrorists/extremists have established numerous Web sites, online forums, and chat rooms to facilitate their propaganda and psychological warfare activities [9]. The Web sites are more vulnerable to hacking or closure by ISPs [7, 9]. They provide a diversity of multilingual digital artifacts such as training manuals, forum postings, images, video clips, and fundraising campaigns [2].

In recent years, there have been studies of how terrorists/extremists use the Web to facilitate their activities [2, 6, 14, 15, 17 18]. For example, researchers at the Institute for Security Technology Studies (ISTS) have analyzed dozens of terrorist/extremist organizations' Web sites and identified five categories of terrorists' use of the Web: propaganda, recruitment and training, fundraising, communications, and targeting. These usage categories are supported by other studies such as those by Thomas [14], and Weimann [17]. However, except for anecdotal information, none of the studies have provided empirical evidence of the levels of technical sophistication or compared terrorist/extremist organizations' cyber capabilities with those from other organizations' Web sites. Since technical knowledge required to maintain innovative Web sites provides an indication of terrorist/extremist organizations' technology adoption strategies [8], we believe it is important to analyze the technologies required to maintain terrorist/extremists' Web sites from the perspectives of technical sophistication, media richness, and Web interactivity.

2.2 Dark Web Collection Building

Previous research from the digital library community suggested automatic approaches to collect Web pages in particular domains. Albertsen [1] used a Web spider program in the "Paradigma" project to archive Norwegian legal deposit documents on the Web. The "Political Communications Web Archiving" group employed a semiautomatic approach to collecting Web sites [12]. Domain experts provide seed URLs as well as typologies for constructing metadata that can be used in the spidering process. Their project's goal is to develop a methodology for constructing an archive of broadspectrum political communications over the Web. For the September 11 and Election 2002 Web Archives projects, the Library of Congress' approach was to manually collect seed URLs for a given theme [13]. The seeds and their immediate neighbors (distance 1) are then crawled. To ensure the quality and comprehensiveness of our terrorist/extremist Web collection, we believe that an approach that combines automatic Web spidering and human experts' knowledge is needed.

2.3 Dark Web Content Analysis

In order to reach an understanding of the various facets of terrorist/extremist Web usage and communications, a systematic analysis of the Web sites' content is required. Demchak and Friis [4] provide a well-defined methodology for analyzing communicative content in government Web sites. Their work focuses on measuring "openness" of government Web sites. To achieve this goal they developed a Web site Attribute System (WAES) tool that is basically composed of a set of high level attributes such as transparency and interactivity. Each high level attribute is associated with a second layer of attributes at a more refined level of granularity. For example, the right "operational information" and "responses" on a given Webpage can induce an increase in the openness level of a government Web sites.

Demchak and Friis' framework is an example of a well-structured and systematic content analysis exercise. It provides guidance for the present study. However, the "openness" attributes used in their work were designed specifically for e-Government studies. In order to study the technical advancement and effectiveness of terrorists' use of the Internet, a new set of attributes must be identified. Researchers in e-Commerce, e-Government, and e-Education domains have proposed several sets of attributes to study Internet usage.

Palmer and Griffith's [10] study identified a set of 15 attributes (called "technical characteristics") to evaluate two aspects of e-Commerce Web sites: technical sophistication and media richness. More specifically, the technical sophistication attributes measures the level of advancement of the techniques used in the design of Web sites. For example, "use of HTML frames," "use of Java scripts," etc. The media richness attributes measure how well the Web sites use multimedia to deliver information to their users, e.g., "hyperlinks," "images," "video/audio files," etc.

Another set of attributes called Web interactivity has been widely adopted by researchers in e-Government and e-Education domains to evaluate how Web sites facilitate the communications among Web site owners and users. Two organizations, the United Nations Online Network in Public Administration and Finance (UNPAN; www.unpan.org) and the European Commission's IST program (www.cordis.lu/ist/) have conducted large-scale studies to evaluate the interactivity of government Web sites of major countries in the world. The web interactivity attributes can be summarized into three categories: one-to-one-level interactivity, community-level interactivity, and transaction-level interactivity.

The one-to-one-level interactivity attributes measure how well the Web sites support individual users to give feedback to the Web site owners (e.g., provide email contact, provide guest book functions, etc.). The community-level interactivity attributes measure how well the Web sites support the two-way interaction among site owners and multiple users (e.g., use of forums, online chat rooms, etc.). The transaction-level interactivity measures how well users are allowed to finish tasks electronically on the Web sites (e.g., online purchasing, online donation, etc). Chou's [3] study proposed a detailed four-level framework to analyze e-education Web site's level of advancement and effectiveness. Attributes in the first level (called Learner-interface interaction) of Chou's framework are very similar to the technical sophistication attributes used in Palmer and Griffith's [10] study. Attributes in the other three levels (learner-content interaction, learner-instructor interaction, and learner-learner interaction) of Chou's framework are similar to the three-level Web interactivity attributes used in the e-Government evaluation projects as mentioned above.

To date, no study has employed the technical sophistication, media richness, and Web interactivity attributes as well as the WAES framework in the terrorism domain. We believe that these Web content analysis metrics can be applied in terrorist/extremist Web site analysis to deepen our understanding of the terrorist's tactical use of the Web.

3 Proposed Methodology

The research questions postulated in our study are:

1) What design features and attributes are necessary to build a highly relevant and comprehensive Dark Web collection for intelligence and analysis purposes?

2)   For terrorist/extremist Web sites, what are the levels of technical sophistication in their system design?
3)   For terrorist/extremist Web sites, what are the levels of media richness in their online content?
4)   For terrorist/extremist Web sites, what are the levels of Web interactivity to support individual, community, and transaction interactions?

To study the research questions, we propose a Dark Web analysis methodology which contains several components: a systematic procedure for collection building and monitoring Dark Web contents and a Dark Web Attribute System to enable quantitative analysis of Dark Web content (see Figure 1).

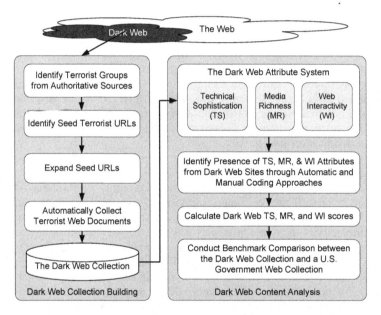

Fig. 1. The Dark Web collection building and content analysis framework

3.1 Dark Web Collection Building

The first step towards studying terrorists' tactical use of the Web is to build a high-quality Dark Web collection. To ensure the quality of our collection, we propose to use a semi-automated approach to collecting Dark Web contents [11].

We start the collection building process by identifying a list of terrorist/extremist groups from authoritative sources such as reports published by government agency and studies published by terrorism research centers. We then manually identify the URLs created by the terrorist/extremist groups from two sources: 1) the authoritative sources and literatures aforementioned and, 2) search results from major online search engines using group names and leader names as queries. The identified set of terrorist group URLs serve as the seed URLs.

After identifying the seed URLs, in-links of the seed URLs were automatically extracted through Google in-link search service and serve as additional seed URLs. We then filter out irrelevant and bogus Web sites based on evidence and clues from the Web sites. All the contents of identified terrorist/extremist Web sites are automatically download by a Web spider toolkit developed by our team. The automatic downloading method allows us to effectively build Dark Web collections with millions of documents. This would greatly increase the comprehensiveness of our Dark Web study.

3.2 Dark Web Content Analysis: The Dark Web Attribute System (DWAS)

Instead of using observation-based qualitative analysis approaches [14], we propose a systematic framework to enable the quantitative study of terrorist/extremist groups' use of the Web. The proposed Dark Web Attribute System focuses on identifying three sets of attributes from terrorist/extremist Web contents which could help us better understand the level of advancement and effectiveness of terrorists' Web usage. These three sets of attributes are the technical sophistication attributes, the media richness attributes, and the Web interactivity attributes. Based on our literature review, we selected 13 technical sophistication attributes, five media richness attributes, and 11 Web interactivity attributes for our DWAS framework. A list of these attributes is summarized in Tables 1a-1c.

1) Technical sophistication (TS) attributes: The technical sophistication attributes can be grouped into four categories as shown in Table 1a. The first category of four attributes, called basic HTML technique attributes, measures how well the basic HTML layout techniques are applied in Web sites to organize Web contents. The second category, called embedded media attributes, measures how the Web sites deliver their information to the user in multimedia formats. The third category of three attributes, called advanced HTML attributes, measures how well advanced HTML techniques such as DHTML and SHTML are applied to implement security and dynamic functionalities. The last category, called dynamic Web programming attributes, measures how dynamic Web programming languages such as ASP and JSP are utilized to implement dynamic interaction functionalities such as user login and online transaction processing. The four technical sophistication attributes and the associated sub-attributes are present in most of the Dark Web sites we collected.

2) Media richness (MR) attributes: In traditional media richness studies, researchers only focused on the variety of media used to deliver information [10, 16]. However, to have a deep understanding of the richness of Dark Web contents, we would like to measure not only the variety of the media but also the amount of information delivered by each type of media. In our study, we expand the media richness concept by taking the volume of information into consideration. More specifically, as shown in Table 1b, we calculated the average number of four types of Web elements: hyperlinks, downloadable documents, images, and video/audio files, as the indication of Dark Web media richness.

Table 1a. Technical Sophistication Attributes

TS Attributes	
Basic HTML Techniques	Use of Lists
	Use of Tables
	Use of Frames
	Use of Forms
Embedded Multi-media	Use of Background Image
	Use of Background Music
	Use of Stream Audio/Video
Advanced HTML	Use of DHTML/SHTML
	Use of Predefined Script Functions
	Use of Self-defined Script Functions
Dynamic Web Programming	Use of CGI
	Use of PHP
	Use of JSP/ASP

Table 1b. Media Richness Attributes

MR Attributes	Scores
Hyperlink	# Hyperlinks
File/Software Download	# Downloadable documents
Image	# Images
Video/Audio File	# Video/Audio Files

3) Web interactivity (WI) attributes: For the Web interactivity attributes (see Table 1c), we followed the standard built by the UNPAN and the European Commission's IST program as well as Chou's [3] work to group the attributes into three levels: the one-to-one interactivity level, the community level interactivity, and the transaction level interactivity. The one-to-one level interactivity contains five attributes that provide basic one-to-one communication channels for Dark Web users to contact the terrorist Web site owners (see Table 1c). The community-level interactivity contains three attributes that allow Dark Web site owners and users to engage in synchronized many-to-many communications with each other. The transaction-level interactivity contains three attributes that allow Dark Web users to complete tasks such as donating to terrorist/extremist groups, applying for group membership, etc. The presence of these attributes in the Dark Web sites indicates how well the terrorists/extremists utilize Internet technology to facilitate their communications with their supporters.

Table 1c. Web Interactivity Attributes

WI Attributes	
One-to-one Interactivity	Email Feedback
	Email List
	Contact Address
	Feedback Form
	Guest Book
Community-level Interactivity	Private Message
	Online Forum
	Chat Room
Transaction-level Interactivity	Online Shop
	Online Payment
	Online Application Form

We developed strategies to efficiently and accurately identify the presence of the DWAS attributes from Dark Web sites. The TS and MR attributes are marked by HTML tags in page contents or file extension names in the page URL strings. For example, an HTML tag "<image>" indicates that an image is inserted into the page content. We developed programs to automatically analyze Dark Web page contents and URL strings to extract the presence of the TS and MR attributes. Since there are no clear indications or rules that a program could follow to identify WI attributes from Dark Web contents with a high degree of accuracy, we developed a set of coding scheme to allow human coders to identify their presence in terrorist/extremist groups' Web sites. Technical sophistication, media richness, and Web interactivity scores are calculated for each Web site based on the presence of the three set of attributes to indicate how advanced and effective the site is in terms of supporting terrorist/extremist groups' communications and interactions.

4   Case Study and Preliminary Results

To test our methodology, we conducted a case study to collect and analyze the Web presence of major Middle Eastern terrorist/extremist groups such as Al Qaeda and Palestinian Islamic Jihad. We collected a large collection of Middle Eastern terrorist/extremist Web sites and compared the terrorist/extremist Web sites to a collection of U.S. government Web sites to better understand the status of terrorists/extremists' exploitation of the Internet.

The Middle Easter terrorist/extremist Web collection was created in June of 2004. Following our collection building approach, we identified and collected about 222,000 multimedia Web documents from the 86 Middle Eastern terrorist/extremist Web sites. The Benchmark U.S. government Web collection was built in July of 2004. It contains about 277,000 multimedia Web documents collected from 92 federal and state government Web sites listed under Yahoo! "Government" category.

Following the DWAS framework, presence of the technical sophistication, media richness, and Web interactivity attributes was extracted from the collections. For each Web site in the two collections, three scores (technical sophistication, media richness, and Web interactivity) were calculated. The advancement/effectiveness scores achieved by the terrorist/extremist collection were compared to those of the U.S. government collection. The results are presented in the following sub-sections.

4.1 Benchmark Comparison Results: Technical Sophistication

The technical sophistication comparison results are shown in Table 2. The results showed that the U.S. government Web sites are more advanced than the terrorist Web sites in terms of basic HTML techniques. We also found that the U.S. government Web sites are significantly more advanced than the terrorist Web sites in terms of utilizing dynamic Web programming languages. However, we found no significant difference between the terrorist Web sites and the U.S. government Web sites in terms of applying advanced HTML techniques. Furthermore, the results showed that the terrorist Web sites have a significantly higher level of embedded media usage than the U.S. government Web sites. When taking all four sets of attributes into consideration, there is no different between the technical sophistication of the Middle-Eastern terrorist Web and the U.S. government Web sites.

Table 2. Technical Sophistication Comparison Results

TS Attributes	Weighted Average Score	
	U.S.	**Terrorists**
Basic HTML Techniques	**0.9130434**	0.710526
Embedded Multimedia	0.565217	**0.833333**
Advanced HTML	1.789855	1.771929
Dynamic Web Programming	**2.159420**	1.407894
Average	1.356884	1.180921

4.2 Benchmark Comparison Results: Media Richness

The media richness comparison results are summarized in Table 3. The results showed that the U.S. government Web sites provided significantly more hyperlinks, downloadable documents, and video/audio clips than the terrorist/extremist Web sites. On the other hand, the U.S. government Web sites provided more images than the terrorist/extremist Web sites; but the difference is not significant. Overall, the terrorist/extremist Web sites are not as good as the U.S. government Web sites in terms of media richness because the volumes of contents in terrorist/extremist Web sites are often smaller than U.S. government Web sites.

Table 3. Media Richness Comparison Results

MR Attributes	Average Counts per Sites	
	U.S.	Terrorists
Hyperlink	**3513.254654**	3172.658483
Downloaded Documents	**400.9674532**	151.868427
Image	582.352456	540.0484563
Video/Audio File	**91.55434783**	50.9736828

4.3 Benchmark Comparison Results: Web Interactivity

Table 4 summarizes the Web interactivity comparison results. The results showed that, in terms of supporting one-to-one interactivity, the U.S. government agencies are doing significantly better than terrorist/extremist Web sites by providing their contact information (e.g., email, mail address, etc.) on their sites. Because of their covert nature, terrorist/extremist groups seldom disclose their contact information on their Web sites. However, in terms of support community-level interactivity, terrorist/extremist Web sites are doing significantly better than government Web sites by providing online forums and chat rooms. Few government agencies provided such online forum and chat room support in their Web sites. Our experts did not identify transaction-level interactivity in terrorist/extremist Web sites, although such interactivity might be hidden in their sites. Taking both one-to-one and community level interactivity into consideration, we did not find significant difference between the terrorist/extremist Web sites and the U.S. government Web sites.

Table 4. Web Interactivity Comparison Results

WI Attributes	Weighted Average Score	
	U.S.	Terrorist
One-to-one	**0.342857**	0.292169
Community	0.028571	**0.168675**
Transaction	0.3	*Not presented*
Average (Transaction not included)	0.185714	0.230422

5   Conclusions and Future Directions

In this study, we proposed a systematic procedure to collect Dark Web contents and a Dark Web Attribute System (DWAS) to enable quantitative analysis of terrorists' tactical use of the Internet. The automatic collection building and content analysis components used in the proposed methodology allow the efficient collection and analysis of thousands of Dark Web documents. This enables our Dark Web study to achieve a high level of comprehensiveness than previous manual approaches. Furthermore, the DWAS is a systematic framework that, we believe, brings more insights into terrorist/extremist groups' Internet usages than previous observation-based studies provided.

Using the proposed collection building procedure and framework, we built a high-quality Middle Eastern terrorist/extremist groups Web collection and benchmarked it against the U.S. government Web site collection. The results showed that terrorist/extremist groups adopted similar levels of Web technologies as U.S. government agencies. Moreover, terrorists/extremists had a strong emphasis on multimedia usage and their Web sites employed significantly more sophisticated multimedia technologies than government Web sites. We also found that terrorists/extremists seem to be as effective as the U.S. government agencies in terms of supporting communications and interaction using Web technologies.

We believe that the proposed Dark Web research methodology could contribute to the terrorism research domains and to help enrich our understanding of terrorists/extremists' Internet usage, online propaganda campaigns, and their psychological warfare strategies. Moreover, results from our case study could also help policy-making, and intelligence communities to apply counter-terrorism measures on the Web.

We have several future research directions to pursue. First, we plan to collaborate with other terrorism domain experts to better interpret our study results and gain more insights. Second, we plan to cooperate with Web technology experts to further improve the DAWS by incorporating additional attributes and adjusting the relevant weights. Third, we plan to expand the scope of our study by conducting a comparative analysis of terrorist/extremist groups' Web sites across different regions of the world. We also plan to conduct a time series analysis study on the Dark Web to analyze the evolution and diffusion of terrorist/extremist groups' Web presence.

Acknowledgements

This research has been supported in part by the following grants:

- NSF, "COPLINK Center: Information & Knowledge Management for Law Enforcement," July 2000-September 2005.
- NSF/ITR, "COPLINK Center for Intelligence and Security Informatics Research – A Crime Data Mining Approach to Developing Border Safe Research," September 2003-August 2005.
- DHS/CNRI, "BorderSafe Initiative," October 2003-March 2005.

We would like to thank Dr. Joshua Sinai formerly at the Department of Homeland Security, Al Qaeda expert Dr Marc Sageman, Dr. Chip Ellis from the Memorial Institute for the Prevention of Terrorism, and all the other anonymous domain experts for their insightful comments and suggestions on our project. We would also like to thank all members of the Artificial Intelligence Lab at the University of Arizona who have contributed to the project, in particular Homa Atabakhsh, Cathy Larson, Chun-Ju Tseng, and Shing Ka Wu.

References

1. Albertsen, K.: The Paradigma Web Harvesting Environment. 3rd ECDL Workshop on Web Archives, Trondheim, Norway (2003)
2. Chen, H., Qin, J., Reid, E., Chung, W., Zhou, Y., Xi, W., Lai, G., Bonillas, A. A., Sageman, M.: The Dark Web Portal: Collecting and Analyzing the Presence of Domestic and International Terrorist Groups on the Web. Proceedings of International IEEE Conference on Intelligent Transportation Systems (2004)
3. Chou, C.: Interactivity and interactive functions in web-based learning systems: a technical framework for designers. British Journal of Educational Technology 34(3) (2003) 265-279
4. Demchak, C., Friis, C., La Porte, T. M.: Webbing Governance: National Differences in Constructing the Face of Public Organizations. Handbook of Public Information Systems. G. D. Garson. NYC, Marcel Dekker (2001)
5. Denning, D. E.: Information Operations and Terrorism. Journal of Information Warfare (draft) (2004) http://www.jinfowar.com.
6. ISTS: Examining the Cyber Capabilities of Islamic Terrorist Groups. Report, Institute for Security Technology Studies (2004) http://www.ists.dartmouth.edu/
7. Delio, M.: Al Qaeda Web sites Refuses to Die. Wired (2003) http://www.wired.com/news/infostructure/0,1377,58356-2,00.html?tw=wn_story_page_next1
8. Jackson, B. J.: Technology Acquisition by Terrorist Groups: Threat Assessment Informed by Lessons from Private Sector Technology Adoption. Studies in Conflict & Terrorism 24 (2001) 83-213
9. Jesdanun, A.: WWW: Terror's Channel of Choice. CBS News (2004)
10. Palmer, J. W., Griffith, D. A.: An Emerging Model of Web Site Design for Marketing. Communications of the ACM 41(3) (1998) 45-51
11. Reid, E., Qin, J., Chung, W., Xu, J., Zhou, Y., Schumaker, R., Sageman, M., Chen H.: Terrorism Knowledge Discovery Project: a Knowledge Discovery Approach to Addressing the Threats of Terrorism. Proceedings of 2nd Symposium on Intelligence and Security Informatics, ISI 2004 (2004)
12. Reilly, B., Tuchel, G., Simon, J., Palaima, C., Norsworthy, K., Myrick, L.: Political Communications Web Archiving: Addressing Typology and Timing for Selection, Preservation and Access. Proceedings of 3rd ECDL Workshop on Web Archives (2003)
13. Schneider, S. M., Foot, K., Kimpton, M., Jones, G.: Building thematic web collections: challenges and experiences from the September 11 Web Archive and the Election 2002 Web Archive. Proceedings of the 3rd ECDL Workshop on Web Archives (2003)
14. Thomas, T. L.: Al Qaeda and the Internet: The Danger of 'Cyberplanning. Parameters, (2003) 112-23 http://carlisle-www.army.mil/usawc/Parameters/03spring/thomas.htm.
15. Tsfati, Y. Weimann, G.: www.terrorism.com: Terror on the Internet. Studies in Conflict & Terrorism 25 (2002) 317-332
16. Trevino, L. K., Lengel, R. H., Daft, R. L.: Media symbolism, media richness, and media choice in organizations: A symbolic interactionist perspective. Communication Research, 14(5) (1987) 553-574
17. Weimann, G.: www.terror.net: How Modern Terrorism Use the Internet. Special Report, U.S. Institute of Peace (2004) http://www.usip.org/pubs/specialreports/sr116.pdf.
18. Zhou, Y., Reid, E., Qin, J., Chen, H., Lai, G.: U.S. Domestic Extremist Groups on the Web: Link and Content Analysis. IEEE Intelligent Systems Special Issue on Homeland Security 20(5) (2005) 44-51

Multi-lingual Detection of Terrorist Content on the Web

Mark Last[1,*], Alex Markov[1], and Abraham Kandel[2]

[1] Department of Information Systems Engineering, Ben-Gurion University of the Negev,
Beer-Sheva 84105, Israel
{mlast, markov}@bgu.ac.il
[2] Department of Computer Science and Engineering, University of South Florida,
Tampa, FL 33620, USA
kandel@csee.usf.edu

Abstract. Since the web is increasingly used by terrorist organizations for propaganda, disinformation, and other purposes, the ability to automatically detect terrorist-related content in multiple languages can be extremely useful. In this paper we describe a new, classification-based approach to multi-lingual detection of terrorist documents. The proposed approach builds upon the recently developed graph-based web document representation model combined with the popular C4.5 decision-tree classification algorithm. Evaluation is performed on a collection of 648 web documents in Arabic language. The results demonstrate that documents downloaded from several known terrorist sites can be reliably discriminated from the content of Arabic news reports using a simple decision tree.

1 Introduction

Terrorist organizations are actively using the web for propaganda, disinformation, and other purposes. Under such circumstances, the ability to detect terrorist content automatically can be extremely useful for counter-terrorism experts around the globe. In this paper, we show how web content mining methods can contribute to this task.

Web sites classification became a very important sub-field of document categorization in the last decade due to rapid growth of the Internet. Most web categorization methods build upon the traditional text classification techniques that use only inner text of documents for classification model induction. Such approach is not optimal for web documents. It totally ignores the fact that web documents contain markup elements (HTML tags), which are an additional source of information. Thus, HTML tags can be used for identification of hyperlinks, title, underlined or bold text etc. This kind of structural information may be critical for the accurate web page classification.

Most existing works related to document classification have been evaluated on English language documents only. In fact, it is difficult to estimate their performance for non-English document collections. Machine translation of documents into English is generally not recommended due to semantic distortions often caused by such tools.

---

* Corresponding author.

H. Chen et al. (Eds.): WISI 2006, LNCS 3917, pp. 16–30, 2006.

In this paper we study the ability of a novel hybrid (graph and vector based) classification technique [6] to recognize automatically terror web sites in multiple languages. Our paper is organized as follows. In Section 2, we formally define the document classification task. Traditional models of document representation are reviewed in Section 3. Sections 4 and 5 present the proposed methodology for document representation and classification respectively. A case study based on a collection of authentic web sites in Arabic is described in Section 6 and some conclusions are drawn in Section 7.

2 Document Categorization and Classification

Document categorization may formally be defined [8] as the task of assigning a Boolean value to each pair $\langle d_j, c_i \rangle \in D \times C$, where D is a domain of document and $C = \{c_1, c_2, ..., c_{|c|}\}$ is a set of predefined categories. The value T (true) assigned to $\langle d_j, c_i \rangle$ indicate the decision to associate a document d_j with the category c_i, and the value F (false) indicates the reverse. In text mining two assumptions are usually taken by text categorization techniques: (1) the categories are just symbolic labels and no additional knowledge of their meaning is available, (2) no external knowledge, such as metadata, document type, publication date, publication source, is available – classification is based on document content only.

In some applications |c| category labels may be assigned to each document. Cases when |c| > 1 are called *multi-labeled classification* whereas the case where exactly one category must be assigned to each document – *single label classification*. A special case for single label classification is a *binary classification*, in which each document should be assigned to either category c or its complement $\bar{c}$. Terrorist content detection is a binary problem, because the goal is to classify document into the *terrorist* category or its complement – *non-terrorist*. This categorization task has the following two features: (1) *imbalanced categories* (much more documents belong to non-terror than to terror) and (2) *unevenly characterized categories* (e.g. the terror content can be characterized much easier than the non-terror one).

Multi-lingual document classification relates to the case where documents, written in different languages should be classified under the same category labels simultaneously as opposed to *cross-lingual classification systems* that can work with different languages but not simultaneously. Those systems usually integrate machine translation techniques with classification methods.

With the rapid growth of the Internet, the World Wide Web has become one of the most popular mediums for the distribution of multilingual information. Ability to distribute multilingual information has increased the need to automatically mediate across multiple languages, and in the case of the Web, finding foreign language pages. This is a *cross-lingual query matching* problem. Authors of [3] try to solve this problem for English and Arabic languages. The goal is to enable users to retrieve documents from an English document collection using queries in the Arabic language. To achieve this, a query should be translated as accurately as possible. Two machine translation techniques are compared in the article in terms of retrieval quality. Solutions for other languages are proposed in [30, 31].

3   Traditional Representation of Text and Web Documents

Standard data mining classifiers get an attribute table as input for classification model induction. Each row of this table refers to a pre-classified data item and each column is an item attribute, where each cell is a value of an attribute related to the specific column for a data item represented by the specific row. Consequently, documents in their original format cannot be used as input for classifier and need to be converted into such table. In order to perform those conversions, a set of attributes common for all documents in the training set should be defined. For a text document, this is a problem of choosing a meaningful textual unit – a term. In information retrieval techniques the *vector space model* [20] is typically used for document representation. A set of terms (features) $T(t_1,...,t_{|t|})$ that occurred in at least one document of the *document corpus*, serves as an attribute set and each document d_j is represented as a vector $d_j(w_1,...,w_{|t|})$ where w_i is a weight (significance) of term t_i in document d_j. The set T is usually called *vocabulary* or *dictionary*. Differences between various approaches are: (1) in the way of defining a term and (2) in the way of calculating the weight of a term.

3.1   Traditional Text Models

In traditional information retrieval techniques single words are used as a terms [11, 19, 9, 10]. According to this "bag of words" approach, vocabulary is constructed from all words that take place in the training set documents. Though this simple approach provides relatively good classification accuracy results, its weaknesses are obvious. This popular method of document representation does not capture important structural information, such as the order and the proximity of term occurrence or the location of a term within the document. The experiments of join noun phrases and words in a term set performed in [21] seem to be more effective in terms of classification accuracy. It is impractical and useless to insert all phrases into the T set so only phrases that occurred more than three times in positive examples of the training set were used.

As to the term weight calculation, *TF * IDF* (term frequency * inverse document frequency) measure [22] is most frequently used and defined as

$$w_{ij} = TF \times IDF = TF_{ij} \times \log \frac{N}{n}$$

where:

w_{ij} = weight of Term t_j in Document d_i

TF_{ij} = frequency of Term t_j in Document d_i

N = number of Documents in collection

n = number of Documents where term t_j occurs at least once

Such calculation assigns the highest weight to the terms that occur frequently in one document but do not occur at all in most other documents. Alternatively, documents may be represented by binary vectors, with each element indicating the presence or absence of the corresponding term in a given document.

3.2 Web Document Models

Most applications of web document classifiers still make use of the standard text representation techniques that were originally designed for plain-text documents. There are several reasons why such approach is not optimal. First - text classification methods make no use of external knowledge, such as metadata, publication source, etc. That is problematic for web documents where metadata is almost always available. Second and more important, web documents contain HTML tags which are not found in plain-text documents. These elements determine document's layout and can be a source of additional knowledge about the documents. Traditional text document representations ignore this important information. We assume that a representation that holds more information about a document should bring us to more accurate classification results.

In [26] five different classification approaches were presented and compared. The typical vector space model used for document representation but HTML tags were treated differently in each technique. First, *no hypertext* approach made use of web document text only for classification. No additional information was extracted from HTML tags. In *encyclopedia* approach, authors assume that all documents linked to a classified document relate to the same category and use its words as attributes for classification. The same assumption was taken in *co-referencing* regularity but words from original document receive higher weights than words from linked documents. Available information about already classified documents was used in the *pre-classified* approach. For instance, if we know that document d belong to category c then it makes sense that linked with d document d_l can be classified under c too. Under the last, *metadata* method only title and words under metadata tags are used for categorization. Experiments show that all methods that make use of HTML tags information outperform standard text representation techniques. Disadvantage of those particular methods is that each of them is limited to only one type of metadata, while their combination can provide even better results.

4   Graph Based Representations of Web Documents

The graph-based representations described in this section are part of a novel, graph-theoretic methodology designed especially for web document clustering and classification [23]. The main benefit of the graph-based techniques is that they allow us to keep the inherent structural information of the original document. Before we describe the graph-based methodology, the definition of a graph should be given. A graph G is a 4-tuple: $G = (V, E, a, b)$, where V is a set of nodes (vertices), $E \subseteq V \times V$ is a set of edges connecting the nodes, $\alpha : V \rightarrow \sum v$ is a function labeling the nodes, and $\beta : V \times V \rightarrow \sum e$ is a function labeling the edges ($\sum v$ and $\sum e$ being the sets of labels that can appear on the nodes and edges, respectively). For brevity, we may abbreviate G as G= (V, E) by omitting the labeling functions.

When creating a graph model from the Web document, a series of pre-processing steps will be taken. **First** - all meaningless words (stop words such as "the", "of", and "and" in English) will be removed from text. Those words do not bring information about document's topic so they are not needed in order to classify or cluster documents. **Second** – stemming will be done to bring all words with identical stem into one form (e.g. "students" and "student"). Stemming, or normalization, is often used in information retrieval to reduce the size of term vectors by conflating those terms which are considered to be identical after the removal of their suffixes or prefixes. **Third** and optional is extraction of document's most frequent words. In order to reduce the graph size and, consequently, the computational complexity, only N most frequent words can be chosen for creation of graphs. The first two steps are language-specific, while the third step can be applied automatically to a "bag of words" in any language.

All graph representations proposed in [23] are based on the adjacency of terms in an HTML document. Under the *standard* method each unique term (keyword) appearing in the document becomes a node in the graph representing that document. Distinct terms (*stems, lemmas*, etc.) can be identified by a stemming algorithm and other language-specific normalization techniques. Each node is labeled with the term it represents. The node labels in a document graph are unique, since a single node is created for each keyword even if a term appears more than once in the text. Second, if word a immediately precedes word b somewhere in a "section" s of the document, then there is a directed edge from the node corresponding to term a to the node corresponding to term b with an edge label s. An edge is not created between two words if they are separated by certain punctuation marks (such as periods). Sections defined for the standard representation are: *title*, which contains the text related to the document's title and any provided keywords (meta-data); *link*, which is the "anchor text" that appears in hyper-links on the document; and *text*, which comprises any of the visible text in the document (this includes hyperlinked text, but not text in the document's title and keywords). Thus, the same pair of nodes may be connected by up to six directed edges (one per each section and order of corresponding terms). Graph representations are language-independent: they can be applied to a normalized text in any language. An example of a standard graph representation of a short English web document is shown in Fig. 1.

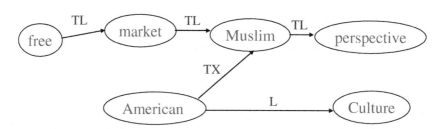

Fig. 1. Example of a Standard Graph Representation

The second type of graph representation is a "simple" representation. It is basically the same as the standard representation, except that we look at only the visible text on the page (no title or meta-data is examined) and we do not label the edges between nodes. Thus we ignore the information about the "section" of the HTML document where the two respective words appear together. Several ways to modify the Standard and the Simple graph representations are shown in [23].

Available similarity measures between two graphs allow us to classify graphs with some distance-based *lazy algorithms*[1] like *k-NN* [24]. Computational complexity of such algorithms is typically very high. This is very problematic in terms of execution time and, thus, lazy algorithms cannot be used for online massive web document classification. On the other hand, we cannot induce even a simple classification model from a graph structure using available data mining algorithms, which need an attribute table as input for the induction process. Consequently, graphs need to be converted into an attribute table for classification model induction with some classifier. To achieve this, terms should be defined and extracted from the web document graph structure. In the next section, we will present two methods of term extraction designed specifically for the classification task.

5   Multi-lingual Web Document Classification with Graphs

5.1   Representation and Classification Process

Our process for multi-lingual classification models induction and classification of previously unseen documents is shown in Figures 2 and 3 respectively. The first, model induction stage begins with a training set of pre-classified web documents $D = (d_1, ..., d_{|d|})$ and a set of categories as $C = (c_1, ..., c_{|c|})$, where each document $d_i \in D$; $1 \leq i \leq |d|$ belongs to one category $c_v \in C$; $1 \leq v \leq |c|$. Then parsing of HTML documents is done and all parts relevant for document representation are extracted. We used the *standard* method for graph document representation (see Section 4 above), so relevant document parts are title, document text, and "anchored text" of hyperlinks. Next, document language is identified. This stage is needed because the preprocessing stage is language-dependent. While preprocessing we remove from the text all stopwords and perform stemming for remaining words. Obviously, stemming rules and stopwords list are defined separately for each language. It is important to keep the original order of words in the document because it is meaningful for graph creation. Afterwards indexing is performed. During this stage we relate unique numeric index to each word and simply replace the word with its index. Vocabularies of original words in every language and their corresponding indexes are saved in language-specific index files. Since we deal with multi-lingual documents and different formats (ASCII or Unicode), it is easier to represent words in any language by numbers rather than handling each character set separately. Next step is the graph construction. Every document is converted into graph, where we label the nodes with word indexes instead of words themselves, and a set of labeled graphs $G = (g_1, ..., g_{|d|})$ is obtained.

---

[1] Algorithms that do not create a model in order to classify a data item.

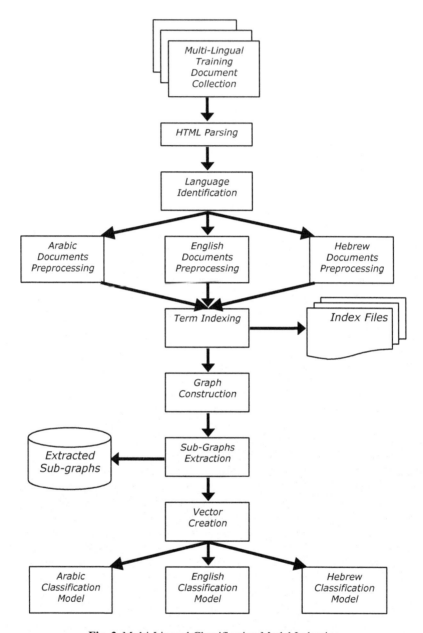

Fig. 2. Multi-Lingual Classification Model Induction

Sub-graphs relevant for classification are extracted with either *smart* or *naïve* method (see sub-section 5.2 below) and a set of sub-graph terms $T(t_1,...,t_{|T|})$ is obtained. Extracted sub-graphs are saved for classification of previously unseen documents. Then we represent all document graphs as vectors of Boolean features

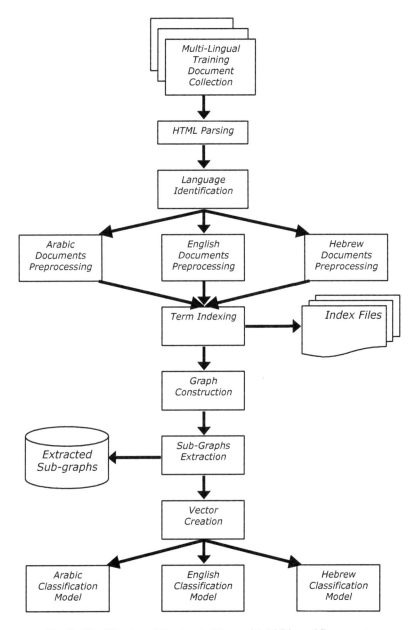

Fig. 3. Classification of Previously Unseen Multi-Lingual Documents

corresponding to every term in T ("1" – a sub-graph from the set appears in a graph). Such vector collection can be processed by one of conventional classification algorithms. Examples of available classification algorithms include decision trees [19, 28, 29], IFN - info-fuzzy networks [28], artificial neural networks, NBC - Naïve

Bayes Classifier [11], and many others. Classification model for documents in each language is the output of this stage.

The classification process begins with a set of previously unseen documents and first stages are similar to those of model induction process. A difference begins after construction of graphs. We use previously extracted sub-graphs as terms for vectors creation so we need to identify them in the set of document graphs. Then each document vector is labelled with a classification model related to its language.

Index files can be used for converting sub-graphs back into a readable structure by replacing indexes with words and translating them into another language (e.g., from Arabic to English) as needed. It can help to understand which words or sentences were more relevant for classification than others (see the case study in Section 6 below).

5.2 Term Extraction Methods

Before explaining our term extraction method, *sub-graph* and *term* should be defined. A graph $G_1 = (V_1, E_1, a_1, b_1)$ is a *sub-graph* of a graph $G_2 = (V_2, E_2, a_2, b_2)$, denoted $G_1 \subseteq G_2$, if $V_1 \subseteq V_2$, $E_1 \subseteq E_2 \cap (V_1 \times V_1)$, $\alpha_1(x) = \alpha_2(x)$ $\forall x \in V_1$ and $\beta_1(x, y) = \beta_2(x, y)$ $\forall (x, y) \in E_1$. Conversely, graph G_2 is also called a super-graph of G_1. *Terms* are sub-graphs selected to represent the document. The term selection procedure is described below.

The Naïve method presented in [6] is based on a simple postulate that an attribute explains the category best if it is frequent in that category, but in real-world situations it is not necessarily true. For example if a sub-graph g is frequent in more than one category, it can be chosen to be an attribute but cannot help us to classify instances belonging to those categories. The "Smart" sub-graph extraction method has been developed by us to overcome this problem.

Like in the naïve representation, all graphs representing the web documents should be divided into groups by the class attribute value. In order to extract sub-graphs relevant for classification of each group, several measures are defined.

SCF – Sub-graph Class Frequency: $SCF\left(g'_k(c_i)\right) = \dfrac{g'_kf(c_i)}{N(c_i)}$

where:

$SCF\left(g'_k(c_i)\right)$ - Frequency of sub-graph g'_k in category C_i.

$g'_kf(c_i)$ - Number of graphs that contain sub-graph g'_k.

$N(c_i)$ - Number of graphs in category C_i.

ISF - Inverse Sub-graph Frequency:

$$ISF\left(g'_k(c_i)\right) = \begin{cases} \log_2\left(\dfrac{\sum N(c_j)}{\sum g'_kf(c_j)}\right) & \text{if } \sum g'_kf(c_j) > 0 \\ \log_2\left(2 \times \sum N(c_j)\right) & \text{if } \sum g'_kf(c_j) = 0 \end{cases} \qquad \{\forall c_j \in C;\ j \neq i\}$$

where:

$ISF(g'_k(c_i))$ - Measure for inverse frequency of sub-graph g'_k in category C_i.

$N(c_j)$ - Number of graphs belonging to all categories except of C_i.

$g'_k f (c_j)$ - Amount of graphs that contains g'_k belonging to all categories except C_i.

And finally: _CR – Classification Rate:_ $CR(g'_k(c_i)) = SCF(g'_k(c_i)) \times ISF(g'_k(c_i))$

where:

$CR(g'_k(c_i))$ - Classification Rate of sub-graph g'_k in category C_i.

Implication of this measure is how good g'_k can explain category C_i. $CR(g'_k(c_i))$ will reach maximum value when every graph in category C_i contains g'_k and graphs in other categories do not.

According to the *smart* method, CR_{min} (minimum classification rate) is specified by the user and only sub-graphs with CR value higher than CR_{min} are chosen as terms and stored in the vocabulary.

5.3 Frequent Sub-graph Extraction Problem

The input of the sub-graph discovery problem, in our case is a set of labeled, directed graphs and parameter t_{min} such that $0 < t_{min} < 1$. The goal of the frequent sub-graph discovery is to find all connected sub-graphs that occur in at least ($t_{min}*100$) % of the input graphs. Additional property of our graphs is that a labeled vertex is unique in each graph. This fact makes our problem much easier than the standard sub-graph discovery case [25, 27] where such restriction does not exist. The most complex task in frequent sub-graph discovery problem is the *sub-graph isomorphism identification*[2]. It is known as NP-complete problem when nodes in the graph are not uniquely labeled but in our case it has a polynomial $O(n^2)$ complexity. We use *breadth first search* (BFS) approach and simplify the algorithm given in [25] for sub-graph detection.

6 Case Study: Identification of Terrorist Web Sites in Arabic

Our graph based representation technique has already been successfully evaluated on three web documents collections in English [6] with a lazy *k-NN* classification algorithm. In this work we present classification results obtained with C4.5 decision-tree classifier [29] and documents in Arabic. Decision tree models are widely used in machine learning and data mining, since they can be easily converted into a set of humanly readable if-then rules [1] [2].

---

[2] Means that graph is isomorphic to a part of another graph.

6.1 About Document Collection

In this case study we try to classify real-world web documents into two categories (Boolean classification approach): *terrorist* and *non-terrorist*. Our collection consists of 648 Arabic documents where 200 belong to terrorist web sites and 448 to non-terrorist categories. We took more non-terrorist sites because of the Boolean classification properties that were presented in section 2. The collection vocabulary contains 47,826 distinct Arabic words (after normalization and stopword removal).

Non terrorist documents were taken from four popular Arabic news sites: www.aljazeera.net/News, http://arabic.cnn.com, http://news.bbc.co.uk/hi/arabic/news and http://www.un.org/arabic/news. We automatically downloaded about 200 documents from each web site and then manually chose 448 documents while verifying that they are not belonging to the terror category. We also made sure that at least 100 documents from each web site are included into this group to ensure content and style diversity.

Terror content documents were downloaded from http://www.qudsway.com and http://www.palestine-info.com/, which are associated with Palestinian Islamic Jihad and Hamas respectively according to the SITE Institute web site (http://www.siteinstitute. org/). A human expert, fluent in Literary Arabic, has manually chosen 100 pages from each web site and labeled them as terror based on the entire *content* of each document rather than just occurrence of any specific keywords.

6.2 Preprocessing of Documents in Arabic

Text analysis of the Arabic language is a big challenge, as Arabic is based on unique grammar rules and structure, very different from the English language [33]. For example, orthographic variations are prevalent in Arabic; characters may be combined in different ways. For example, sometimes in glyphs combining HAMZA or MADDA with ALIF, the HAMZA or MADDA is excluded. In addition, broken plurals are common, so the plural form might be very dissimilar to the single form.

Another problem is that many Arabic words have ambiguous meaning due to the three or four-lateral root system. In Arabic, a word is usually derived from a root containing three to four letters that might be dropped in some derivations. Also, short vowels are omitted in written Arabic and synonyms are very common. Each word can assume a very large number of morphological forms, due to an array of complex and often irregular inflections. Furthermore, prepositions and pronouns are attached as an integral part of the word.

The first stage in text analysis is term extraction. We have defined a subset of Arabic characters in the Standard Unicode Table to be considered by the text analysis tool. The extracted terms are later stored in a data structure (array, hash table) which is called "term vocabulary". We tend to make the vocabulary as small as possible to improve run-time efficiency and data-mining algorithms accuracy. This is achieved by normalization and stop words elimination, which are standard dimensionality reduction operations in information retrieval.

Our normalization process for Arabic is based on the following rules:

1. Normalize the initial Alif Hamza in the word to plain Alif.
2. Normalize Waw with Hamza to plain Waw.
3. Normalize the Alif Maksura to plain Ya.
4. Normalize the feminine ending, the Ta-Marbuta, to Ha.
5. Removal of Kashida (a calligraphic embellishment that has no associated meaning).
6. Removal of vowel marks (the short vowels: Fatha, Damma and Kasra).
7. Normalize original Arabic ("Hindi") numerals to their Western ("Arabic") counterparts.
8. Remove Shaddah, which is a consonant doubler.
9. Removal of certain letters (such as: Waw, Kaf, Ba, and Fa) appearing before the Arabic article THE (Alif + Lam).

Next, each term was compared to a list of pre-defined stop words containing several hundred terms. If the term was not found in that list, it was added to the vocabulary of terms, provided that this term was not already in the list.

6.3 Experimentation and Evaluation of Results

In order to evaluate our classification approach we used the C4.5 decision-tree classifier. The goal was to estimate classification accuracy and understand how it is affected by user-defined parameters such as document graph size N, t_{min} in case of the Naïve and CR_{min} in case of the Smart approach. We used graphs limited to 30, 40, 50 and 100 nodes in our experiments.

We used *ten fold cross validation* method to estimate classification accuracy. According to this method, the training set is randomly divided into ten parts with approximately equal number of items. Then a classification algorithm is executed ten times where each time one different part is used as a validation set and the other nine

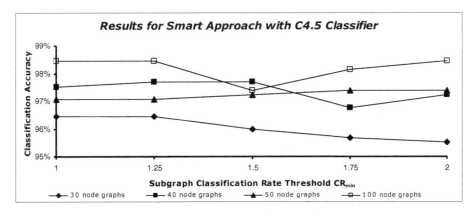

Fig. 4. C4.5 Classification accuracy for the Smart Approach

parts as the training set. The percentage of correctly classified documents is reported as the classification accuracy rate. Our experimental results for the Smart approach are presented in Figure 4.

Using the Smart method, 100 nodes graph was found optimal bringing us almost 98.5% classification accuracy with the minimum classification rate CR_{min} value equal to 1.25. The resulting decision tree is shown in Figure 5. The tree contains five binary attributes: four attributes representing single-node subgraphs (the words "The Zionist" in two forms, "The martyr", and "The enemy") and one two-node subgraph ("Call [of] Al-Quds" in the document text, standing for the alias name of the Hamas web site). This simple decision tree can be easily interpreted as follows: if *at least one* of these five terms appears in an Arabic web document, it can be safely classified as "terrorist". On the other hand, a document that contains *none* of these terms should be classified as "non-terrorist". The results of the Naïve approach [6] for this corpus were nearly the same and, thus, we are not showing them here.

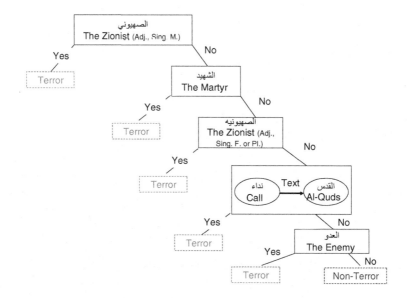

Fig. 5. C4.5 Decision Tree for Classification of Web Pages in Arabic

7   Conclusions

In this paper we present a multi-lingual document classification methodology, which can help us to identify automatically terrorist content on the WWW. The proposed approach is based on the novel, graph-theoretic representation of web documents. Our hybrid classification techniques were evaluated on a collection of real-world web documents in Arabic with the C4.5 classification algorithm. The results of initial experiments show that the graph-based document classification methods can be used for accurate terrorist content detection on the Internet. Finding the optimal Graph Size N, the Minimal Subgraph Frequency Threshold t_{min} and the Minimal Classification

Rate Threshold CR_{min} is a subject for our future research. We also plan to compare the performance of the hybrid representation to classification results of the same classification algorithm (C4.5, Naïve Bayes, etc.) with the vector-space representation.

Acknowledgment

This work was partially supported by the Fulbright Foundation that has awarded Prof. Kandel the Fulbright Senior Specialists Grant at Ben-Gurion University of the Negev in November-December 2005. We are grateful to Dror Magal, an expert in Arabic, for his valuable help with analysis of Arabic web sites and to Slava Kiselevich, a graduate research assistant, for his collaboration on execution of experiments presented in this paper.

References

1. J. Han, M. Kamber, "Data Mining Concepts and Techniques", Morgan Kaufmann, 2001.
2. T. M. Mitchell, "Machine Learning", McGraw-Hill, 1997.
3. M. Aljlayl, O. Frieder, "Effective Arabic-English Cross-Language Information Retrieval via Machine-Readable Dictionaries and Machine Translation", Tenth International Conference on Information and Knowledge Management, October 2001.
4. L. S. Larkey, F. Feng, M. Connell, V. Lavrenko, "Language-Specific Models in Multilingual Topic Tracking", 27th Annual International Conference on Research and Development in Information Retrieval, July 2004.
5. R. Larson, F. Gey, A. Chen, "Harvesting Translingual Vocabulary Mappings for Multilingual Digital Libraries", 2nd ACM/IEEE-CS joint conference on Digital libraries, July 2002.
6. A. Markov and M. Last, "A Simple, Structure-Sensitive Approach for Web Document Classification", in P.S. Szczepaniak et al. (Eds.), Advances in Web Intelligence, Proceedings of the 3rd Atlantic Web Intelligence Conference (AWIC 2005), Springer-Verlag, LNAI 3528, pp. 293–298, Berlin Heidelberg 2005.
7. K. Ramakrishna and S. S. Tan (Eds.), "After Bali, the Threat of Terrorism in Southeast Asia", World Scientific, 2003.
8. F. Sebastiani, "Machine Learning in Automated Text Categorization", ACM Computing Surveys, 1999.
9. N. Maria, M. J. Silva, "Theme-based Retrieval of Web news", 23rd Annual International ACM SIGIR Conference on Research and Development In Information Retrieval, July 2000.
10. R. Carreira, J. M. Crato, D. Gonçalves, J. A. Jorge, "Evaluating Adaptive User Profiles for News Classification", 9th International Conference on Intelligent User Interface, January 2004.
11. A. McCallum, K. Nigam, "A Comparison of Event Models for Naive Bayes Text Classification", AAAI–98 Workshop on Learning for Text Categorization, 1998.
12. D. Reis, P. Golgher, A. Leander, A. Silva, "Automatic Web News Extraction Using Tree Edit Distance", 13th International Conference on World Wide Web, 2004.
13. G. Amati, F. Crestani, "Probabilistic Learning for Selective Dissemination of Information", Information Processing and Management 35, 5, 633–654, 1999.

14. D. Tauritz, J. Kok, I. Sprinkhuizen-Kuyper, "Adaptive Information Filtering Using Evolutionary Computation", Information Sciences 122, 2–4, 121–140, 2000.
15. S. Dumais, H. Chen, "Hierarchical classification of Web content", 23rd Annual International ACM SIGIR Conference on Research and Development in Information Retrieval, July 2000.
16. M. Eirinaki, M. Vazirgiannis, "Web Mining for Web Personalization", ACM Transactions on Internet Technology (TOIT), February 2003.
17. M. Mulvenna, S. Anands, A. Buchner, "Personalization on the Net Using Web Mining", Communications of the ACM, August 2000.
18. M. Eirinaki, M. Vazirgiannis, I. Varlamis, "Sewep: Using Site Semantics and a Taxonomy to Enhance the Web Personalization Process", Ninth ACM SIGKDD International Conference on Knowledge Discovery and Data Mining, August 2003.
19. S. M. Weiss, C. Apte, F. J. Damerau, D. E. Johnson, F. J. Oles, T. Goetz and T. Hampp, "Maximizing Text-Mining Performance", IEEE Intelligent Systems, Vol.14, No.4. Jul. /Aug. 1999. Pp.63–69.
20. G. Salton, A. Wong, and C. Yang, "A Vector Space Model for Automatic Indexing", Communications of the ACM, 18(11):613–620, 1971.
21. K. Tzeras, S. Hartmann, "Automatic Indexing Based on Bayesian Inference Networks", 16th Annual International ACM SIGIR Conference on Research and Development in Information Retrieval, July 1993.
22. G. Salton, C. Buckley, "Term Weighting Approaches in Automatic Text Retrieval", Technical Report: TR87-881, 1987.
23. A.Schenker, H. Bunke, M. Last, A. Kandel, "Graph-Theoretic Techniques for Web Content Mining", World Scientific, Series in Machine Perception and Artificial Intelligence, Vol. 62, 2005..
24. Schenker, M. Last, H. Bunke, A. Kandel, "Classification of Web Documents Using Graph Matching", International Journal of Pattern Recognition and Artificial Intelligence, Special Issue on Graph Matching in Computer Vision and Pattern Recognition, Vol. 18, No. 3, pp. 475-496, 2004.
25. M. Kuramochi and G. Karypis, "An Efficient Algorithm for Discovering Frequent Subgraphs", Technical Report TR# 02-26, Dept. of Computer Science and Engineering, University of Minnesota, 2002.
26. Y. Yang, S. Slattery, R. Ghani, "A Study of Approaches to Hypertext Categorization", Journal of Intelligent Information Systems, March 2002.
27. X. Yan, J. Han, "gSpan: Graph-Based Substructure Pattern Mining", IEEE International Conference on Data Mining (ICDM'02), December 2002.
28. J.R. Quinlan,"Induction of Decision Trees", Machine Learning, 1:81–106, 1986.
29. J.R. Quinlan,"C4.5: Programs for Machine Learning", 1993.
30. Ahmed, C. James, F. David, O. William, "UCLIR: a Multilingual Information Retrieval tool", Multilingual Information Access and Natural Language Processing, November 2002.
31. B. Ripplinger, "The Use of NLP Techniques in CLIR", Revised Papers from the Workshop of Cross-Language Evaluation Forum on Cross-Language Information Retrieval and Evaluation, September 2000.
32. O. Maimon and M. Last, *Knowledge Discovery and Data Mining – The Info-Fuzzy Network (IFN) Methodology*, Kluwer Academic Publishers, Massive Computing Series, 2000.
33. L.S. Larkey, L. Ballesteros, M.E. Connell, Improving Stemming for Arabic Information Retrieval: Light Stemming and Co-occurrence Analysis"" SIGIR 2002.

INEXT: An Investigative Search Tool for Knowledge Extraction

Zhen Sun and Ee-Peng Lim

Centre for Advanced Information Systems, School of Computer Engineering,
Nanyang Technological University, Singapore 639798, Singapore
{aseplim, sunz0001}@ntu.edu.sg

Abstract. In this paper, we present an investigative search tool called
INEXT for searching documents relevant to some terrorism related information seeking tasks. Given a set of seed entities, INEXT conducts
information extraction on the documents, and ranks them based on
the amount of novel entities and relations they contain. With users interacting with INEXT throughout the search process, documents are
re-ranked to identify other relevant documents based on revised document relevance scores. In this paper, we present the overall system
architecture and its component modules including the named entity
recognition module, entity co-reference module, domain entity and relation extraction module, document ranking module, and entity and
relation annotation module. These modules are designed to address the
different sub-problems in the entire search process.

Keywords: Document ranking, knowledge extraction.

1 Introduction

Searching news articles and reports about terrorism and analysing them represent an important information seeking task that has not been well supported by
the existing document retrieval systems. The existing document retrieval systems
usually assume that each user query (keyword based or attribute based) is independent of other queries, and the main objective is to find documents relevant to
a given user query. The way a user analyses the returned documents is however
completely beyond their scope. We therefore call these systems *task-oblivious*.
From a terrorism analyst's standpoint, document searching is an integral part
of a larger investigative or research task. The task entails finding documents
and extracting from them knowledge about some event, people, organisation,
etc.. We call this an *investigative search task*. A *task-aware* document retrieval
system will therefore have to return documents that contain the required knowledge and to support the knowledge extraction requirement of the investigative
search task.

In this paper, we present a novel system, known as INtelligent EXplorer for
Terrorism knowledge (INEXT) to support investigative search tasks. The system
supports both finding relevant documents relevant to a specific terrorism event
and extracting entity and relation information describing the event from the
returned documents.

H. Chen et al. (Eds.): WISI 2006, LNCS 3917, pp. 31–37, 2006.

2   System Architecture

This section presents the overall system architecture of INEXT. It assumes the existence of a collection of documents on which investigative search is to be conducted. At present, only documents containing natural language plain text can be handled.

INEXT consists of a *named entity recognition (NER) module* that extracts named entities of general classes from the text documents. These named entities include person names, organisation names, place names and others that can appear in documents from any domains.

The *coreference resolution (CR) module* is responsible for matching semantically equivalent pronouns and named entities found within the input documents. This is necessary as the same named entity (e.g., person name) may be referred multiple times either as pronouns or as other named entities. Once the antecedent named entity is identified for a given pronoun or a given named entity, it is necessary for this coreferenced entities to be maintained in the extracted object knowledge base.

The extraction of domain specific entities and relations are performed by a *domain entity and relation extraction (DERE) module*. It relies on a combination of single-slot and multi-slot extraction patterns to assign semantic roles to entities and to determine inter-relationships among the extracted entities respectively.

The *document ranking (DR) module* provides the core search functions required by investigative search tasks. The idea here is to use extracted domain specific entities and relations and user given seed query terms to compute document relevance scores. Instead of a purely content-based approach to rank documents, the module uses extracted domain specific entities and relations as well as entities and relations already known to the user to derive document scores. The highly ranked documents are therefore expected to contain many domain specific named entities and relations that have not yet been examined by the user yet.

The user can manually annotate one or more highly ranked documents using a INEXT's *entity and relation annotation (ERA) module*. With intelligent document ranking, the highly ranked documents selected by the user are to contain new domain entities and relations. The annotation module allows them to be marked up and added to the extracted object knowledge. These annotated objects can be further used in training the extraction patterns used by domain entity and relation extraction module.

3   Named Entity Recognition and Coreference Resolution

Our NER module extracts named entities from text documents. To save some efforts in implementation, we have adopted GATE for extracting the entities of following types: person names and organization names [1].

In general, we observe that there are some limitations in the existing NER packages. Firstly, some NER packages only extract partial name from a piece of text. This is considered as incomplete name extraction. Secondly, incorrect name splitting refers to names splitted into multiple parts and each part is recognized as an individual named entity. Lastly, name title and designation, which is applicable to person names only, refers to names recognized with some job titles (e.g., "President Lee"), or courtesy titles (e.g., Mr, Miss).

All the above limitations are also found in GATE. Instead of replacing GATE, we propose a post-processing algorithm on the NER results of GATE to address the limitations. The algorithm identifies missing name components and incorrectly splitted name components of a named entity by the noun phrases right before and after the named entity. Once a noun phrase that is found right before and after a named entity is concatenated to it. Furthermore, to address the third limitation, we extracted in total 27,695 job titles from the U.S. Department of Labor website[1]. In addition, we also added some titles in the terrorism domain, such as "Terrorist", "Militant", etc.. For each named entity extracted, we check the name from our list and remove any existence of titles in it.

Coreference resolution refers to determining the identity relationships among objects within documents. In INEXT, the objects involved are pronouns and named entities. In the following, we describe our approach to resolve both pronoun and name coreferences in the context of person and organisation names. These are currently the two types of entities handled by our coreference resolution module.

Pronoun coreference resolution is a well studied problem. In INEXT, we adopt the GATE's pronoun coreference resolution implementation. GATE can determine for pronouns such as "it", "its", "he", "she", etc., the appropriate named entities found in the same document[1].

Name coreference resolution is conducted after the pronouns are resolved. A given person name or organisation name may appear in different forms and determining their equivalence is not always trivial. In INEXT, we adopt a simple approach that resolves a name with a more complete name that appears before the former. This assumes that the names are processed according to order they appear. For each name to be resolved also known as the target name, we first tokenize it into a string a tokens. A search is then performed on the other names that appears before the target name. These names are tokenized and compared with the target name token string using string comparison. The nearest name with token string containing the target name token string will be chosen to resolve the target name.

4   Domain Entity Relation Extraction and Document Ranking

To begin with an investigative search on a document collection, a user is required to provide some initial query terms, known as *seeds*, representing some initial set of entities and relations that are part of the knowledge to be constructed. INEXT

---

[1] http://www.bls.gov/ncs/ocs/ocsm/commain.htm

then ranks documents in the collection based on these seeds. Nevertheless, the document ranking module differs from the normal document retrieval engine in several ways:

- It not only looks out for documents containing seeds, but also documents with rich domain relevant entities and relations.
- It supports an iterative search process which allows the user's annotation in the previous search iteration to influence the document ranks in the next search iteration.

Figure 1 illustrates the query window of INEXT. Suppose the seed textbox contains some query terms relevant to the beheading event that happened in Iraq. Domain entity relation extraction involves determining the domain specific entities and inter-relationships among them as opposed to general named entity recognition. A set of extraction patterns based on common linguistic structures is used to extract the domain entities and relations. INEXT will then rank the documents according to an *initial score function*. As mentioned earlier, the score function is designed to give higher ranks to documents containing seeds as well as the amount of domain relevant entities and relations. Figure 1 shows that the scored documents will be listed in the document result panel ordered by decreasing scores together with their snippets. In the document snippets, seeds found are marked up by ⟨'s and ⟩'s.

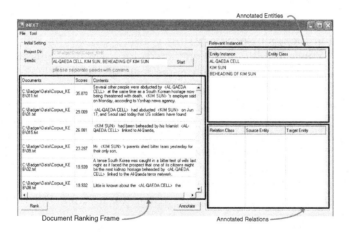

Fig. 1. Query Interface of INEXT

Documents can be selected from the result window and be annotated by the user. Relevant domain entities and relations from the selected documents can be manually annotated to extract further knowledge. A detailed description of the annotation module can be found in Section 5. The two panels on the right of Figure 1 show the sets of entities and relations subsequently are currently known to be relevant. They include the seeds initially, and other entities and relations subsequently annotated by the user.

After some new entities and relations from a selected resultant document are annotated, our document ranking module will revise the document scores by applying a different *partial match score function* that considers the following ranking criteria:

- Number of seeds found in the documents
- Number of new entities and relations linked to the already known annotated (i.e., relevant) entities and relations.

Readers can refer to [2] for details about the *initial score function* and *partial match score function*.

5   Entity and Relation Annotation

When one of the highly ranked documents is selected for annotation, the entity and relation annotation module will be activated helping the user to annotate the selected document. Figure 2 depicts the annotation user interface where the selected document is displayed in the left panel.

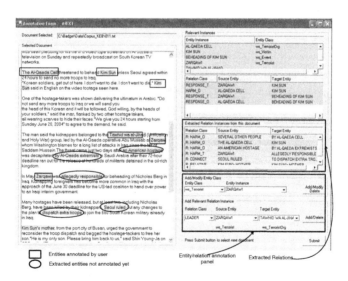

Fig. 2. User annotation windows of INEXT

Within the document panel, the domain entities extracted by INEXT are highlighted to allow the user to easily recognize potentially relevant entities. The user can select any noun phrases from the document and annotate them as relevant entities.

Once annotated, the entities will highlighted differently in the document panel to distinguish them from the ones extracted by INEXT. The user can further assign (and also update) entity classes to the annotated entities within the annotation window (see the entity/relation annotation panel of Figure 2). Within the annotation window, the relations extracted by INEXT are shown in the list box on the right as shown in Figure 2. The user can annotate a relation similar to that of entity.

Once the user completes the annotation of the selected document, he or she can return to the document ranking window giving the annotated entities and relations as feedback to the document ranking module. As mentioned in Section 4, the partial match document scoring function will then be used to re-rank the documents.

As shown in Figure 3, the previously annotated document, is now given a smaller score as it does not contain many entities or relations which are not already seen (or annotated) by the user. Instead, some other documents are now given higher ranks.

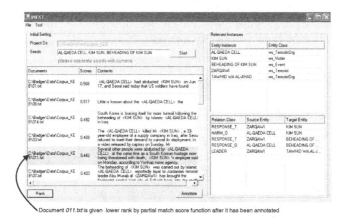

Fig. 3. Revised Document Ranking

6   Conclusions

We have presented a novel document retrieval system call INEXT which supports investigative search tasks. An overview of the system design and user interface is given. The system provides named entity recognition, coreference resolution, pattern based extraction and document ranking functions for uncovering knowledge from the text content. In this paper, we describe some of the algorithms used in processing and scoring documents. INEXT is an ongoing implementation efforts and it has incorporated some existing NER and information extraction packages such as GATE and Crystal. It is currently equipped with extraction patterns to extract entities and relations relevant to terrorism events.

References

1. K. Bontcheva, V. Tablan, D. Maynard, and H. Cunningham. Evolving GATE to Meet New Challenges in Language Engineering. *Natural Language Engineering*, 10(3/4), 2004.
2. Zhen Sun, Ee-Peng Lim, Kuiyu Chang, Teng-Kwee Ong, and Rohan Kumar Gunaratna. Event-driven document selection for terrorism information extraction. In *Proceedings of IEEE International Conference on Intelligence and Security Informatics*, 2005.

Cybercrime in Taiwan – An Analysis of Suspect Records

WenYuan Jen[1], Weiping Chang[2], and Shihchieh Chou[2]

[1] Department of Information Management, Overseas Chinese Institute of Technology,
Taichung, Taiwan 40724
denise@ocit.edu.tw
[2] Department of Information Management, National Central University,
Chung-Li, Taiwan 32054
{wpchang, scchou}@mgt.ncu.edu.tw

Abstract. This paper explores the increasing number of cybercrime cases in Taiwan and examines the demographic characteristics of the criminals responsible for the criminal activity. The report is based upon data taken from the Criminal Investigation Bureau of Taiwan cybercrime database over the interval of 1999 through 2004. The paper defines cybercrime, addresses cybercrime case statistics and examines profiles of the suspects' characteristics. The findings show that the top five categories of crime committed over the past six years are sex trading or sex trading on the Internet, Internet fraud, larceny, cyber piracy and cyber pornography. As for the suspects' characteristics, the findings show that 81.1% were male; 45.5% had some senior high school education exposure; 63.1% acted independently; 23.7% were currently enrolled students; and 29.1% were in the 18-23 age bracket which was the majority group. Finally, this paper proposes four recommendations to governments, society, schools, and researchers to reduce cycbercrime.

1 Introduction

Cybercrime is becoming ever more serious; hindering personal, societal, and national security. Many studies have noted that cybercrime also negatively impacts e-commerce [1, 5, 8, 9, 10]. An effort to raise public awareness of cybercrime cases and offenders' demographic characteristics increases the likelihood that laws will be updated, educational institutes will be endorsed and funded, and industry will receive funding to further develop various cybercrime detection tools.

Compilation of official statistics for Taiwan cybercrime was initiated in 1999. All cyber criminal records are sent to the Criminal Investigation Bureau (CIB), and the data is entered into a database. According to Taiwan police regulations, each cybercrime case is recorded on a criminal record form that contains information such as field event time and suspect's birth date, education, gender and vocation. This paper uses the CIB database as a window through which readers may clearly see the trends and changes in cybercrime between 1999 and 2004. The cybercrime suspect database helps us understand cybercrime's historical change and this paper's findings serve as a reference for cybercrime professionals, educational institutes, and the government policy makers.

H. Chen et al. (Eds.): WISI 2006, LNCS 3917, pp. 38–48, 2006.

The paper is organized as follows. First, cybercrime is defined. Next, based on the Taiwan CIB database, detailed cases are discussed. Then, the characteristics of cybercrime criminal suspects are discussed. Finally, the results of the analysis and implications for cybercrime prevention are discussed and recommendations to reduce and control cybercrime are proposed.

2   Cybercrime

"Cybercrime" is defined as any illegal activity conducted through a computer. However, authorities disagree on where cybercrime takes place. Park considers any information system (which may not be computerized) as the channel through which cybercrime is committed [12]. In contrast, Philippsohn views cybercrime as appearing mainly on the Internet [13]. This study follows Thomas and Loader [17] in defining cybercrime as "illegal computer-mediated activities that often take place in the global electronic networks."

Cybercrime is a major problem faced by businesses attempting to establish and maintain an online presence [16]. Cybercrime attacks can potentially be just as damaging to a nation's infrastructure as attacks by classical criminals. Wilson [19] cites the need to combat computer crime, cyber terrorism and information warfare on parallel paths. Development of effective security countermeasures for each type of attack are needed to control potential threats.

With a 64 percent annual growth rate for cyberattacks, cybercrime plays a primary role in hindering growth of e-commerce [14, 15]. For instance, piracy in foreign countries resulted in substantial losses to the U.S. motion picture industry, and piracy threatens the industry's survival. International Intellectual Property Alliance (IIPA) pointed out that production rates of pirated optical disks in Taiwan have been among the highest in Asia for at least two decades [7]. IIPA also reported an estimated loss of US$42 million for American firms. Is cybercrime so serious in Taiwan? The issue is valuable to be explored.

The most common categories of cybercrime are experienced throughout the world on a common basis. To increase national public awareness and to help people avoid becoming victims of cybercrime, cybercrime statistical reports may be examined. This paper's purposes are to delineate the trends of Taiwan's cybercrime and analyze the characteristics of the criminals that are responsible. Hence, according to Taiwan CIB database (1999-2004), this study explores the detailed in the following way:

(1) the overview of cybercrime cases and suspects.
(2) the overview of top five cybercrime cases.
(3) the overview of cybercrime in group, gender and student status.
(4) the overview of education level of cybercrime suspects.
(5) the overview of age range of cybercrime suspects.

3   The Cases and Suspects of Cybercrime in Taiwan

Table 1 summarizes the rapid growth seen in Taiwan's Internet user population [4] and the staggering growth in cybercrime cases and suspects for the years 1999 through 2004. We see that cybercrime cases and suspects have been increasing at an average annual rate 136.5% and 119.7% respectively. These changes have occurred during a period of time when the overall population growth was nearly zero.

Table 1. The overview of cybercrime cases and suspects in Taiwan

Year	Total Population	Internet Population	Number of	
			Cases	Suspects
1999	22,034,096	4,800,000	116	187
2000	22,216,107	6,260,000	427	516
2001	22,405,568	7,820,000	1,009	1,249
2002	22,520,776	8,230,000	3,118	3,740
2003	22,604,550	8,800,000	4,346	5,786
2004	22,689,122	9,160,000	5,633	7,306
Average Annual Growth	0.6%	14.3%	136.5%	119.7%

The Taiwan government decontrolled the use of fixed network telecommunication markets in 2001, thus Internet population increased quickly. It should be noted that the numbers of cybercrime cases and suspects increased because some related broadband Internet applications such as online games and Internet cafés then became fully accessible. Many young Internet users are addicted to online games and related entertainment. However, not all Internet users are equal. There are bad as well as good Internet users. Furthermore, Internet regulations were not clear and not taught to most of them. Therefore, it results in many various and new type criminal behaviors.

Based on cybercrime case data, Table 2 shows the top five cybercrime cases. The greatest number of cybercrime cases are money laundering (1999), cyber piracy (2000), spreading message of sex trading or sex trading on the Internet (2001, 2002), larceny (2003), Internet fraud (2004). They are respectively against the Control Act, Copyright Law, Child and Youth Sexual Prevention Act, Larceny and Fraud or Breach of Trust in Taiwan.

Both cyber pornography and spreading message of sex trading or sex trading on the Internet are listed in the top five cybercrime cases every year.

Table 2. The overview of top 5 cybercrime cases in Taiwan

Cybercrime case	1999	20000	2001	2002	2003	2004
Money Laundering	22.5%		5.6%			
Cyber pornography	16.0%	15.5%	8.9%	5.0%	4.7%	5.6%
Cyber piracy	13.4%	30.4%	15.9%	4.3%		
Spreading message of sex trading or sex trading	9.6%	20.0%	41.3%	33.8%	20.4%	22.6%
Internet fraud	9.1%	9.1%		13.3%	27.0%	49.2%
Gambling		4.7%				
Larceny			4.6%	32.0%	28.5%	1.7%
Against Personal Liberty					4.6%	
Computer misuse						12.2%
The percentage of the top 5 cybercrime case occupied	70.6%	79.7%	76.3%	88.4%	85.2%	91.3%

Among spreading message of sex trading or sex trading on the Internet cases, many suspects committed "Relations for Allowances" – a beautified name for prostitution. "Relations for Allowances" originated from Japanese middle-aged men who give money or expensive gifts to young girl students in exchange for sexual relationships. It is noted that many Taiwan police disguised themselves as whoremongers to arrest the suspects who committed "Relations for Allowances" in 2001 and 2002, and who were against the child and youth sexual prevention act.

Because of the prevalence of on-line gaming, the proportion of criminal offences of stealing fictitious treasure is about 30% of all cybercrime cases in 2002 and 2003. Criminal law was revised in 2003 to reclassify theft of this type to be "Against Computer Misuse". This reclassification results in a reduction of the reported larceny annual rate to 1.7% in 2004, and a commensurate rise in the classification of "Against Computer Misuse" up to 12.2%.

In 2004, the number of Internet fraud cases accounted for half of all cybercrime cases. With the growth of Internet fraud cases, more Internet users have become increasingly aware of the potential dangers of making purchases over the Internet. The U.S. Federal Bureau of Investigation (FBI) and the Computer Security Institute (CSI) reported that Internet fraud losses in the US alone were approximately $299 million [14]. Smith [15] pointed out that cybercrime directly affects consumers in negative ways, and the cybercrime threat is a hindrance to e-commerce. The high growth of Internet fraud cases is of major concern.

4 The Characteristics of Cybercrime Suspect

This study analyzes cybercrime suspects' records with regard to complicity, gender, student status, educational level, and age range. In order to understand the difference between "Total crime report to the police" [11] and "Cybercrime", this stduy lists the proportion of both in Table 3,4,5 . Results of the analysis follow.

Table 3. The overview of cybercrime in group, gender and student status in Taiwan

Year	Complicity		Gender		Student Status	
	Alone	**Group**	**Male**	**Female**	**Non-Stu.**	**Student**
1999	43.8%	56.2%	84.0%	16.0%	90.9%	9.1%
	(N/A)	*(N/A)*	*(85.2%)*	*(14.8%)*	*(92.7%)*	*(7.3%)*
2000	29.6%	71.4%	79.1%	20.9%	84.1%	15.9%
	(N/A)	*(N/A)*	*(86.1%)*	*(13.9%)*	*(93.7%)*	*(6.3%)*
2001	68.8%	31.2%	75.2%	24.8%	81.3%	18.7%
	(N/A)	*(N/A)*	*(86.0%)*	*(14.0%)*	*(93.8%)*	*(6.2%)*
2002	75.6%	24.4%	83.9%	16.1%	68.4%	31.6%
	(N/A)	*(N/A)*	*(83.8%)*	*(16.2%)*	*(93.8%)*	*(6.2%)*
2003	73.8%	26.2%	89.3%	10.7%	69.2%	30.8%
	(N/A)	*(N/A)*	*(84.7%)*	*(15.3%)*	*(93.5%)*	*(6.5%)*
2004	86.9%	13.1%	75.1%	24.9%	83.8%	16.2%
	(N/A)	*(N/A)*	*(85.5%)*	*(15.5%)*	*(94.8%)*	*(5.2%)*
1999-2004 cybercrime	63.1%	36.9%	81.1%	18.9%	76.3%	23.7%
1999-2004 Total crime	*(N/A)*	*(N/A)*	*(85.2%)*	*(14.8%)*	*(93.7%)*	*(6.3%)*

( ) stands for the percentage of total crime report to the police

Complicity
About 37% of suspects acted as part of a group, and most crimes were Internet fraud, Larceny, spreading message of sex trading or sex trading, Internet Gambling and Cyber piracy. Although about 63% of suspects acted alone, in most of these cases the suspects committed spreading message of sex trading or sex trading, larceny, Internet fraud, cyber pornography and cyber piracy. It is interesting to note that the cases have no significant difference except in ranking.

In the Table 3, we find that 63% of cybercrime suspects in Taiwan who acted independently increased from 43.8% (1999) to 86.9% (2004). We considered the suspects may place themselves in different locations. For instance, a suspect posted pornography on websites; the other suspects deal with logistics in different city or countries. In another word, the lower rate (37%) in complicity, it is possible that the complicity cases are more difficult to be detected. Hence, we tend to explain the trend of independent perpetration is involved with group perpetration.

Gender
Table 3 shows that the majority of cybercrime suspects in Taiwan were male (81.1%). With an growth rate of 24.9% in 2004, the number of female suspects grew at a rate much greater than preceding years. In 2004, 1539 female suspects committed Internet Fraud, 7 times the 188 female suspects in 2003. Internet Fraud and spreading message of sex trading or sex trading are the top two types of cybercrime for male and female suspects respectively in Taiwan.

Student Status
Table 3 shows that the number of currently enrolled students who committed cybercrime increased dramatically in 2002 and 2003. Approximately one-fourth of suspects (23.7%) were currently enrolled students, most of whom were stealing virtual equipment and money from online games. This caused larceny and Internet fraud cases to increase. The next most prevalent type of cybercrime was student suspects spreading sex trading messages on Internet. For non-student suspects, Internet Fraud ranked first among all cybercrime cases. Among all cybercrime suspects, almost 25% were currently enrolled students; in contrast, currently enrolled students accounted for only 6.3% of all crimes. The large number of student involvement in cybercrime is extremely serious, and all government agencies and educational institutes have to pay attention to this problem.

Education Level
Table 4 shows the distribution by cybercrime suspects' education level in Taiwan. The majority of suspects held senior high school diplomas (45.5%), the second largest group was with Bachelor's degrees (27.8%), the third group was with junior high school diplomas (17.9%) and other groups comprised the remaining 8.9%. For those suspects at the senior high school education level, the proportion of larceny case was higher than other cases. Among the suspects with Bachelor's degree, spreading message of sex trading or sex trading cases were most prevalent. In the junior high school group, Larceny was again the most widespread.

From 1999 to 2004, 80% of cybercrime cases were committed by junior high school, senior high school and college students. In contrast, total crimes reported to the police were dominated by elementary school, junior high school and senior high school. The differentiation reveals cybercrime is attracting intellectuals to commit crime activities. For instance, cybercrime suspects with elementary education level were only 5.3%, but the rate of total crimes reported to the police was up to 13.0%. In addition, only 8.0% suspects of total crime report to the police was with Bachelor's degrees, but over one-fourth of cybercrime suspects (23.7%) were Bachelor's degrees.

Table 4. The overview of education level of cybercrime suspects in Taiwan

Year	Elementary	J. High	S. High	College	Graduate School	Unlisted
1999	14.4%	12.8%	46.0%	25.1%	1.6%	0.0%
	(13.7%)	(44.8%)	(30.7%)	(5.6%)	(0.4%)	(4.8%)
2000	1.7%	15.5%	41.9%	37.6%	1.0%	2.3%
	(13.6%)	(43.9%)	(33.3%)	(7.4%)	(0.3%)	(1.5%)
2001	3.0%	17.4%	44.4%	33.0%	1.5%	0.6%
	(13.8%)	(41.6%)	(34.2%)	(7.9%)	(0.3%)	(2.3%)
2002	1.4%	20.8%	47.4%	27.7%	1.6%	1.1%
	(13.9%)	(38.1%)	(36.2%)	(8.8%)	(0.3%)	(2.8%)
2003	1.4%	23.1%	50.8%	21.6%	1.3%	1.8%
	(11.9%)	(38.4%)	(38.2%)	(9.1%)	(0.3%)	(2.0%)
2004	9.6%	17.8%	42.5%	21.7%	1.8%	6.5%
	(10.9%)	(38.8%)	(39.6%)	(8.9%)	(0.4%)	(1.4%)
1999-2004 cybercrime	5.3%	17.9%	45.5%	27.8%	1.5%	2.0%
1999-2004 Total crime	(13.0%)	(40.9%)	(35.4%)	(8.0%)	0.3%	2.5%

( ) stands for the percentage of total crime report to the police

Age Range

Among the age ranges shown in Table 5, the age range 18-23 had the highest rate (29.1%), and the second group was the 24-29 age range (24.7%). The juvenile range and the 18-23 age range combined for a total of 44.8% among all ranges. In the juvenile group, the year 2003 had the highest proportion (29.7%), and the year 2002 was ranked top two (27.8%) as well. After 2002, the percentage of total crime report to the police was compared with cybercrime, the juvenile criminal percentage was much more serious than total crime report.

From 1999 to 2004, juveniles committed 3,664 cybercrime cases. Among the juvenile cases, the first ratio, 36.4% (1,333), were larceny cases, the second ratio, 19.3% (707), were Internet fraud and the third ratio 10.3% (377) is computer misuse. It may be that the above three cases are related to online gaming. In order to steal virtual property, criminals defraud Internet users or hack into victims' computers. After online games being popular in 2002, many young students became addicted to role-playing games where novices are easily cheated by experienced users. Moreover, this role-playing experience was brought into real life, causing problems and troubles. That juveniles committed cybercrime in order to get more virtual property when playing

Table 5. The overview of age range of cybercrime suspects in Taiwan

Year	juvenile	18-23	24-29	30-39	40-49	50-59	60+
1999	6.0%	25.4%	29.5%	28.7%	7.5%	2.2%	0.7%
	(12.2%)	(18.1%)		(69.7%)			
2000	8.1%	26.6%	32.1%	24.2%	6.8%	1.2%	1.0%
	(10.3%)	(17.8%)		(71.9%)			
2001	9.8%	32.6%	30.4%	20.5%	5.3%	1.1%	0.3%
	(9.7%)	(15.4%)	(19.6%)	(27.9%)	(18.7%)	(6.0%)	(2.7%)
2002	27.8%	36.7%	18.7%	13.2%	2.5%	0.9%	0.2%
	(8.7%)	(15.1%)	(18.2%)	(26.6%)	(19.7%)	(7.6%)	(4.1%)
2003	29.7%	31.5%	19.7%	14.4%	3.9%	0.7%	0.2%
	(8.0%)	(14.8%)	(20.0%)	(27.2%)	(19.7%)	(7.3%)	(3.0%)
2004	12.6%	21.9%	17.8%	21.5%	13.7%	8.1%	4.4%
	(6.2%)	(12.6%)	(21.8%)	(28.6%)	(20.2%)	(7.6%)	(3.0%)
1999-2004 cybercrime	15.7%	29.1%	24.7%	20.4%	6.6%	2.4%	1.1%
1999-2004 Total crime	(8.1%)	(14.5%)	(19.9%)	(27.6%)	(19.6%)	(7.1%)	(3.2%)

( ) stands for the percentage of total crime report to the police

online games is hardly surprising. Unfortunately, some juveniles believed committing cybercrime did not actually harm anyone. Young Internet users spend greater time playing online games, communicating in chat rooms and utilizing other entertainment services relative to older people. As shown in Table 5, the years 2002 and 2003 had a higher proportion of both juvenile and 18-23 age group suspects.

In Table 5, almost 30% cybercrime cases were dominated by the age range 18-23 suspects; however, total crime report to the police were dominated by the age range 30-39 suspects. The percentage portrays the differentiation in age structure. According to Table 5, the age range percentage of cybercrime suspects was younger than suspects of total crime reported to the police, for instance, the juvenile had higher rate (15.7%), but the juvenile had lower rate (8.1%) in total crime reported to the police. Competing with the juvenile, the age range 40-49 had lower rate (6.6%) in cybercrime, but the age range 40-49 had higher rate (19.6%) in total crime report to the police. We consider that the age range 40-49 suspects lack of computer knowledge is the main reason to hinder them from committing cybercrime. The statistics reported in Table 5 show 44.8% of all suspects were younger than 24. This proportion is a clear indication that efforts to control cybercrime should be focused upon the young suspect.

5 Conclusions

Based on cybercrime suspect records from 1999 to 2004, this study portrays the cybercrime cases and suspects' characteristics as follows.

Cybercrime cases. In decreasing order, the top five types of cybercrime in Taiwan were spreading message of sex trading or sex trading on the Internet, Internet fraud, larceny, cyber piracy and cyber pornography. The statistics reported 44.8% of all suspects were younger than 24; hence, we can clearly see the need for more active measures to prevent young people committing cybercrime.

Suspect characteristics. Among all cybercrime suspects in Taiwan, 81.1% were male; 45.5% had a senior high school education level; 63.1% committed cybercrime alone; 23.7% were currently enrolled students; and 29.1% were 18-23 age range, which was the majority group.

In our portraits of cybercrime suspects, we found that currently enrolled students often committed Larceny case, Internet fraud, or spreading message of sex trading or sex trading on the Internet. For instance, 45.2% of all Larceny cases were committed by juvenile suspects. According to the juvenile suspect's growth rate, it is noted that the related problems of juvenile cybercrime are serious.

6 Recommendations

Based on the cybercrime suspect records of the Criminal Investigation Bureau, this study proposes four recommendations to government agencies, social groups, schools and researchers.

Government. Both updating existing laws and enhancing specialized task forces are needed [2]. To prevent cybercrime, government agencies have to update out-of-date laws and recruit more qualified investigators. Basically, cybercrime criminals are fond of committing crime in cyberworld because of less stringent laws. More complete laws will help law enforcement fight cybercrime. Judicial decisions are influenced by soundness of evidence, and the previous criminal record of the suspect. Hence, our computer forensics labs need more investigators with technical and legal knowledge so that they might collect digital evidence for fighting cybercrime. Government agencies should provide updated laws and anti-cybercrime investigating institutes to protect the public's property and privacy.

Society. Goodman [6] pointed out that only 1% of intrusion cases were filed. Why do we see such a high percentage of unreported cybercrime? One reason is the lack of information security awareness, and the other is a desire to maintain a business reputation. Whiteman and Mattord [18] believe that information security awareness is important to information security. With high information security awareness, people will discover more cybercrime. After discovering cybercrime, people and companies should report it to authorities. However, some companies are unwilling to report cybercrime for fear of damaging their reputation. If more cybercrime cases go ignored or unreported, the successful attacks may challenge other criminals to repeat the crime.

Hence, this study suggests that law enforcement set up safeguards for the attacked companies or individuals. Ensuring victim safety will encourage others to willingly report cybercrime.

Schools. In the past cases, students who committed cybercrime and were arrested by police replied to the police they didn't know laws had been violated. Students not only need to learn how to use computer but also should learn basic law. In recent years, privacy and ethical behavior have received increased emphasis. Electronic data security is a relatively high growth area, so information ethics is especially important in e-society. We know the dangers of the cyberworld, and we should ask students to be informed about the ethical use of technological tools in the cyberworld. There is an urgent need for information ethics and ethical education programs, and more scholars, researchers and schools need to become involved. It is never too late to educate our students and Internet users, regardless of their age.

Researchers. Scholars need to increase their research into cybercrime causal factors and to discover methods of preventing cybercrime. More advanced research and new information security tools will help to sift through tons of criminal related information and to create a safe cyberworld.

References

1. Cordy, E.D.: The Legal Regulation of E-Commerce Transactions. Journal of American Academy of Business 2, 2(2003) 400-407
2. Chang, W., Chung, W., Chen, H. and Chou S.: An International Perspective on Fighting Cybercrime. Lecture Notes in Computer Science 2665, (2003) 379-384
3. DS-MOI, Department Statistics, Ministrey of the Interior (2005, January). Annual population census. Retrieved October 5, 2005 from http://www.moi.gov.tw/stat/index.asp
4. FIND, Focus on Internet News and Data. (2005, June). The statistics report of Taiwan Internet Users. Retrieved October 5, 2005 from http://www.find.org.tw/0105/howmany/usage_1.asp
5. Geer, D.: Security Technologies Go Phishing. Computer, 38, 6(2005)18-21.
6. Goodman, M.: Making Computer Crime Count. FBI Law Enforcement Bulletin, 70, 8(2001) 10-17
7. IIPA.: Special 301 Report on Global Copyright Protection and Enforcement. Washington, DC: International Intellectual Property Alliance, 303-322
8. McCrohan, K. F.: Facing the Threats to Electronic Commerce. The Journal of Business & Industrial Marketing 18, 2/3(2003) 133-145
9. MacInnes, I., Musgrave, D., Laska, J.: Electronic Commerce Fraud: Towards An Understanding of the Phenomenon. In: 2005 Proceedings of the 38th Annual Hawaii International Conference, (2005)
10. McCusker, R.: E-Commerce, Business and Crime: Inextricably Linked, Diametrically Opposed. The Company Lawyer 23, 1(2002) 3-8
11. Ministry of the Interior. (2005, Oct.). The statistics report of National Police Agency. Retrieved October 5 2005 from http://www.npa.gov.tw/stats.php
12. Parker, D.B.: Fighting Computer Crime: A New Framework for Protecting Information. Wiley Computer Publishing, (1998)

13. Philippsohn, S.: Trends in Cybercrime - An Overview of Current Financial Crimes on the Internet. Computers & Security 20, 1(2001) 53-69
14. Saban, K.A., McGivern, E. and Saykiewicz, J.N.: A Critical Look at the Impact of Cyber Crime on Consumer Internet Behavior. Journal of Marketing Theory and Practice 10, 2(2002) 29-37
15. Smith, A.D.: Cyberciminal Impacts on Online Business and Consumer Confidence. Online Information Review 28, 3(2004) 224-234
16. Smith, A.D. and Rupp, W.T.: Issues In Cybersecurity: Understanding the Potential Risks Associated with Hackers/Crackers. Information Management and Computer Security 10, 4(2002) 178-83
17. Thomas, D. and Loader, B.D.: Introduction - Cybercrime: Law Enforcement, Security and Surveillance in the Information Age. In Cybercrime: Law Enforcement, Security and Surveillance in the Information Age. Taylor & Francis Group, New York, (2000)
18. Whitman, M.E. and Mattord, H.J.: Management of Information Security. Boston, (2004)
19. Wilson, C.: Holding Management Accountable: A New Policy for Protection Against Computer Crime. In: National Aerospace and Electronics Conference, Proceedings of the IEEE 2000, (2000) 272-281

Analysis of Computer Crime Characteristics in Taiwan

You-lu Liao[1] and Cynthia Tsai[2]

[1] Associate professor of Criminal Investigation Department, Central Police University,
56 Shu Jen Road, Ta Kang Chun, Kuei San, Taoyuan, 333 Taiwan, R.O.C.
ylliaw@mail.cpu.edu.tw
[2] Lecturer of Center for General Education, Central Police University,
56 Shu Jen Road, Ta Kang Chun, Kuei San, Taoyuan, 333 Taiwan, R.O.C.
Cynthiatsai@walla.com

Abstract. This study is intended to uncover the characteristics of computer crimes happening in Taiwan. Applying frequency distribution analysis to the 165 cases collected from the authorities concerned, we find some interesting facts with respect to the crimes' properties. First, regarding the crimes' features, a majority of the crimes were related to transmission of pornography and unauthorized copying of proprietary works. Most of them took place at residences. The illegal acts, mainly for profit, usually continued until they were detected. As to the criminals, most of them were male, young, unemployed and college-educated. They tended to commit the crime alone, possessed no prior records and mostly resided in urban areas. Some of them were disabled people, which could be attributed to their difficulties of being employed. The number of cases reported and investigated was increasing, yet, due to certain practical problems, such as the police agency's limited capability over the offenses or judicial systems' huge workload, a Funnel Effect emerged in the meantime, resulting in the loss of some cases in each processing phase. In addition, there was a propensity for the judicial system to impose lenient punishment on the violators, e.g. probation and financial penalty instead of imprisonment.

1 Introduction

Throughout humans' survival history, poverty, disease, and crime are the three most difficult problems they face. However, along with the development of economy, the problem of poverty has almost been eliminated from the earth except for some areas in the third world. As to disease, due to advancements in medical science, the number of incurable disease is also decreasing. In comparison with these great achievements, the problem of crime has been increasing, ironically with the help of high-technological developments. To name some, criminal instruments are becoming more refined, ways of covering up or escaping from detection are more skilful, and the damage to society is more serious and extensive. [15]

Every new technology is introduced into a society with both good and bad, and the bad parts usually come into existence later than the good. [4] The computer is no exception. The invention of the computer first brought people comfort and convenience in life, but later provided people with more delicate tools and complicated skills to commit illegal acts in a deft manner.

H. Chen et al. (Eds.): WISI 2006, LNCS 3917, pp. 49–57, 2006.
© Springer-Verlag Berlin Heidelberg 2006

Computer crime, a recently emerging crime type with computers used by some people to commit various kinds of unlawful acts, has become one of the most troublesome problems of the world and is now the most important subject of study in criminology. The reason is facilitated by its powerful Internet function. The computer has become such a useful instrument that almost all the modern societies in the world rely on it to conduct their businesses or transmit, process and store their vital information. With such a close relationship between humans and computers, it's not hard to imagine how severe the loss or damage might be if a computer crime should happen. [6]

Apart from the harm that has been caused to the workplace, piracy and pornography activities on the Internet have become so rampant and unbearable that it has been strongly suggested the law enforcement agency build a cyber police force to tackle the ever-worsening problem or include the cyberspace in police routine patrol areas. [10] Some scholars even predict that crimes happening in the near future, except for sexual and physical abuse, could all be accomplished by way of certain computer-related skills. [1] In a sense, computers have evolved to be the most powerful criminal instrument next to firearms. Coupled with high technology, computer crimes surely will become one of the most devastating problems for humans before long. This problem can no longer be neglected.

2 Background

This section will be devoted to showing the seriousness of domestic computer crime. Ever since the 1960s, the number of computers employed in governmental agencies as well as private corporations has been increasing. However, illegal activities concerning computers also began to appear and boom in the meantime.

Reportedly, only 8 computer crimes occurred countrywide before September 1993, comprising both simple cases like input manipulation and complex ones like code interception. [16] This number appeared small and insignificant compared with the 342 sabotage and data misuse cases recorded in Japan during the same period of time. [5]

However, thanks to the efficient information education and increasingly widespread use of the Internet, computer crime here also underwent some enormous changes. Not only did the case number make a sharp increase, but the damage it caused also mounted to such a great extent that it has aroused deep concern and anxiety of people here. Below are some of the famous cases that happened in the last decade, which might serve as good examples.

In 1995, an email with an obvious intention of threat was sent to the American White House from Taiwan, addressed to ex-President Clinton. Almost at the same time, the homepage of the Kuomintang, the then ruling party of Taiwan, was invaded, with the late founder, Dr. Sun Yet-sen's electronic portrait replaced with an obscene picture. In 1996, a graduate of National Taiwan University was accused of launching a slandering attack on two professors on the school's bulletin board system, using a fake identity. In 1997, a computer peripheral plant was reported to suffer a great financial loss because of the sabotage act of one of its ex-employees, which not only caused the production of a great number of defective integrated circuits, but also resulted in subsequent loss of orders to the rival company.

In 1998, a bank worker, taking advantage of an auditing loophole, input fake transactional information and created an account in a branch agency. He successfully stole nearly 30 billion dollars for the purpose of personal stock investment, which definitely inflicted a great shock on financial circles. In 1996, the incidence in which two computers crashed simultaneously at the Muzha Mass Rapid Transit Station was believed to be a case of intentional vandalism, which not only exposed the company's weakness cornering their computer security, but also aroused great concern about the police's ability to handle such crimes.

Other than the illegal acts mentioned above, computers were also connected to cases like software piracy, anonymous blackmailing, weapon dealing, instruction of bomb making, hacking into personal or corporate computers to interfere with their normal functions, etc. In 1997 a computer crook was caught for planting and spreading CIH viruses, which not only caused a lot of precious data to be lost, but also nearly paralyzed computer systems internationally. In 1999, the sensitive relations across the Taiwan Strait were made even intense because of some hackers' exchanging provocative remarks. In 1998, a girl from a vocational school was arrested because she tried to swindle money out of some well-educated males on the net. In 1999, a programmer, taking the opportunity of rewriting computer programs for a bank, counterfeited the customers' ATM cards and got away with a big sum of money. In 1997, the Taipei District Court had its computers intruded by some hackers intending to alter someone's jail term that was soon to be handed down. The suspects haven't been found yet. Last but not the least, in 1998, a staff member of Central Police University was jailed for changing exam scores through computers in return for candidates' bribes.

3   Research Orientation

Local computer crime research, though treating various subjects, can be split into two categories. One category aimed at exploring the occurrence and process of computer crime incidents. [2], [7], [14] The other focused on measures that can be taken to ensure computer security. [3], [12], [13] As a result, essays or empirical studies treating prevention and investigation matters from legal or criminological perspectives have been neglected, which to some extent took responsibility for the present limited effectiveness in curbing the crime. Facing such a rampant crime, ignorance of the crime is worrisome, and so is a lack of relevant theories.

Luckily, thanks to previous studies, we have harvested some basic understanding of the crime. Dubbed as a wise crime, computer-related offenses were found to be prone to cause extensive damage, hard to detect or prosecute, attractive to white collar workers, requiring expertise, often conducted repeatedly, and carrying a big dark figure of crime. In addition, studies also found numerous similarities between computer crimes and traditional ones, including criminal motive, goal, and nature. That means about 90% of the crimes can be handled with traditional investigative techniques if our investigators are equipped with enough skills, advanced knowledge and a strong mind to tackle them. [11]

Yet, to fight for a clean cyber space, there is clearly room for improvement in many areas, including conducting more theoretic and empirical research about the crime, improving preventive and investigative techniques, establishing better and faster judicial procedures, etc. This study is motivated by the awareness of the problems and inadequacies just highlighted.

4 Data Collection and Analysis

The data we analyzed were collected from the following main sources:

- Court: including criminal indictments, written verdicts, etc.
- Police agency: including reporting records, interrogating records, etc.
- Prosecutors' office: including records concerning investigating and issuing search and arrest warrants, etc.
- Miscellaneous: including media reports or newspaper clippings, stock transactional records, telecommunication records, etc.

All the data collected were sorted, and input according to a codebook and then statistically analyzed employing frequency distribution. The results are shown and discussed below.

5 Results of Analysis

5.1 Types of Computer Crime

The paper published by the U.S. President's Working Group on Unlawful Conduct on the Internet [9] classified computer crimes into three main categories: crimes with computers used as communication tools, crimes with computers used as storage media, and crimes with computers being the main target. For the purpose of comparison, we also divided the 165 cases collected in the same way. All of the crimes did fall into three categories. Yet, to better display the crime nature, the crimes were further classified into 10 types and 27 patterns, among the 27 patterns, crime combining pornography and piracy topped the list by possessing the most cases (25) and the highest percentage (15.3%), followed by porn website (23 cases and 14%), slander (17 cases and 10.4%) and pirate CD (16 cases and 9.7%). Of the total 10 types, distribution of pornography has the highest proportion (26.8%), followed by copyright infringement, 14.5%. Within the three categories, computers used as storage media wins with a majority of 56.6%.

5.2 Crime Scene

To demonstrate the distinguished characteristics of computer crime, crime scene is another essential element. Totally 6 kinds of sites were found. As was expected, a vast majority of computer crimes took place at criminals' residences (75.5%). The second most common scene is the criminals' workplace (13%) while the least popular one is the Internet café (0.7%), a surprising fact to find. Though unpopular presently, the Internet café is certain to become a hotbed of computer crime sooner or later due to the good equipment and anonymous environment it provides.

5.3 Cases Solved over a Four-Year Period

The numbers of computer crimes handled by the police and judicial systems were on the rise over the four-year period (from 1997 to 2000) and March was the month when the most cases were dealt with, which probably resulted from the large scale crackdown on porn websites and pirate software launched by the authorities concerned.

5.4 Lasting Time of the Criminal Actions

The time for which computer-related criminal acts lasted ranged from one month to 5 years. The average length was 6.7 months. More than half of the crimes (60.9%) got detected within 4 months after they began. Their common feature was they all lasted until they were found or busted.

5.5 Motives of Crime

Various reasons motivate the illegal acts relating to computer. Profit (Swindle and Embezzlement included) alone represents 64.1% of the cases, followed by curiosity (9.7%), and revenge (5.5%). It's not hard to note the financial gain-oriented nature of computer crime.

5.6 Victim Analysis

Some of the computer crimes were victimless, that is, causing no harm to others. They include drug dealing, gambling, illegal multi-level marketing, porn website, sex procurer, pasting obscene pictures, etc, totally comprising 31.5% of the crimes. Victimless crimes, though no direct or immediate harm caused through them, would inflict severe hardship and suffering onto society in the long run, due to their evil nature morally.

5.7 Complicity

Though hard and complex, most of the crimes were committed alone (86%), presumably because of the offenders' assumption that the fewer people there were who knew about the crime or participated in it, the less chance there would be for the crime to be discovered. For those involving more than one offender, it was usually for the reason of acquiring expertise and for the purpose of "profit-sharing." And the one who was often implicated or asked help from was the close friend or relative of the chief criminal.

5.8 Profile of Computer Criminal

Gender
Conspicuous proportions (90.5%) of the criminals were male. Crimes with women playing the dominant roles were not only rare but also mostly non-profit-related.

Age
From our data we found nearly half of the crimes were conducted by people between the ages of 23 and 30 (average age: 27). The main factor contributing to this might be the common unemployment problem facing those who are just discharged from the army. Under great financial stress and being idle, these people either resort to illegal means to make a living or immerse themselves in computer-related activities, culminating in the commitment of computer crimes. Since there were 8 criminals, 4.3%, older than 40 years of age, computer crime was hardly an unlawful act exclusively for the young. The explanation for the small proportion of offenders aged 41 to 50 (only 4.3%) may be that these people were not 'interested' in conducting computer-related activity and the reason was simply because they lacked the advanced expertise or knowledge required.

Occupation
One-fourth of the cyber criminals (25.1%) were students, outnumbering the unemployed, 17.5%, and all the others occupying certain positions in government or private agencies. One unfortunate and also surprising fact is there were 4 with a teaching background, i.e., people who were responsible for educating and were supposed to possess a higher moral standard.

Education
With respect to education, those who were involved in the crimes were predominantly college-educated (66.7%), followed by senior high graduates (21.1%), who unexpectedly outnumbered graduate students, 5.3%, an interesting fact worth noting.

Previous Criminal Record
Big proportions (80.4%) of the offenders were first offenders, meaning most of them had no previous record. For the remaining roughly 20%, their previous convictions consist of larceny, gambling, distribution of porn CDs, copyright infringement, drug dealing, fraud, embezzlement, etc.

5.9 Geographical Distribution

Taipei City and Taipei County, the two most important administrative regions in northern Taiwan, had more than half of all the cases, approximately 58%. Computer offenders tended to live in urban areas probably for two reasons: better economic development and easier access. Yet, the situation is going to change along with the improved availability of both computer education and equipment throughout the nation. It is predictable that computer crime will pose an equal challenge for all areas in Taiwan in the near future, thus the urgent needs for all local law enforcement agencies to equip their staff with necessary knowledge and skills.

5.10 Involvement of Disabled People in Computer Crime

The number of disabled people (totally 6) involved in the computer-related crimes was quite small, compared with the 'normal' ones. Though the figure is immaterial and out of proportion (3.2%), plus mostly of misdemeanor nature, the commission of computer crime by disabled people is still a noteworthy phenomenon for authorities concerned because most of them resort to illegal ways of making a living simply because they couldn't get employed through normal channels.

5.11 Judicial Process of Computer Crime

Investigative Agency
All the cases we studied, 62.3% of them were handled by the Criminal Investigative Bureau (CIB), followed by Criminal Investigative Squad of Taipei Municipal Police Headquarters (TMPH), 29%. That most of the cases went to the CIB could be attributed to the fact that it was the oldest, most experienced and best-equipped specialized investigative unit for both computer and traditional crime.

Prosecuting Agency
According to our data, the Taipei District Prosecutors' Office had charged most of the computer crime cases we studied. Though these crimes were spread throughout the island, the fact that the Taipei District Prosecutors' Office had jurisdiction over the cases occurring in the south and that the Office had a host of experienced veteran prosecutors resulted in its high charging rate.

Sentence
For these computer offenders, penalties handed down ranged from life imprisonment to reprimand, with a vast majority of them receiving fixed term sentence, averaging 7.2 months in jail. The one receiving the longest term and also the heaviest penalty-life imprisonment, was the offender involved in a police entrance examination scandal. Most offenders sentenced to jail received 4 to 6 months of imprisonment.

However, cases in which offenders received probation instead of prison terms were numerous, amounting to 84.6%. In the cases with offenders still studying at school, substitute punishments like safeguard restriction or commutation to fines was often adopted instead of jail term too. Although the fines that the criminals were ordered to pay seemed high, probably because of the big profit they made through racketeering, yet, compared to the threat that those computer crimes posed and the damage they caused, the punishments for the offenders were no doubt too lenient to act as a deterrent to breaking the law again.

Funnel Effect
Although the number of computer crimes investigated over the last few years appeared to be increasing, a 'funnel effect' emerged in the meantime. The term is used here to describe a situation in which the crimes that are detected or reported to the law enforcement agencies outnumber those that are finally prosecuted or convicted by the judicial systems. In other words, not all crimes get through the entire process from investigation to conviction.

Of all the cases reported, only 94.5% were handled and succeeded in having suspects arrested. Moving onto the second phase, only 90.4% remained, that is, being referred to the prosecution agencies. Proceeding to the third stage, only 70.8% stuck around or were prosecuted, while in the last stage, only 66% 'survived', being convicted. The reasons for losing some cases in each phase were various, including the crimes being too complex for the investigators to handle, the victims or the prosecutors unwilling to file the charges because of having reached a compromise, charges withdrawn, dropped, or dismissed for lack of evidence or suitable legal provisions, cases committed by servicemen being referred to military courts, etc.

5.12 Criminal Instrument and Evidence

This part is meant to introduce other important discoveries about computer crime.

Criminal Instrument
The instruments most often used in these cases were as follows:

1. Computer: mainframe, server, PC, notebook, and palm computer.
2. Peripherals: CD recorder, copy machine, scanner, and digital camera.
3. I/O device: monitor, keyboard, mouse, and printer.
4. Communication facility: MODEM, router, hub, and telephone line.
5. Storage media: HD, diskette, CD (program, pornography, blank), magnetic tape, and videotape.
6. Other apparatus: slot timer, label printer, card reader, and video recorder.

Major Evidence Collected
The major things that were collected to determine the existence of a crime and also served as the evidence to file a charge against an offender are listed below:

1. Electromagnetic record (printout): website content, Email, newsgroup discussion, BBS, IRC, message left on boards, program source code, virus code, data interpreted from HD, BBS registration data, audit log.
2. Postal receipt.
3. Bank statement, ATM card, credit card bill, check.
4. Picture, name list, stamp, fax, letter.

6 Conclusion

This paper has aimed to observe computer crime from a criminological perspective. Besides conducting a short review of related literature, we also observed computer crime based on the data, mainly the 165 cases we collected from a variety of sources that occurred in Taiwan during the recent decades. A statistical analysis was exploited on the cases. The results obtained provided us a fuller understanding of the crime, with respect to its type, crime scene, lasting time of the criminal action, motive, victimhood, profile of the criminal, complicity, geographical distribution, involvement of disabled people, judicial process, criminal instrument and evidence, etc. These findings will be of great help to us in developing preventive and combating strategies for the crime. The funnel effect we found is also a good reminder for the authorities concerned to develop a good solution as soon as possible.

This study tops previous research in data quantity and quality, and can serve as a good reference point for future studies on similar subjects, although admittedly, computer crime is so complicated that we simply could not treat all the important issues on one try. Therefore, we need to work harder in the future to explore the problem further, hoping that we can help get rid of the evil that does now and will continue to plague people here and all over the world.

References

1. Bawden, B.: International symposium on the prevention and prosecution of computer crime. *Computer Law and Security Report* (1992, May-June) 7-11
2. Chen, W. D.: *A study of cyber crime pattern analysis and its prevention and investigation.* Thesis of Information Management Graduate Institute of Central Police University (2000)
3. Cheu, C. D.: *An automatic system for crime information filtering on Internet.* Thesis of Information Management Graduate Institute of Central Police University (1999)
4. Hollinger, R. C. (ed.): *Crime, deviance and the computer.* England: Dartmouth (1997)
5. Japanese Police Administration: *Police white paper* (1994)
6. Li, B. H., Liao, Y. L.: The problems and tactics of computer crime. *Police Science Quarterly,* 26(6) (1996) 141-154
7. Lin, W. X.: *A study on computer crime pattern analysis.* Thesis of Police Science Graduate Institute of Central Police University (1998)
8. Liu, S. Y.: *Cyber hacker- Security practice of e-commerce.* Taipei: Yatai (1998)
9. President's Working Group on Unlawful Conduct on the Internet: *The Challenge of Unlawful Conduct Involving the Use of Internet* (2000, March) Retrieved August 14, 2001, from http://www.usdoj.gov/criminal/cybercrime/unlawful.htm
10. Sterling, B.: Good cop, bad hacker. *Wired,* 3 (1995) 122-129
11. Tipton, H.: Computer crime- Investigating inside the corporation. *Computer Fraud & Security Bulletin,* 4 (1993, February)
12. Tseng, Y. K.: *The study of SYN flooding defense- Based on traffic control.* Thesis of Information Management Graduate Institute of Central Police University (1999)
13. Wang, J. H., et al.: *A study of automated search system on cyber crimes.* Telecommunication Bureau of Ministry of Traffic and Communication (1999)
14. Wu, K. C.: A survey of police computer crime and prevention measures. *The Fourth Conference on Information Management and Its Applications on Law Enforcement* (2000) 201-215
15. Zou, Z. O.: *Criminological sociology.* Taipei: Liming Book Store (1993)
16. Zung, Z. J.: A study of the investigation and enactment of computer crime. Unpublished paper (1994)

A Cross Datasets Referring Outlier Detection Model Applied to Suspicious Financial Transaction Discrimination

Tang Jun

School of Computer Science and technology, Wuhan University of Technology,
Wuhan 430063, China
School of Information, Zhongnan University of Economics and Law,
Wuhan 430074, China
James_tang97@yahoo.com.cn

Abstract. Outlier detection is a key element for intelligent financial surveillance systems which intend to identify fraud and money laundering by discovering unusual customer behaviour pattern. The detection procedures generally fall into two categories: comparing every transaction against its account history and further more, comparing against a peer group to determine if the behavior is unusual. The later approach shows particular merits in efficiently extracting suspicious transaction and reducing false positive rate. Peer group analysis concept is largely dependent on a cross-datasets outlier detection model. In this paper, we propose a cross outlier detection model based on distance definition incorporated with the financial transaction data features. An approximation algorithm accompanied with the model is provided to optimize the computation of the deviation from tested data point to the reference dataset. An experiment based on real bank data blended with synthetic outlier cases shows promising results of our model in reducing false positive rate while enhancing the discriminative rate remarkably.

1 Introduction

Intelligent finance surveillance and anti-money laundering (AML) monitoring system are attracting highly focused attention among mainland China nowadays for the rampant nation-wide corruption, bribery and other economic crimes, which seriously influence the national economic security and stability. It is estimated more than RMB200 billion yuan (US$125 billion) involved to money laundering every year in China. At least RMB 600 billion yuan (US$73 billion) laundered to other countries, of which more than 500 billion yuan (US$ 62 billion) was obtained through corruption. Every branch of commercial banks is obliged to regularly report large value and suspicious transaction data to the intelligence department. But the data reporting system does not work well by its enormous results volume and high false positive rate which shows very few intelligence merits for the investigators. The current monitoring system works mainly by establishing a fixed threshold or by matching known money laundering patterns. Such methods are always accompanied with two connatural limits: First, pre-established rules may be easily eluded by the money

H. Chen et al. (Eds.): WISI 2006, LNCS 3917, pp. 58–65, 2006.

launders while those normal businesses may frequently trigger the thresholds resulting false positive reports. Second, they only own the ability to discover specific money laundering behaviors that have been found before with the new appeared pattern ignored. Thus all those systems suffer from a very high false positive rate and low discriminative rate.

Customer behavior pattern recognition methods are introduced to improve the situation. These methods could find out some unusual behaviors while false positive rate still stays relative high because a lot of unusual cases could prove to be normal given the economic cycle fluctuation and the continuously changing environment. To solve the problem we conceive a new adaptive profiling during our procedure of developing new generation anti-money laundering system for the bank regulator in south central area of China. The profiling first comparing every transaction against its corresponding account history to determine if the behavior is unusual. It then compares the transaction against a peer group for further analysis of risk. The later step will remarkably decrease the false positive rate. In this paper an outlier detection model is put out to express the procedure of peer group comparison. The model provides a set of formal symbol definition system to determine the outlier decision criteria. Such definitions are mainly based on data points distance measurement and statistical theory. To be more practical, an estimation algorithm to speedup the comparison process by neighbor points counting is also given.

The rest of the paper is organized as below: section 2 discusses the importance of cross datasets comparison in reducing the false positive rate and discovering unrevealed suspicious dealing during self historic records analysis. Section 3 presents the formal symbol definition for outlier detection through a cross datasets referring process. To be more practical, an estimation algorithm to speedup the comparison process by neighbor points counting is given in section 4. Section 5 gives the verification experiment prototype, methods and results based on the simulated data sets provided by a commercial bank. And in the last, section 6 are the conclusion and further jobs to be fulfilled.

2   Background and Related Work

2.1   Peer Group Comparison Procedure

The new generation intelligent monitoring system is effective at discovering suspicious transaction by two fold comparisons--self comparison and peer group comparison. Self comparison means comparing every transaction against its corresponding account history to determine if the behavior is unusual. The second step is to compare the transaction against a peer group for a further analysis. This process greatly reduces the number of false positives and provides a clearer understanding of actual risk. For example, if a customer makes a fixed low amount deposit into an account over the past 11 months, then suddenly makes a high amount deposit in the last month, this could appear unusual according to the account history. But when compared to the peer group, the suspicion will be released because the peer group has the same fluctuation and a year-end bonus is the explanation. Conversely, the peer group analysis can also discover risk that the account history review would not. Since most businesses involved with money laundering do not care about profit making and seldom conduct real operations, the account always appears smoothly with no lulls or busy periods. A look at the account history would not reveal suspicious activity. While comparing the transactions against a peer group, the account suddenly appeared very suspicious for the lack of fluctuation featured by the economic cycle. Thus a peer group analysis surely owns two fold advantages: reduces false positives and enhances the ability of discrimination.

2.2   Related Work on Outlier Detection

A well quoted definition of outliers is firstly given by Hawkins [1], "An outlier is an observation that deviates so much from other observations as to arouse suspicious that it was generated by a different mechanism". Exclusive focus has been put on the solution of detect deviants in a single set of observations, which is corresponding to the finance account self history analysis. Very few literatures in explicitly considering outlier detection through datasets comparison could be found to the best of our knowledge[2-7]. [8] Deals with the problem the general relationship of one multi-dimensional dataset with respect to another. It only explores correlations between datasets but fails to identify outlying points. [9] considers the problem of selectivity estimation of spatial joins across two points sets. Spiros Papadimitriou and Christos Faloutsos of Carnegie Mellon University conceived a formulated definition to describe the cross outlier detection process [10] which is the only literature we could find to express the concept of cross datasets comparison explicitly for the first time. However, it only applies the approach to astronomy datasets and gives no consideration to finance surveillance.

3   A Cross Datasets Comparison Outlier Detection Model Definition

Given two datasets $\mathbb{P}$ and $\mathbb{R}$, we want to discover points $p \in \mathbb{P}$ that "appear significant deviation" with respect to points $r \in \mathbb{R}$. Here we employ $\mathbb{P}$ as the primary set and $\mathbb{R}$ as the reference set. Points in both set are composed by multi-dimensional features vector. It is accepted that an outlier is an object if it is in some way "significantly different" from its "neighbours". As listed in table 1, we develop a set of formal definitions to solve the outlier definition using the concepts from statistical theory and pattern recognition techniques.

We will give specifications to the two symbols of distance $d(p,q)$ and locality parameter α in order to well understand the definitions. There are no particular requirements to distance definition. Arbitrary distance functions are allowed, which may incorporate with financial domain expert knowledge. Locality parameter α is a key factor introduced by LOCI algorithm [11] to solve the problems caused by the singularity in distance distribution. Parameter α is usually set to $1/2^l$ (l is a positive integer).

Table 1. Symbols and definitions for cross datasets outlier detection

Symbol	Definition
$\mathbb{P}$ p_i	Primary set of points $\mathbb{P}=\{p_1,...,p_b,....,p_N\}$
$\mathbb{R}$ r_i	Reference set points $\mathbb{R}=\{r_1,...,r_b,....,r_M\}$
N,M	Point set sizes
K	Dimension of the data sets
D(p,q)	Distance between points p and q
$R_{\mathbb{P}}, R_{\mathbb{R}}$	Range (diameter) of each point set, $R_{\mathbb{P}}=\max_{p,q \in \mathbb{P}}d(p,q)$.
$N_p(p,r)$	The set of r-neighbors of p from the point set P: $N_p(p,r)=\{q \in \mathbb{P}|d(p,q) \leq r\}$
$n_p(p,r)$	The number of r-neighbors of $p \in \mathbb{P}$, for brevity, we use n instead of $n_p(p,r)$.
α	Locality parameter, see [11] for details.
$\hat{n}_{\mathbb{P},\mathbb{R}}(p,r,\alpha)$	Average of $n_R(p,\alpha r)$ over the set of r- neighbors of $p \in \mathbb{P}$, i.e., $$\hat{n}_{\mathbb{P},\mathbb{R}}(p,r,\alpha)=\frac{\sum_{q \in N_{p(p,r)}}n_R(q,\alpha r)}{n_p(p,r)}$$ For brevity, we use $\hat{n}$ instead of $\hat{n}_{\mathbb{P},\mathbb{R}}$.
$\hat{\sigma}_{\mathbb{P},\mathbb{R}}(p,r,\alpha)$	Standard deviation of $n_R(p,\alpha r)$ over the set of r-neighbors of $p \in \mathbb{P}$, we use $\hat{\sigma}$ for brevity. $$\hat{\sigma}_{\mathbb{P},\mathbb{R}}(p,r,\alpha)=\sqrt{\frac{\sum_{q \in N_{p(p,r)}}(n_R(q,\alpha r)-\hat{n}_{p,R}(p,r,\alpha))^2}{n_p(p,r)}}$$
k_σ	Determine what is significant deviation, a point $p \in \mathbb{P}$ is flagged as an outlier iff $|\hat{n}_{\mathbb{P},\mathbb{R}}(p,r,\alpha)\text{-}n_R(p,\alpha r)|>k_\sigma \ \hat{\sigma}_{\mathbb{P},\mathbb{R}}(p,r,\alpha)$ k_σ is a human heuristic value, typically is set to 3
C(p,r, α)	Set of cells in grid, with cell side $2\alpha r$
$N_p(p,\mathbf{C_j})$	Number of cells
$c_{p,j}$	Count of points from set P within the cell C_j
$s_P^q(p,r,\alpha)$	Sum of cell counts from set P to the q-th power,, $s_P^q(p,r,\alpha)=\sum_{C_j \in C(p,r,\alpha)}c_{P,j}^q$
$P_{P,R}^q(p,r,\alpha)$	Sum of cell count products from sets P and R $$P_{P,R}^q(p,r,\alpha)=\sum_{C_j \in C(p,r,\alpha)}c_{P,j}\cdot c_{R,j}^q \quad \text{Note that } s_P^q=P_{P,P}^{q-1}$$

As a similar method often adopted in statistical theory, we first compute the parametrical values of average and standard deviation, then compare the distance of the point to be detected to a human set threshold value, if the deviation is significant enough, the point will be determined as an outlier.

4 A Fast Estimation Algorithm on Distance Distribution

Considering both the enormous transaction data sizes and data dimensionality dealt by each bank everyday, the distance distribution computation would easily exceeds a computer's limits. The computing complexity mainly comes from the $\hat{n}(p,r,\alpha)$, which calls for recursive computation summing up to be overwhelmed. To improve the situation, we adopt a trade off by inferring the $\hat{n}(p,r,\alpha)$ through an estimation scheme. This concept is derived from the k nearest neighbor counting.

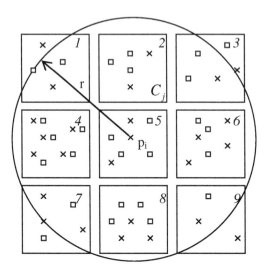

Fig. 1. Illustration of the approximate estimation Point in source dataset $\mathbb{P}$ is denoted by "×", point in referring dataset $\mathbb{R}$ is denoted by "□". In this sample, *C(p,r, α)* will only count box 2,4,5,6,8 while other boxes will be neglected.

As shown in Figure 1, we divide the r neighbor space into a grid composed of cells with side $2\alpha r$ over both sets $\mathbb{P}$ and $\mathbb{R}$. Within each cell, we note down counts of points it contains from $\mathbb{P}$ and $\mathbb{R}$. For each cell C_j in the grid, compute the counts $c_{P,j}$ and $c_{R,j}$, of the number of points from $\mathbb{P}$ and $\mathbb{R}$, respectively, in the cell. Since each point $p \in P \cap C_j$ has $c_{R,j}$ neighbours from R, the total number of R neighbours over all points from P in C_j is $c_{P,j} * c_{R,j}$. *C(p,r, α)* denotes those boxes which are completely covered by the r-neighbor of point p_i. Thus, counting the sum of $c_{P,j}$ in *C(p,r, α)* will get an approximate estimation of the r-neighbor to point p_i. The approximation process is illustrated in Figure 1. A fast estimation algorithm is derived as below:

First, $P_{P,R}(p,r,\alpha) = \displaystyle\sum_{C_i \in C(p,r,\alpha)} c_{P,j} \cdot c_{R,j}$, where the total number of

points in set P is approximately computed by the sum of $c_{P,j}$, namely $s_P^1(p,r,\alpha)$, then $\hat{n}_{P,R}(p,r,\alpha)$ and $\hat{\sigma}_{P,R}(p,r,\alpha)$ can be deduced out as:

$$\hat{n}_{P,R}(p,r,\alpha) = \frac{P_{P,R}^1(p,r,\alpha)}{s_P^1(p,r,\alpha)}$$

$$\hat{\sigma}_{P,R}(p,r,\alpha) = \sqrt{\frac{P_{P,R}^2(p,r,\alpha)}{s_P^1(p,r,\alpha)} - \left(\frac{P_{P,R}^1(p,r,\alpha)}{s_P^1(p,r,\alpha)}\right)^2}$$

The outlier then could be discriminated by the above average and standard deviation. The computation complexity is reduced to linear related to the dataset size and vector dimensions.

5 Experiment

5.1 Data Set Description

A real financial transaction record database set acquired from Wuhan Branch of Agriculture Bank in south central China is adopted in the experiment. It comprises 5000 accounts, 12 million records transactions over 7 months from the year 2003 to 2004. The main structure of database is like below:

Table 2. The database structure of raw data sets

ACCOUNT	CUSTOMER-ID	INDUSTRY	CAPITAL (million)	DEALING -DATE	SUM	BALANCE
1408010000195	801001	Manufacture	5	20030108	1,000,000.00	369,877.00
1408010000300	801021	Service	1	20030110	12,2200.00	12,2260.48
......	......	....	......	......	......	......

As a tested dataset, only 3 distinctive features to describe the customer's background including account, industry and registered capital are kept, more other detailed identification features are omitted.

By clustering analyses using the shared nearest method propose in [11] first we divide the datasets into some neighbouring groups. In next step we will apply the cross datasets comparison method.

We construct a test dataset $\mathbb{P}$ by mixing the raw dataset with 80 deliberately simulated unusual accounts whose business cycle features are obviously deviated from those of peer groups. Since no real money laundering cases data could be acquired, and the purpose of intelligent system is not to find out the real money laundering action but the suspicious transaction for the staff to investigate. A normal transaction dataset $\mathbb{R}$ is also derived by clustering division as described in [11].

5.2 Experiment Results

Using the current pre-rule based system in the bank, we will get a result of 18663 records of which triggered the thresholds. Using the two-class SVM(Support Vector) algorithm of self comparison outlier detection provided in the package by libsvm[12], 1343 unusual records were detected to show the obvious deviation. Then we test the outlier detection by our cross datasets approach. Set $\alpha = 1/4$, k=3, we can estimate $\hat{\sigma}_{\mathbb{P},\mathbb{R}}(p,r,\alpha)=4/341$, and 271 cases are detected out.

From the reporting data, we examined our 80 synthetic accounts, out of which 2, 9 and 52 are detected in the three methods. Through cross dataset comparison method, the 65% detection ratio gives promise for our proposal. Table 3 gives the comparison of the 3 methods.

Table 3. The experiment result

	pre-defined rule	SVM	Cross datasets
reporting cases	18663	1347	271
detected cases	2	9	52
false positive cases	18661	1338	219

6 Conclusions

Conventional outlier detection approaches don not handle peer comparison involved in financial suspicious behaviour recognition. In this paper we present a cross datasets outlier detection mode to fulfil the void. The further research jobs we shall undertake include probabilistic estimation algorithm, algorithm efficiency evaluation and real datasets experiments analysis.

Acknowledgement

This work is supported by the Research Foundation of National Science and Technology Plan Project (2004BA721A02), China.

References

[1] Hawkins,D. Identification of outliers. London:Chapman and Hall,1980
[2] Faloutsos, C., Seeger, B., Jr.,C.T.,Trainar,A.,:Spatial join selectivity using power laws. In: Proc. SIGMOD. (2000)177-188
[3] E.Knorr,R,Ng. Algorithms for mining distance-based outliers:Properties and computation. Kdd'97,pp.219-222,1997
[4] Knorr, E.M., Ng, R.: Algorithms for mining distance-based outliers in large datasets. In: Proc. VLDB 1998. (1998) 392–403
[5] Knorr, E., Ng, R.: Finding intentional knowledge of distancebased outliers. In: Proc. VLDB. (1999) 211–222
[6] Knorr, E., Ng, R., Tucakov, V.: Distancebased outliers: Algorithms and applications. VLDB Journal 8 (2000) 237–253
[7] S.Ramaswarmy,R.Rastogi,S.Kyuseok. Efficient Algorithms for Mining Outliers from Large Datasets. SIGMOD'00,pp93-104,2000
[8] Traina, A., Traina,C., Papadimitriou, S., Faloutsos,C.:Tri-plots:Scalable tools for multidimensional data mining. In Proc.KDD.(2001) 184-193

[9] Spiros Papadimitriou.Cross-Outlier Detection. http://www.db.cs.cmu.edu/Pubs/Lib/sst
d03cross/sstd03.pdf

[10] S.Ramaswarmy,R.Rastogi,S.Kyuseok. Efficient Algorithms for Mining Outliers from
Large Datasets. SIGMOD'00,pp93-104,2000

[11] L. Eltoz, U Steinbach,V. Kumar,A new shared nearest neighbor clusteing algoithm and its
applications, AHPCRC, Tech. Rep, pp. 134, Aug. 2002.

[12] http://www.csie.ntu.edu.tw/~cjlin/libsvm

Detecting Novel Network Attacks with a Data Field

Feng Xie[1,2] and Shuo Bai[1]

[1] Software Department, Inst. of Computing Tech.,
Chinese Academy of Science, Beijing, 100080, P.R. China
[2] Graduate School, Chinese Academy of Science,
Beijing, P.R. China
xiefeng@software.ict.ac.cn

Abstract. With the increased usage of computer networks, network intrusions have greatly threatened the Internet infrastructures. Traditional signature-based intrusion detection often suffers from an ineffectivity to those previously "unseen" attacks. In this paper, we analyze the network intrusions from a new viewpoint based on data field and propose branch and bound tree to lessen computation complexity. Finally, we evaluated our approach over KDD Cup 1999 data set.

1 Introduction

Recently, many international organizations and governments as well as enterprises have been attacked by hackers or malicious users who want to get secret information or destroy target systems, which causes a great loss to whole society. According to CERT report[1], the incidents have increased rapidly since 2000. Therefore, a powerful tool is needed to monitor and possibly prevent intrusion attempts to protect our system and network resources, which is called intrusion detection system (IDS). In essential, IDS is a system that collects and extracts security-related information from different sources including network traffic and host system, and then analyzes them in order to find intrusion attempts.

There are generally two types of approaches taken toward network intrusion detection: *signature-based*, in which audit data are searched for patterns known to be intrusive, or *anomaly-based*, in which aberrations from normal usage patterns are searched for. A significant limitation of traditional signature-based detection approach is that they cannot detect novel attacks. In addition, the knowledge of attack signatures is provided by human experts, which may require enormous time. In order to address these problems, machine learning and data mining are being investigated for IDS [2, 6, 7, 3, 1, 4]. The key idea to use these techniques is to discover consistent and useful patterns of features that describe network behavior, and use them to build classifiers that can recognize network intrusions.

---

[1] http://www.cert.org/stats/

H. Chen et al. (Eds.): WISI 2006, LNCS 3917, pp. 66–72, 2006.
© Springer-Verlag Berlin Heidelberg 2006

 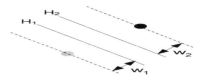

(a) In general, traditional classification always finds the separating hyperplane with
the largest margin (H_1)

(b) We substitute two hyperplanes (H_1
and H_2) for previous H_1. The region
between them is anomaly region.

Fig. 1. The idea of our modified classification algorithm

Traditional classification algorithm, however, only labels the data as known
categories that are presented in the training set, which makes it unable to find
those data of new category. Fig. 1(a) shows a usual classification criterion: it
always seeks for the hyperplane to separate the data from two categories. To
adapt to anomaly detection, we modify the criterion as follows: rather than to
find the separating hyperplane with the largest margin, we introduce a region
to represent anomaly. It is illustrated in Fig. 1(b), in which H_1 and H_2 are hyperplanes separating the two different points. It is important to notice that w_1
and w_2 may be different margins relied on the type of point. In this paper, we
propose data field and influence function as a case of this separation.

2 Data Field Based Classification Algorithm

In physics, we often represent a region in space as a field, in which objects are
interacting with each other by some effect forces. The forces are inversely propor-
tional to the square of the separation distance between the two objects. Similarly,
we introduce a new field, data field, to discriminate network activities. Our approach is based on the idea that each data point has an influence region around it,
in which each other point is affected. The influence decreases with the increase of
distance between two points and can be modeled formally using a mathematical
function which we call influence function. Whether a test data point is normal or
not can then be determined by calculating the force at that point.

In essence, influence function is a function of position quantifying the influence of a data object in the field. Formally, we can define it as follows.

Let F^N be the N-dimensional feature space. The influence function of a data
object $y \in F^N$ is a function $f_y : F^N \rightarrow R_0^+$ which is defined in terms of a basic
function ϕ

$$f_y(x) = \phi(x, y) \tag{1}$$

In our experiment, we use Gaussian function to describe it, that is,

$$f_y(x) = \phi(x, y) = e^{-\frac{d^2(x, y)}{2\sigma^2}} \tag{2}$$

where $d(x, y)$ is the distance from x to y, and σ is called influence factor determining the influence scope of y.

We also call the influence magnitude at a given position p as the potential energy at that position, or simply potential.

Furthermore, the influence function of a data field D can be defined as follows.

$$f_D(x) = \sum_{y \in D} f_y(x) = \sum_{y \in D} e^{-\frac{d^2(x,y)}{2\sigma^2}} \tag{3}$$

To perform detection, we introduce sign to represent the difference of potential produced by points of different categories. We provide that the potential is positive only if the point producing that field is normal, otherwise it is negative. Note that the sign of the potential is used only in determining the type of a test point, not the magnitude of the potential.

If the total potential of a point obtained from the field D is negative, we think such point is more near to the attack samples and label it as "attack". If the potential is rough equal to zero, we think it isn't similar with any known behavior and may be a new attack or a rare behavior and label it as "anomaly". In general, the magnitude of potential determines the confidence of the judgment and the sign determines the class of given testing sample.

The basic steps of algorithm are shown in Fig. 2. It is important to note that we are only interested in those data within "3σ" region. An important reason is that for a field conforming to Gaussian distribution, there are up to 99.7 % energy within the sphere with the radius of 3σ, which is the famous "3σ criterion". We, therefore, only focus on those objects inside this range and ignore others, which will save a lot of computations.

OUTPUT: Label input point P as normal, known-attack or anomaly
step 1. normalize $P, f_+ \leftarrow 0, f_- \leftarrow 0$;
step 2. for each sample Q in training set D
    if $d(P,Q) > 3\sigma$ continue;
    compute the influence at P generated by Q and add it to f_+ if Q is normal, otherwise add it to f_-;
step 3. according to f_+ and f_-, judge P's type and label it;

Fig. 2. Data field based classification algorithm

3   Branch and Bound Tree

A significant weakness of the approach above is computation complexity. It is very difficult and time-consuming to compute the potential of a given data point obtained from the data field D according to Eq. (3). We can, however, get the same results from another viewpoint. In fact, a point is mainly affected by other points within "3σ" region which are called the neighbors of such point. Therefore, we only need to find all neighbors of the input point instead of all points in training set. Here, we use branch and bound tree to perform the search.

This method is firstly proposed to find nearest neighbor by Fukunaga [5]. We, however, add some pruning rules according to our requirements. The whole process is as follows. First, data point set is divided into k subsets, moreover each subset is divided into k subsets again. By applying this procedure recursively, the search tree is constructed. Each node of the tree corresponds to a subset, while each leaf of the tree contains a minimal number of points. Node p has four parameters $\langle S_p, N_p, \mu_p, r_p \rangle$. S_p is the set of samples associated with node p, N_p is the number of samples in S_p, μ_p is the mean value of samples of S_p, and r_p is the distance from μ_p to the farthest sample in S_p.

When an unknown input x is given, the neighbors are found by searching this tree by depth first search. Among the nodes at the same level, the node which has smaller distance $d(x, \mu_p)$ is searched earlier. Using the pruning rules based-on triangular inequality, the number of nodes and samples are restricted, and fast search is realized.

3.1 The Pruning Rules

Let M be the point set, let μ_p be center of a node p, let S_p be point set of node p, i.e. $S_p \subset M$, let r_p be the radius of p, i.e., $r_p = \max_{s \in S_p} d(s, \mu_p)$, and let ϵ be the influence radius, i.e. $\epsilon = 3\sigma$. Therefore we can get the following 4 rules.

Rule 1	$\forall x \in M$	$d(x, \mu_p) > \epsilon + r_p \Rightarrow \forall s \in S_p \quad d(x, s) > \epsilon$
Rule 2	$\forall x \in M, \forall s \in S_p$	$d(s, \mu_p) > d(x, \mu_p) + \epsilon \Rightarrow d(x, s) > \epsilon$
Rule 3	$\forall x \in M, \forall s \in S_p$	$d(s, \mu_p) < d(x, \mu_p) - \epsilon \Rightarrow d(x, s) > \epsilon$
Rule 4	$\forall x \in M$	$d(x, \mu_p) + r_p \leq \epsilon \Rightarrow \forall s \in S_p \quad d(x, s) \leq \epsilon$

In preprocessing time the algorithm builds two different structures: the distance table and the search tree. The distance table stores the distances between every point in the dataset and the centers of subsets these points belong to.

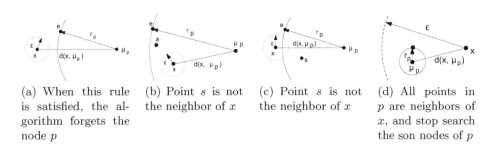

(a) When this rule is satisfied, the algorithm forgets the node p

(b) Point s is not the neighbor of x

(c) Point s is not the neighbor of x

(d) All points in p are neighbors of x, and stop search the son nodes of p

Fig. 3. Illustration of all pruning rules. (a)~(d) corresponds to rule 1~4, respectively.

3.2   The Tree Construction and Search Algorithm

We apply recursively K-means clustering algorithm to construct the search tree. The centroid provided by the algorithm is used as the mean of each node.

The whole search process is actually traversal of tree, meanwhile using pruning rules above to avoid the traversal of some parts of the tree. The search algorithm is illustrated in Fig.4.

Thus, the learning stage complexity is $O(Nlog_2N)$, while the search complexity is $O(log_2N)$. Here, N denotes the number of points in the training set.

FUNCTION   search (tree_node t, input point x)

step 1. if t can be pruned by Rule 1, then return;   /* the samples in ACK list must be neighbors of x.*/

step 2. if t can be pruned by Rule 4, then add all samples in t to ACK list and return;

step 3. if t is a leaf, then check each point in t by Rule 2 and 3, and add left samples to candidate list;

step 4. if t is a node, compute all distances between x and the center of each child of t and sort them into ascending order. Search each child recursively according to short distance-prior criterion.

Fig. 4. The search algorithm

4   Experimental Evaluation

The experimental data we used are the KDD Cup 1999 Data[1] which includes 494019 labeled connections for training and 311029 connections for testing. In the test set, there are more than 160000 "smurf" samples which belong to known DOS attacks. Therefore, we get rid of most of such samples to prevent "smurf" from dominating the test set, which will ensure the results more fair. Otherwise, if we can detect "smurf" attacks, the detection rate will become very high. Apparently, it is unreasonable. Table 1 shows the description of intrusion examples in our test dataset.

Table 1. The description of intrusion set for test in our experiment

Attack Category	PROBE	DOS	U2R	R2L
Total Number of Samples	4166	59054	228	16189
Proportion of Novel Attacks	42.9%	11.1%	82.9%	63%

Both Fig. 5 and 6 show the potential distributions of all attacks in test set obtained from the data field[2]. We can see that most of PROBE, DOS and U2R samples can be identified correctly while only a few are mislabeled. Since there are too few U2R samples in training set, and novel U2R attacks account for 82.9% of total U2R test samples, they achieve tiny negative potential. Thus we would label them as "anomaly", which is what we desire.

---

[1] http://kdd.ics.uci.edu/databases/kddcup99/kddcup99.html.

[2] Since the thresholds are often set between -1 and 1, we highlight the results within this scope.

The detection performance of R2L attacks, however, is very poor surprisingly. Fig. 6 shows a lot of R2L attacks obtain the high positive potential and are recognized as "normal" according to our judgment criterion. We analyze the results in detail and find that most of mislabeled R2L attacks are *snmpgetattack* and *snmpguess* which account for rough 62.7% of all testing R2L samples. In fact, they are almost identical with normal examples and hardly detected only by the connection information. Except for these two types of attacks, many other R2L attacks can be discriminated correctly in our data field.

In addition, we compare our results with other approaches including bayes [2], decision tree [2], PNrule [1], boosting [7] and so on[3]. The results are shown in Fig. 7. It can be seen that our approach drastically outperforms others, especially in detection of PROBE and U2R[4].

Fig. 8 shows the performance of branch and bound tree in reducing candidate neighbors. The number of candidates selected by proposed approach is slightly more than that of real neighbors. Therefore, it is very effective to reduce the computation complexity.

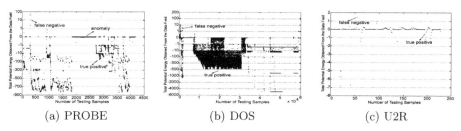

(a) PROBE   (b) DOS   (c) U2R

Fig. 5. The obtained potential distribution of different samples. (a)~(c) corresponds to PROBE, DOS and U2R attacks, respectively.

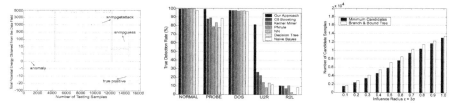

Fig. 6. The obtained potential distribution of R2L samples

Fig. 7. The comparison of proposed approach with other methods

Fig. 8. The performance of branch and bound tree in reducing candidates

5   Concluding Remarks

This paper views the network intrusions from a new standpoint. Rather than to find the hyperplane to maximize the separating margin, we keep a region to

---

[3] Some results come from http://www-cse.ucsd.edu/users/elkan/clresults.html.

[4] For simplicity, we use true detection rate to represent the ratio of correct detection, i.e., it means true negative rate for normal samples and true positive rate for attacks.

represent anomaly and propose the specific method based on data field. Furthermore, we lessen the computation complexity by branch and bound tree. The good experimental results prompt us to do more researches on it in the future.

References

1. R. Agarwal, and M. V. Joshi. PNrule: A New Framework for Learning Classifier Models in Data Mining. SIAM conference on Data Mining, 2000.
2. N. B. Amor, S. Benferhat, and Z. Elouedi. Naive Bayes vs. Decision Trees in Intrusion Detection Systems. ACM Symposium on Applied Computing, 2004.
3. L. Ertoz, E. Eilertson, and A. Lazarevic. The MINDS - Minnesota Intrusion Detection System. Workshop on Next Generation Data Mining, 2004.
4. E. Eskin, A. Arnold, M. Prerau, L. Portnoy, and S. J. Stolfo. A Geometric Framework for Unsupervised Anomaly Detection: Detecting Intrusions in Unlabeled Data. Application of Data Mining in Computer Security, Kluwer, 2002.
5. F. Fukunaga and P. M. Narendra. A Branch and Bound Algorithm for Computing K-Nearest Neighbors. IEEE Trans. Computers, 1975.
6. W. Lee, S. J. Stolfo, and K. W. Mok. A Data Mining Framework for Building Intrusion Detection Models. IEEE Symposium on Security and Privacy, 1999.
7. B. Pfahringer. Winning the KDD99 Classification Cup: Bagged Boosting. SIGKDD explorations, 2000, Vol. 1(2): 65-66.

Improving Authentication Accuracy of Unfamiliar Passwords with Pauses and Cues for Keystroke Dynamics-Based Authentication

Seong-seob Hwang, Hyoung-joo Lee, and Sungzoon Cho

Department of Industrial Engineering, Seoul National University,
San 56-1, Shillim-dong, Kwanak-gu, 151-744, Seoul, Korea
{hss9414, impatton, zoon}@snu.ac.kr

Abstract. Keystroke dynamics-based authentication (KDA) is to verify a user's identification using not only the password but also keystroke patterns. The authors have shown in previous research that uniqueness and consistency of keystroke patterns are important factors to authentication accuracy and that they can be improved by employing artificial rhythms and tempo cues. In this paper, we implement the pause strategy and/or auditory cues for KDA and assess their effectiveness using various novelty detectors. Experimental results show that improved uniqueness and consistency lead to enhanced authentication performance, in particular for those users with poor typing ability.

1 Introduction

The password-based authentication is the most commonly used in identity verification. However, they become vulnerable when they are stolen. Keystroke dynamics-based authentication (KDA) was proposed to provide additional security [1,2]. KDA was motivated by the observation that a user's keystroke patterns are repeatable and distinct from those of other users. Its potential applications include internet banking, ATM machines, digital doorlocks, cellular phones, and so forth which require high security. It is possible to complement the password-based authentication using other biometric attributes such as fingerprint, iris, and voice [3,4]. However, these methods require very expensive devices [5]. In addition, users may be reluctant to provide those biometric data. On the other hand, KDA needs no additional device and keystroke data can be collected relatively easily.

There are three steps involved in KDA as illustrated in Fig. 1. First, a user enrolls his/her keystroke patterns. A password of m characters is transformed into a $(2m+1)$-dimensional timing vector. A "duration" denotes a time period during which a key is pressed while an "interval" is a time period between releasing a key and stroking the next key. Second, a classifier is built using the keystroke patterns. Third, when a new keystroke pattern is presented, it is either accepted or rejected based on the classification made by the classifier.

One of the most obvious difficulties in KDA is that impostor patterns are usually not available when building a classifier. Thus it is not possible to train a binary

H. Chen et al. (Eds.): WISI 2006, LNCS 3917, pp. 73–78, 2006.

classifier. This limitation can be overcome by the novelty detection framework [6,7]. In novelty detection, the valid user's patterns are designated as normal and all other possible individuals' patterns as novel. A novelty detector learns the characteristics of normal patterns during training and detects novel patterns that are different from the normal ones during test. In a geometric sense, a novelty detector defines a closed boundary around the normal patterns in the input space [8].

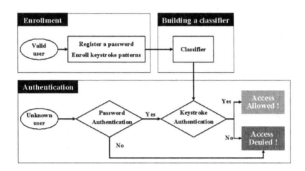

Fig. 1. Three steps are involved in the KDA framework

Another difficulty in KDA stems from the fact that in practice, the number of the valid user's patterns is also limited. Thus, we have to improve the quality of patterns. Recently, it has been shown that uniqueness and consistency are two important factors to the quality and artificial rhythms and tempo cues were proposed to improve them [9,10]. Uniqueness refers to how different the valid user's keystroke patterns are from those of potential impostors. Consistency is concerned with how similar the user's patterns are to those enrolled in the registration stage. For familiar passwords, the valid user's keystroke patterns are both relatively unique and consistent. However, users do change their passwords every once in a while and may use different passwords for different accounts. Therefore, there is a great possibility that a password is newly adopted and/or relatively unfamiliar to the user. Unfamiliar passwords usually translate into inconsistency.

Another paper in this publication [10] has statistically verified the hypothesis that artificial rhythms and tempo cues improve uniqueness and consistency. This paper examines whether improved uniqueness and consistency is actually translated to enhanced authentication performance when artificial rhythms and tempo cues are implemented in real-world applications. Three strategies are considered based on whether pauses or cues are applied: natural, pause, and pause with cues. Five novelty detectors are utilized for the strategies: Gaussian and Parzen density estimators, k-nearest neighbor method, k-means clustering, and one-class support vector machine.

The following section introduces the implementation of pauses and cues in KDA. Section 3 describes the strategies based on pauses and cues and the experimental settings. In Section 4, a number of novelty detectors are applied to keystroke pattern datasets with the strategies and the results are presented. Finally, conclusions and a list of future work are discussed.

2 Typing Strategies: Pause and Cue

KDA works well for familiar passwords that have already been used over a certain period of time. However, uniqueness and consistency tend to deteriorate for unfamiliar passwords, especially if users are not good at typing. In this case, pauses and cues can be employed to improve uniqueness and consistency of keystroke patterns [9,10].

2.1 Pauses

One way to improve uniqueness is to type a password with artificial rhythms that only the user can remember. Pauses are selected among various artificial rhythms since they are simple and easy to control. A user inserts a number of unusually long intervals where he thinks appropriate. The user should determine the following factors: how many pauses are inserted, where the pauses are inserted, and how long the pauses are. Impostors would not even know whether the pauses are inserted, let alone how the three factors are combined. So pauses, if well-executed, can make the valid user's keystroke patterns much more unique.

2.2 Cues

In order to prevent pauses from being inconsistent, tempo cues are provided. Tempo cues work like a metronome helping the user keep the timing, i.e. how long the pauses are. Given the tempo beat, the user only need to remember the number of beats for each pause. Usually they can be provided in three modes: auditory, visual, and audio-visual. In addition, users are allowed to choose the cue tempo which will dictate how fast they type their passwords. It has another advantage of improving uniqueness since only the valid user knows the tempo.

3 Experimental Settings

Three strategies were used in terms of pauses and cues. First, the "natural" strategy indicates that a user types a password with own natural rhythm using neither a pause nor a cue. Second, a user inserts pauses in the middle of typing passwords when he employs the "pause" strategy. In our experiments, users were asked to insert two long pauses. Third, the "pause with cues" strategy is used when a user is provided with auditory cues while the user types a password using the pause strategy. Auditory cues are selected since they can be implemented in a wide range of digital devices.

Four sessions of data collection were conducted. First, 25 users enrolled using the natural strategy familiar passwords which had been used for more than three months. Second, the users enrolled using the natural strategy unfamiliar passwords that were adopted just before data collection. In the third and the fourth experiments, the users enrolled the unfamiliar passwords using the pause and the pause with cues strategies, respectively. We assumed that impostors knew the valid passwords, but were not aware of pauses and cues. For each session, each user generated 30 training patterns in an enrollment session and 24 test patterns in a simulated log-in session. On the

Table 1. Experimental Design: Four data collection sessions were conducted with different passwords and different strategies.

Session	Password	Valid users			Impostors		
		Strategy	Pause	Cue	Strategy	Pause	Cue
1	Familiar	Natural	No	No			
2	Unfamiliar	Natural	No	No	Natural	No	No
3	Unfamiliar	Pause	Yes	No			
4	Unfamiliar	Pause with cues	Yes	Yes			

other hand, each of the other 24 users acted as an impostor. Table 1 presents the settings of the four data collection sessions.

Five novelty detectors were implemented as potential authenticators: Gaussian (Gauss) [11] and Parzen window (Parzen) [12] density estimators, k-nearest neighbor (k-NN) [13], k-means clustering (KMC) [14], and one-class support vector machine (1-SVM) [8]. Any biometrics-based approach including KDA has two types of error, i.e. false acceptance rate (FAR) and false rejection rate (FRR) [15]. Since one type of error can be reduced at the expense of the other by varying a threshold, these models were compared in terms of the equal error rate (EER) where the FRR and the FAR are equal.

4   Experimental Results

Table 2 presents the results from each Session. For 19 out of 25 passwords in Session 1, at least four models produced 0% EERs. On average, the best model is 1-SVM with the EER of 1.41% while the worst is Gauss with 3.77%. In Session 2, compared to the results from Session 1, the errors markedly increased across the board. When the users switched to unfamiliar passwords, the average EERs went up to around 10%. The errors from Session 3 significantly decreased compared with the ones from Session 2. On average, the errors are almost 10% lower than the ones from Session 2. They are slightly lower than even the errors from Session 1 where familiar passwords were used. Obviously, use of the pause strategy resulted in more accurate authentication. The results presented in Table 2 (d) shows that auditory cues can be a solution to inconsistency problem. For most passwords, the EERs are zero. On average, the EERs are about 1/100 of those from Session 2 and about 1/10 of those from Session 3. The highest error is only 0.25% by Parzen. It should be stressed that Gauss gave the EERs of 0% for all passwords. That suggests that a simple model is sufficient for KDA if keystroke patterns are both unique and consistent.

In Table 3, the average EERs by KMC are listed with respect to the users' typing ability. "Good" users are those whose average EERs over the five models were less than 5% in both Sessions 1 and 2 while "poor" users are the rest. KMC always produced errors close to 0% for the good users, regardless of passwords and strategies. The pause strategy reduces the error in Session 3, even lower than the one from Session 1. The pause with cues strategy reduces errors even more, nearly to 0% in Session 4. Other models show essentially the same trends. It is clear that pauses and cues are more beneficial for users with poor typing ability.

Table 2. The Equal Error Rates (%)

User	(a) Session 1					(b) Session 2				
	Gauss	Parzen	k-NN	KMC	1-SVM	Gauss	Parzen	k-NN	KMC	1-SVM
Average	3.77	3.22	1.57	1.70	1.41	15.09	10.92	10.72	11.00	11.00
Best	0.00	0.00	0.00	0.00	0.00	0.00	0.00	0.00	0.00	0.00
Worst	19.05	26.42	14.29	14.29	14.29	62.50	50.00	50.00	54.17	50.00
User	(c) Session 3					(d) Session 4				
	Gauss	Parzen	k-NN	KMC	1-SVM	Gauss	Parzen	k-NN	KMC	1-SVM
Average	2.54	2.33	1.97	1.08	2.03	0.00	0.25	0.08	0.08	0.08
Best	0.00	0.00	0.00	0.00	0.00	0.00	0.00	0.00	0.00	0.00
Worst	25.00	18.06	15.28	12.50	14.58	0.00	4.17	2.08	2.08	2.08

Table 3. The EERs (%) of KMC with respect to the users' typing abilities. Nine good users and 16 poor users are identified based on the EERs from Sessions 1 and 2.

Typing ability	Session 1	Session 2	Session 3	Session 4
Good	0	0.54	0	0
Poor	2.65	16.88	1.69	0.13

5 Conclusions and Discussion

Uniqueness and consistency are two major factors to authentication accuracy in KDA. In order to improve them, pauses and cues were proposed. In this paper, we have experimentally examined the effectiveness of artificial rhythms involving pauses and cues. Decent errors were reported in Session 1 where the users typed their familiar passwords using the natural strategy. However, when the users switch to unfamiliar passwords, the errors increased significantly. Employing the pause strategy reduced the errors to a level comparable to or lower than the ones from Session 1. Providing auditory cues reduced the errors even more to nearly 0%. We can conclude that improved uniqueness and consistency lead to enhanced authentication performance. In particular, pauses and cues are much more beneficial to users who are not good at typing. The performance difference among the five different novelty detectors was negligible. The quality of patterns, user-wise or strategy-wise, is much more important than the novelty detector utilized.

A few limitations and future directions need to be addressed. First, we measured the accuracy in terms of EER. However, EER is a kind of best-case error rates, thus there is no guarantee that one can achieve the EER in practice. For a real-world KDA application, parameter selection should be considered. Second, we included both duration and interval features in the analysis. Some features are more important than others while some features may be useless or even detrimental to authentication accuracy [7]. So, feature selection schemes should be investigated. Third, we assumed that impostors are aware of neither pauses nor cues. If they are, KDA method may become more vulnerable. Through further research, we need to find the effect of impostor awareness. Finally, in this paper, we investigated strategies involving pauses and auditory cues. Other kinds of artificial rhythms, other types of cues and their combinations should also be considered.

Acknowledgement

This work was supported by grant No. R01-2005-000-103900-0 from the Basic Research Program of the Korea Science and Engineering Foundation.

References

1. Gaines, R., Lisowski, W., Press, S., Shapiro, N.: Authentication by keystroke timing: some preliminary results. Rand Report R-256-NSF. Rand Corporation. (1980)
2. Umphress, D., Williams, G.: Identity Verification through Keyboard Characteristics. International Journal of Man-Machine Studies 23 (1985) 263-273
3. Jain, A.K., Bolle, R., Pankanti, S.: Biometrics: Personal Identification in Networked Society. Kluwer, Norwell (1999)
4. Polemi., D.: Biometric Techniques: Review and Evaluation of Biometric Techniques for Identification and Authentication. Technical Report. Institute of Communication and Computer Systems, National Technical University of Athens, Athens, Greece. (1997) Available at ftp://ftp.cordis.lu/pub/infosec/docs/biomet.doc
5. Monrose, F., Rubin, A.D.: Keystroke Dynamics as a Biometric for Authentication. Future Generation Computer System 16(4) (2000) 351-359
6. Cho, S., Han, C., Han, D., Kim, H.: Web Based Keystroke Dynamics Identity Verification Using Neural Networks. Journal of Organizational Computing and Electronic Commerce 10(4) (2000) 295-307
7. Yu, E., Cho, S.: Keystroke Dynamics Identity Verification - Its Problems and Practical Solutions. Computer and Security 23(5) (2004) 428-440
8. Schölkopf, B., Platt, J.C., Shawe-Taylor, J., Smola, A.J., Williamson, R.C.: Estimating the Support of a High-dimensional Distribution. Neural Computation 13 (2001) 1443-1471
9. Cho, S., Hwang, S.: Artificial Rhythms and Cues for Keystroke Dynamics-based Authentication. Lecture Notes in Computer Science (LNCS 3832). Springer-Verlag (2006) 626-632
10. Kang, P., Park, S., Cho, S., Hwang, S., Lee, H.: The Effectiveness of Artificial Rhythms and Cues for Keystroke Dynamics-based User Authentication. Submitted (2006)
11. Barnett, V, Lewis, T.: Outliers in Statistical Data. Wiley and Sons, New York (1994)
12. Bishop C.: Novelty Detection and Neural Network Validation. In: Proceedings of IEE Conference on Vision and Image Signal Processing (1994) 217-222
13. Knorr, E., Ng, R., Tucakov, V.: Distance-based Outliers: Algorithms and Applications. VLDB Journal 8(3) (2000) 237-253
14. Lee, H., Cho, S.: SOM-based Novelty Detection Using Novel Data. Lecture Notes in Computer Science (LNCS 3578). Springer-Verlag (2005) 359-366
15. Golarelli, M., Maio, D., Maltoni, D.: On the Error-Reject Trade-off in Biometric Verification Systems. IEEE Transactions on Pattern Analysis and Machine Intelligence 19(7) (1997) 786-796

Illegal Intrusion Detection Based on Hidden Information Database[1]

Huizhang Shen, Jidi Zhao, and Huanchen Wang

Institute of System Engineering, Shanghai Jiao Tong University, 200052 Shanghai, China
{hzshen, judyzhao33}@sjtu.edu.cn

Abstract. The national information security mainly depends on the security of database. Current database management system provides some security control mechanisms to ensure the data security such as access control and password protection. However, these mechanisms are not sufficient to ensure database security. This research paper presents a pinion-rack encryption/decryption model (P-R model) and its implementation issues using the field of a record from a database as the basic encryption granularity. Based on the P-R model, this paper also presents a technique of hiding concomitant information in the information system, which can be used to detect the intrusion from illegal users. The P-R model can enhance the ability to identify attacks, accelerate encryption/decryption speed, reduce response time and improve real-time efficiency by cutting the length of keys and minimizing the number of necessary encryption operations. This research paper also proposes a "keeping separately and triggering simultaneously" key management strategy to reduce the possibility of modifying sensitive data purposely by legal users.

1 Introduction

National or international information security is becoming one of the most urgent challenges in database encryption research. When looking at a typical activity of a web user and trace the data flow, there are usually two security issues to be addressed. One is client/server communication: When a client user submits her/his personal data, maybe confidential information, through her/his web browser, the data should remain confidential on its way to the web server, the application server, and the backend DB server. The other is secure data storage and access: When the confidential data arrive at the DB server, the data should be stored in such a way that only people with proper authorization can access them.

The secure transmission of data is well studied and well supported in today's Internet market. Confidential information is well protected on its way from a web browser to a web server via an SSL connection [2]. However, once the data arrive at the backend, there is no sufficient support in storing and processing them in a secure way since typical database management system (DBMS) merely protects stored data through access control mechanisms. Cryptology has become a subject of open research since the early 70's. With the enormous popularity of web-hosting

---

[1] This research has been supported by NSFC(70450001).

applications, incorporating cryptographic support into modern database products has become an increasingly important topic [4]. Somewhat surprisingly, despite its fascinating potentials, it seems to be a fairly recent development among industry database providers and is rarely used by the best selling hardware and software products except its very trivial mechanisms like password protection and access control [1][3][6].

2 Database Access Control and Encryption

The most popular access control policies currently used are Mandatory Access Control(MAC), DAC, RBAC, et al. Access control in database security has been well studied and a nice survey of these policies and their application can be found in [5]. Although access control has proven to be useful in today's databases, it is far from sufficient to secure the database because these policies are inoperative against most insider attacks and particularly against database administrator attacks. An Intruder who usurps successfully the identity of an Insider or an Administrator, that is, bypasses the DBMS access controls are also threatening the data confidentiality. All these kinds of attackers will be considered in the rest of the paper. The model in this paper is dedicated to cast off such attacker actions.

Unlike file encryption, database encryption can be performed at various levels of granularity. The apparent encryption granularity choices are (1) table granularity, each table is encrypted separately, (2) page granularity, a smaller achievable granularity, each page is encrypted separately, a typical page in SQL Server is 8 Kbytes and might contain one or multiple records, (3) record granularity, each record in a table is encrypted separately, and (4) field granularity, the smallest achievable granularity based on the field of a record.

The main challenge in database security from a cryptographic view is to introduce security functionality without incurring too much performance overhead, which rests mainly on the choice of appropriate encryption granularity, encryption/decryption functions, reasonable key length and key numbers.

3 Pinion-Rack Encryption/Decryption Model (P-R Model)

We present a database encryption model using the field of a record from a database as the basic encryption granularity and its implementation. The model is referred to as the pinion-rack encryption and decryption model (P-R Model) in terms of the pinion and rack transmission principle. Let us first introduce some definitions to facilitate subsequent discussions.

- Encryption pinion, each tooth of the encryption pinion corresponds to an encryption algorithm and a key.
- Decryption pinion, each tooth of the decryption pinion corresponds to a decryption algorithm and a key.
- Plaintext rack, the database record(s) in plain text are referred to as plaintext rack, each tooth of the plaintext rack corresponds to a plain text field.

– Ciphertext rack, the database record(s) in cipher format are referred to as ciphertext rack, each tooth of the ciphertext rack corresponds to a cyphertext field, or the result of encrypting a plain text field.

During the encryption process, the encryption pinion starts from the beginning position of the plaintext rack and rotates clockwise to the end of the plaintext rack. A tooth in the plain text rack meshes with a tooth from the encryption pinion, and generates the output of a tooth of the cipher rack, as show in Fig. 1. In other words, a plaintext rack becomes a ciphertext rack after the mesh process.

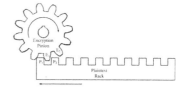

Fig. 1. Pinion-rack encryption process

With this encryption process, the encrypted data in the database enjoys the following advantages: (1) Different data items are encrypted with different encryption algorithms and different keys. (2) The disclosure of a specific encryption algorithm can not help the inference of other encryption algorithms. (3) A key can not inferred from other keys.

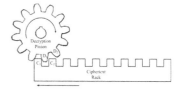

Fig. 2. Pinion-rack decryption process

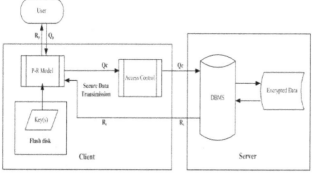

Fig. 3. System architecture based on P-R model and Store Media

Similarly, in the decryption process, the decryption pinion starts from the beginning position of the ciphertext rack and rotates clockwise to the end of the ciphertext rack. A tooth in the cipher text rack meshes with a tooth from the decryption pinion with the output of a tooth of the plain rack, as show in Fig. 2.

We assume a client-server scenario to illustrate the system architecture based on P-R model, as shown in Fig. 3. The client has a combination of sensitive and non-sensitive data stored in a database at the server, with the sensitive data stored in encrypted form. Each client's added responsibility is to protect its sensitive data, i.e., to ensure its confidentiality and prevent unauthorized access. This is accomplished through insulating data encryption, query evaluation and access right in the client components. Basic database operations (insertion, deletion, and update) with the model are implemented as follows. During insertion and update, teeth of the inserting or updated plaintext record (the plain text rack) meshes with teeth of the encryption pinion with the output of the ciphertext record (the cipher rack), and then the ciphertext record is inserted into a corresponding page in the database. Implementation of deletion operations is straight-forward.

When the client user submits a standard SQL form query Q_p, the query is first rewritten into an "encrypted SQL form" Q_c by the P-R model component in the client with keys information from the storage media if there is a sensitive data field. All variables and constants are encrypted $Q_c=E(Q_p, K)$. Then the access control component in the client will authenticate the user's access rights. If the query Q_c doesn't pass the access control, it will be denied instead of being sent to the server. The encrypted form Q_c of a well-formed SQL query is still a well formed SQL query. In the next step, the encrypted result R_c is sent back to the main memory in the client by P-R model. Finally, once decrypted, the records participating in the final result R_p are sent to the terminal users.

4 Computational Complexity and Efficiency of P-R Model

Suppose there are N teeth in the pinion, both the number of the teeth in the encryption pinion and the number of the teeth in the decryption pinion are N. Let R be the number of teeth on the rack, that is, the fields in the database record. Apparently, the number of teeth on the plaintext rack equals the number of teeth on the corresponding cipher text rack.

The number of algorithms (n) in the pinion should definitely satisfies the constraint $1<n\leq N$. If $n=1$, which means only one algorithm is in the pinion, there is no difference between P-R model and traditional encryption method and needs not to discuss its complexity. If $n>N$, the number of algorithms exceeds the teeth in the pinion and some of the algorithms can never be applied in the pinion, discussion of this situation is meaningless.

Let m be the number of the keys, the computational complexity of decrypting P-R model is analyzed as follows:

(1)$n=N=m$, the number of different algorithms equals the pinion teeth and the keys. Let O denotes the upper bound on the running time of additional decryption operations for the attackers besides the decryption of the key in traditional encryption method.

When R mod $N=0$, that is, the length of the rack is a multiple of the length of the pinion, each column in the database has the same algorithm and the same key after the encryption operation. Thus, the number of additional decryption operations is $O((N!)^2)$, the product of the permutation of the number of the algorithms and the permutation of the number of the keys,

When R mod $N\neq0$, the length of the rack is not a multiple of the length of the pinion, the algorithm and the key for the decryption of a field in the database after the encryption operation has no apparent rules to follow up. Thus, the number of additional decryption operations is $O((N!)^3)$.

(2)$n=m<N$, the number of different algorithms equals the number of keys but is less than the number of the teeth in the pinion. In this situation, the additional decryption operations for the permutation of the pinion incur further additional decryption operations than in above situations.

If record level encryption is used and only one out of the several attributes needs to be kept confidential, a considerable amount of computational overload would be incurred due to un-necessary encryption and decryption of all other attributes. The encryption granularity in this paper is field level, thus it is feasible to separate sensitive from non-sensitive fields when encrypting. In this situation, the number of teeth in the encryption pinion equals the number of teeth in the decryption pinion (N) and the length of the rack (R). There is no corresponding encryption and decryption operation and keys for the non-sensitive teeth on the plaintext rack record, the plaintext is copied to the cipher text rack.

In traditional encryption methods, the security is usually ensured by improving the length of the keys. However, in P-R model, the security relies mainly on the number of the encryption pinion teeth and the rack teeth, not merely on the algorithms and the key length. Therefore, the model can speed up the encryption and decryption process through reducing the length of the keys and predigesting the complexity of the encryption/decryption algorithms, so as to shorten the system response time.

5 Implementation of Hidden Information and Key Management

A detection file, which corresponds to a specific business database file and is created to store the operation information, the characteristics of legal users' behavior, the sensitive data needing special monitor, and other information, is under the control of security administers. When the specific business database file is operated, the users' behavior is synchronously recorded in the detection file. Neither illegal users nor legal users can have access to the content of the detection file stored in the application system, that's the reason why we use the term of hidden information. Only the security administers have the privilege of operating the detection file. In order to improve the security of the detection file, another pair of pinion and rack, *coaxial* with the above pair for encrypting the business database file, is used to encrypt the detection file. Here the word "*coaxial*" means to realize the synchronous operations of both the business databases file and the detection file.

The prescribed hidden information is input by legal users. It demands users to input some specific authentication information through a non-interactive way, which means to ask users to input authentication information at certain steps instead of inputting the accounts and passwords with dialogue windows at the beginning of application. The content of authentication information is not displayed on the screen. Where, when, what to input are the arrangement illegal users have no idea of. When illegal users do not input the authentication information as expected, they will feel nothing strange, for the system gives no response, and they can continue their operations. The detection procedure will then affirm that the databases are operated by the illegal users for not receiving the authentication information. In precondition of no response to illegal users, it will send alert to security administers, record all the operation in detection file and accept the operation of illegal users.

Assume there are six sub-keys in the system kept by six different key holders. Later, when it becomes necessary to browse or update the data, these six keys should be gathered and used together to pass the system authentication before any data can be got or modified. These keys may be stored on a storage media such as a smart card or flash disk. The storage of the keys should satisfy the following constraints: The keys stored in a smart card or flash disk in specific file format can not be copied or read with conventional methods even by the key holders. The application system reads the keys directly from the key storage media, the smart card or flash disk. The key holders should use the storage media simultaneously to pass the system authentication before any data can be accessed. Such a mechanism is referred to as the "keeping separately and triggering simultaneously" strategy.

6 Conclusions

This paper presents a P-R model, this model can speed up the encryption and decryption process through reducing the length of the key and predigesting the complexity of the encryption or decryption function. Because the operation and storage of detection file is concealed from the illegal users, especially the prescribed hidden information, the alert will be given in the condition that the illegal users have no sense of being detected. The strategy of key management prevents legal inner users from modifying the confidential data on purpose.

References

[1] Biskup J and Bleumer G. "Cryptographic protection of health information: cost and benefit". http://www.scholar.google.com/url?sa=U&q=http://www.semper.org/sirene/people/gerrit/ papers/protofhealthinfo.pdf. July 2005.
[2] Freier A., Karlton P., and Kocher P. "The SSL Protocol Version 3.0", Internet-Draft. November 1996.
[3] IBM Data Encryption for IMS and DB2 Databases, Version 1.1. http://www-306.ibm.com/ software/data/db2imstools/html/ibmdataencryp.html. 2005.
[4] Iyer B., Mehrotra S., Mykletun E., Tsudik G., Wu Y.H. "A framework for efficient storage security in RDBMS". ADVANCES IN DATABASE TECHNOLOGY - EDBT 2004, PROCEEDINGS, 2004, 2992, pp. 147-164.
[5] Jeong M.A., Kim J.J., Won Y.W. "A flexible database security system using multiple access control policies". DATABASE AND EXPERT SYSTEMS APPLICATIONS, PROCEEDINGS, 2736, pp. 876-885, 2003.
[6] Oracle Corporation: Database Encryption in Oracle9i. oracle.com/deploy/security/ oracle9i

Defender Personality Traits

Tara Whalen and Carrie Gates

Faculty of Computer Science,
Dalhousie University,
Halifax, NS, B3H 1W5, Canada
{whalen, gates}@cs.dal.ca

Abstract. The security community has used psychological research on attacker personalities, but little work has been done to investigate the personalities of the defenders. We surveyed 43 security professionals using a Five Factor Model-based test to reveal common dominant traits. We found that our sampled population demonstrated that they were highly dutiful, achievement-striving, and cautious; in addition, they were high in morality and cooperation, but low in imagination. We conclude that many of these characteristics are appropriate for security professionals, although the low scores in the "openness to experience" domain may indicate difficulties in devising new security defense methods and in anticipating new forms of attack. This potentially leaves large organizations and nation-states vulnerable to attacks.

1 Introduction

Within the security community, psychological research has traditionally been directed towards attackers: for example, the psychology underlying insider threats [8] or criminal hacker behavior[7]. However, another piece of the overall picture is the psychology of the defender who must guard against these threats. It is useful to understand how personality traits influence the effectiveness of security defenders. This in turn might indicate where there may be weaknesses in our defence strategies. In fact, Greenwald *et al.* noted that profiling defenders might be "the most promising solution to the non-acceptance factor: a sensation-seeker is a risk taker, so he/she will not buy an InfoSec software package...."[3].

We present the results from a study of security professionals using the Five Factor Model. This is a continuation of a previous study [1] that used the Myers-Briggs Type Indicator®(MBTI)[1], using a testing instrument that has been more widely adopted in the psychology community than the MBTI. Section 2 describes the Five Factor Model. Section 3 presents our experimental methodology and results while Section 4 provides some concluding analysis.

---

[1] Myers-Briggs Type Indicator and MBTI are registered trademarks of Consulting Psychologists Press, Inc.

H. Chen et al. (Eds.): WISI 2006, LNCS 3917, pp. 85–90, 2006.
© Springer-Verlag Berlin Heidelberg 2006

2   The Five Factor Model

A dominant taxonomy within current personality research is the Five Factor Model (FFM), closely related to the "Big 5" model. Both of these models use five basic domains, containing subfactors (or "facets") that make up each category. The five domains have slightly different names under the two models, but are essentially quite similar. FFM uses the "OCEAN" domains: Openness to experience, Conscientiousness, Extraversion, Agreeableness, and Neuroticism [2]. A person will have different levels of each trait, which are compared to the rest of the population; for example, a person's test results may show that he is less extraverted than the average test subject, but more open to experience. The five FFM domains are described in detail below; the facets are from the International Personality Item Pool Representation of the NEO-PI-R (IPIP-NEO), which was the FFM test used in this study[2].

Openness to Experience: this domain demonstrates a person's comfort with new ideas, abstractions, and imagination. The facets of Openness are emotionality, artistic interests, imagination, adventurousness, liberalism, and intellect. (Note that intellect does not mean intelligence; rather, it refers to enjoyment of playing with ideas rather than with concrete people or things.)

Conscientiousness: this domain deals with impulse control and spontaneity. The facets of Conscientiousness are self-efficacy, orderliness, dutifulness, achievement-striving, self-discipline, and cautiousness.

Extraversion: this domain describes the degree of engagement with the external world. The facets of Extraversion are friendliness, gregariousness, assertiveness, activity level, excitement-seeking, and cheerfulness.

Agreeableness: this domain is focused on how much people value getting along with others. The facets of Agreeableness are trust, morality, altruism, cooperation modesty, and sympathy. (Note that morality in this context does not refer to one's stance on issues of social significance, such as euthanasia, but rather indicate characteristics such as sincerity and lack of guardedness about telling the trust.)

Neuroticism: this domain focuses on the emotional reactions of an individual to a given situation. The facets of neuroticism are anxiety, anger, depression, self-consciousness, immoderation, and vulnerability.

A test subject who takes a Five Factor Model test (such as the IPIP-NEO) is presented with a series of questions to determine the level of a particular facet within each of the five domains. The score is based on a continuum, with subject scores falling along a normal distribution. Approximately half of the questions are keyed positively (towards the high end of the scale) and the other half, negatively; this provides some balance so that the responses are not biased toward one type of response. A person is evaluated in terms of an overall population, giving a comparative score expressed as a percentile.

3 Method

3.1 Sampling Procedure

We conducted a survey of security professionals [9] in order to determine their personality characteristics using the IPIP (International Personality Item Pool) NEO [2][4]. This tool is based on the Five Factor Model, which is widely accepted in mainstream personality psychology [6]. We use a modified version of this test, developed by Dr. Johnson [5]. This version consists of 120 questions about personality traits, which subjects are asked to rate on a 5-point Likert scale from very inaccurate to very accurate. The answers are used to determine scores on 30 facets of personality, which are aggregated into the five broad domains. This particular form of the IPIP NEO has been tested against more than 20,000 respondents to ensure that it has an acceptable measurement reliability.

The on-line questionnaire was converted to a paper format and disseminated with the registration packets at the Annual Computer Security Applications Conference (ACSAC), held in December 2004. There were 177 attendees at this conference, 43 of whom returned completed survey questionnaires, providing a response rate of 24.3%. The attendees at this conference cover a broad spectrum of security professionals, including both researchers and practitioners.

3.2 Analysis

There were 43 responses to the survey: 31 men (72%), ten women (23%) and two people who did not provide their sex. Some questionnaires were either missing results for one or more questions, or had some ambiguous answers (e.g., two responses checked for a single question). In order to include these responses, we determined the personality domain for the missing or ambiguous questions and then removed the results for this user for those domains from further consideration. This left us with $N = 34$ for extraversion, $N = 35$ for neuroticism and openness, $N = 37$ for conscientiousness and $N = 39$ for agreeableness. We calculated percentiles using sex as the only discriminator, where these values were based on responses from 7743 men and 13,524 women [5].

We grouped the percentile scores for each participant into low, medium and high categories, where low indicates that the respondent was below the 30th percentile, high indicates the respondent was above the 70th percentile, with the remainder being the medium. The results from dividing the scores in this manner are presented in Table 1.

We performed a χ^2 test for significance with two degrees of freedom, comparing our actual results for each domain with the expected results given a uniform random distribution. We assume that the expected result fits a uniform random distribution because we are using percentiles, which is a strict ranking.

We examined each domain independently to determine if our respondents differ from the expected values, finding significant differences across two domains. Respondents to our study had unusually high values for conscientiousness ($p = 0.001588$) and unusually low values for openness ($p = 0.01771$).

Table 1. The distribution of results among low, medium and high scores for the five domains and each of their facets

Domain and Facets	Low	Medium	High	Domain and Facets	Low	Medium	High
Extraversion	13	14	7	Neuroticism	14	13	8
Friendliness	12	11	11	Anxiety	11	12	12
Gregariousness	12	15	7	Anger	16	11	8
Assertiveness	4	21	9	Depression	14	13	8
Activity Level	4	13	17	Self-Consciousness	10	16	9
Excitement-Seeking	22	10	2	Immoderation	8	18	9
Cheerfulness	11	13	10	Vulnerability	11	17	7
Agreeableness	5	21	13	Openness to Experience	18	11	6
Trust	6	20	13	Imagination	23	10	2
Morality	4	13	22	Artistic Interests	12	17	6
Altruism	6	22	11	Emotionality	14	14	7
Cooperation	3	15	21	Adventurousness	15	11	9
Modesty	6	20	13	Intellect	8	19	8
Sympathy	12	15	12	Liberalism	8	10	17
Conscientiousness	1	20	16				
Self-Efficacy	8	20	9				
Orderliness	11	12	14				
Dutifulness	3	19	15				
Achievement-Striving	3	17	17				
Self-Discipline	7	17	13				
Cautiousness	2	17	18				

Additionally, four of the five domains had at least one facet that showed a significant deviance from a uniform distribution. We start with the two domains that demonstrated significance: conscientiousness and openness. In the domain of conscientiousness, respondents demonstrated significance across three different facets. Unusually high percentiles were found for dutifulness ($p = 0.01618$), achievement-striving ($p = 0.009718$) and cautiousness ($p = 0.002516$). Thus, as a group, our respondents demonstrate that they have a strong sense of duty and obligation, that they work hard and strive towards excellence, and that they take time before making decisions.

In terms of openness, our respondents demonstrate significance on the facet of imagination. Our results show that the survey respondents have a *very* low score for imagination, with $p = 0.00000973$. This implies that our respondents are very much more oriented towards facts rather than fantasy. Additionally, our responses show a strong tendency towards liberalism, although it is not significant ($p = 0.05136$), where this implies that our respondents tend to challenge authority and traditional values. The low p-value here suggests that a larger sample size might indicate if this is truly a significant trait.

Respondents also exhibited significance on two facets in the agreeableness domain. The percentile scores for morality were unusually high ($p = 0.0006445$), indicating that the respondents tended to be very sincere and straight-forward, demonstrating little need for pretense. Respondents also scored highly for co-operation ($p = 0.0009478$), indicating a high willingness to compromise and a desire to avoid confrontations.

Interestingly, while the percentile distribution for extraversion exhibited no significance, there were three facets within extraversion where there was signifi-cance. These facets were assertiveness ($p = 0.02369$), activity level ($p = 0.01526$) and excitement seeking ($p = 0.00002304$). Respondents showed an unusually high activity level, indicating a busy, fast-paced lifestyle and involvement in a large number of activities. On the opposite extreme, respondents also demonstrated unusually low scores for excitement-seeking, indicating that they do not like commotion and do not tend to be thrill-seeking. The third facet, assertiveness, indicates a person's comfort with speaking out and taking charge. What is in-teresting about this facet is that respondents scored consistently in the middle range, whereas all other facets that were significance exhibited extremes (e.g. unusually high or unusually low scores). Assertiveness is the only facet where respondents were unusually average!

4   Concluding Remarks

Our Five Factor Method analysis of security professionals revealed some in-teresting dominant personality traits. In particular, participants scored high in the conscientiousness domain, and low in the openness domain. Having highly-conscientious defenders appears to be beneficial, as it indicates caution, a ten-dency to plan, and thoroughness. However, it may also be the case the security professionals may not respond quickly in time critical situations such as when an intrusion has occurred. The low score in the openness to experience domain could indicate rigidity of thought, although the questionnaire focuses mainly on artistic sensibilities rather than general acceptance of unusual ideas. However, this aspect is generally high in professors and researchers, which may indicate that security professionals may not be inventive in creating new security mech-anisms. However, it is interesting to note that "research has shown that closed thinking is related to superior job performance in police work." [5] Given that computer security and police work could be considered to be related, this may provide some explanation of the low scores on this particular domain.

Security professionals also demonstrated significant deviances in some of the individual facets within each of the five domains. For example, respondents had a *very* low score for imagination, which is related to the low score on openness to new ideas. Respondents scored very highly on co-operation, which is unusual given that the field is inherently one of conflict, of defenders versus adversaries. The high level of co-operation might be a good trait, indicating the security professionals tend to work well together. Alternatively, it might reflect a weakness given the aversion to conflict. Security professionals also scored unusually high on the facet for activity level, indicating the preference for a busy life-style with the need to balance many activities. If security professionals have positions that mimic their personality preferences, then this could possibly result in the professional being subject to missing important security information due simply to not having the time or inclination to focus on any one particular area.

One additional finding is that the majority of our respondents were not excitement seeking (p = 0.00002304); this indicates a risk-averse population. Again, this may be desirable in a security group: one is attempting to reduce the risk and consequences of a security breach. However, it may also signify that defenders take conservative approaches when they tackle a problem, fearing a negative outcome. It may be necessary to create organizational structures where "contained failure" is supported, so that experimental approaches can be developed without the possibility of actual system damage.

Acknowledgments

The authors would like to thank Dr. John A. Johnson for providing his IPIP-NEO tool and personality statistics, all of the participants from ACSAC 2004 who filled out the personality form, and Josh McNutt for assistance with statistical analysis. The authors gratefully acknowledge the support of the IBM Toronto Centre for Advanced Studies and the Natural Sciences and Engineering Research Council of Canada (NSERC).

References

1. C. Gates and T. Whalen. Profiling the defenders. In *Proceedings of the 2004 New Security Paradigms Workshop*, pages 107–114, Nova Scotia, Canada. 20-23 September 2004.
2. L. Goldberg. A broad-bandwidth, public domain, personality inventory measuring the lower-level facets of several five-factor models. In I. Mervielde, I. Deary, F. D. Fruyt, and F. Ostendorf, editors, *Personality Psychology in Europe*, volume 7, pages 7–28, Tilburg, The Netherlands, 1999. Tilburg University Press.
3. S. J. Greenwald, K. G. Olthoff, V. Raskin, and W. Ruch. The user non-acceptance paradigm: Infosec's dirty little secret. In *Proceedings of the 2004 New Security Paradigms Workshop*, pages 35–43, Nova Scotia, Canada. 20-23 September 2004.
4. International Personality Item Pool. A scientific collaboratory for the development of advanced measures of personality traits and other individual differences. http://ipip.ori.org/, 2001. Last visited: 1 June 2005.
5. J. A. Johnson. IPIP-NEO narrative report. http://www.personal.psu.edu/faculty/j/5/j5j/IPIP/shortipipneo3.cgi, 2005. Last visited: 1 June 2005.
6. R. R. McCrae and P. T. C. Jr. Reinterpretting the Myers-Briggs Type Indicator from the perspective of the Five-Factor model of personality. *Journal of Personality*, 57(1):17–40, 1989.
7. M. Rogers. *A Social Learning Theory and Moral Disengagment Analysis of Criminal Computer Behavior: An Exploratory Study*. PhD thesis, University of Manitoba, 2001.
8. E. Shaw, K. Ruby, and J. Post. The insider threat to information systems: The psychology of the dangerous insider. *Security Awareness Bulletin*, 2-98:1–10, 1998.
9. T. Whalen and C. Gates. Defender Personality Traits. Technical Report 2006-01, Faculty of Computer Science, Dalhousie University, Halifax, NS, 2006.

Mining Criminal Databases to Finding Investigation Clues—By Example of Stolen Automobiles Database

Patrick S. Chen[1], K.C. Chang[2], Tai-Ping Hsing[3], and Shihchieh Chou[4]

[1] Dept of Information Management, Tatung University, No.40, ChungShan North Road, 3rd Section, Taipei City 10452, Taiwan, R.O.C.
chenps@ttu.edu.tw
[2] Information Center, National Police Agency, No. 7, Jhongshiao East Road, 1st Section, Taipei City 10058, Taiwan, R.O.C.
ckco@npa.gov.tw
[3] Dept of Information Management, National Central University, No.300, Jhongda Road, Jhongli City, Taoyuan County 32001, Taiwan, R.O.C.
92443004@cc.ncu.edu.tw
[4] Dept of Information Management, National Central University, No.300, Jhongda Road, Jhongli City, Taoyuan County 32001, Taiwan, R.O.C.
scchou@mgt.ncu.edu.tw

Abstract. While businesses have been extensively using data mining to pursue everlasting prosperity, we seldom consider this technique in public affairs. The government holds a large quantity of data that are records of official operations or private information of the people. These data can be used for increasing benefits of the people or enhancing the efficiency of governmental operations. In this paper we will apply this technique to the data of stolen automobiles to explore the unknown knowledge hidden in the data and provide this knowledge to transportation, insurance as well as law enforcement for decision supports. The data we use are abstracted from 378 thousand records of stolen automobiles in the past eleven years in Taiwan. After constructing a data warehouse, we apply the technique of classification, association rule, prediction, data generalization and summarization-based characterization to discover new knowledge. Our results include the understanding of automotive theft, possibility of finding stolen automobiles, intrigue in theft claims, etc. The knowledge we acquired is useful in decision support, showing the applicability of data mining in public affairs. The experience we gathered in this study would help the use of this technique in other public sectors. Along with the research results, we suggest the law enforcement to consider data mining as a new means to investigate criminal cases, to set up a team of criminal data analysis, to launch a new program to crack down automotive thefts, and to improve the quality of criminal data management.

1 Introduction

Data mining, a newly developed technology in the past few years, help us analyze historical data in order to discover useful knowledge. Businesses accumulate a large quantity of data from their daily operations. These data often contain implicit knowledge or unveiled information that is helpful in decision-making. While businesses

H. Chen et al. (Eds.): WISI 2006, LNCS 3917, pp. 91–102, 2006.

have already found a large variety of applications of data mining, most governmental departments, that hold a lot of critical data, have not fully recognized its value. The same situation exists at some specialized organizations such as law enforcement agencies in Taiwan. The law enforcement agencies have collected large amounts of data from criminal cases and incidents in the past, these data are mostly used through database queries, but they are not available for higher level processing and applications. Addressing the conversion of information to useful and easily understandable knowledge is a powerful aspect of data mining that has so far been missing from most law enforcement information system.

This research is made as one of the first applications of data mining on law enforcement in Taiwan. We noticed that automotive theft has been the most frequently happening crime. According to the experience of criminal investigators, the *modus operandi* of automotive theft can be identified in which many criminals commit their crimes in a fixed manner and using similar technique. They often develop networks in which they form groups or teams to carry out illegal activities. This indicates we are able to develop data mining tools to identify behavioral patterns of automotive theft and, simultaneously, the law enforcement is able to find effective solutions to prevent those crimes in advance.

The data we used in this research is a collection of 378 thousand records of auto thefts[1]. They were collected in the time span from January 1991 to December 2001.

The rest of the paper is organized as follows: In Section 2, we review related literatures and works. In Section 3, we describe our methodology for this research. In Section 4, we present the results of data mining on criminal data for stolen automobiles. In Section 5, we discuss the implications of this research and future research directions.

2 Literature Review

At first, we review the related works of automotive theft. The most famous theories about the automotive theft are social disorganization theory and routine activity theory. Secondly, we review related works about intelligence analysis and data mining for criminal data. We want to know to what extent intelligence analysis and data mining being developed for law enforcement, and try to find where to locate our research in the related field.

2.1 Related Researches on Automotive Theft

It is widely recognized that auto theft represents a major crime problem in Taiwan. In 2004, estimated 217 thousand automobiles are stolen, 65 percent of the total theft cases[2]. The dark figure, arising from the unwillingness of the victims to report to the police, is believed to be higher than the number of reported cases [1].

Historically, the predominant theory of the spatial location of crime was the social disorganization theory. Three exogenous factors—poverty, racial and ethnic

---

[1] We thank for the support from National Police Agency in Taiwan for providing the data for research purpose under strict secrecy protection regulations.

[2] http://www.npa.gov.tw accessed in October, 2005.

heterogeneity, and residential mobility—are hypothesized to result in a withdrawal in community social control activities and an increase in delinquent and criminal activities, including auto theft [2][3]. The application of social disorganization theory to auto theft is especially interesting because contrary to other street crimes, auto theft has long been believed to be concentrated among the socially advantaged and thus seems to negate the hypothesis of social disorganization theory. Sanders [4] typified what has commonly been believed where he wrote, "Automobile theft is generally committed by white middle-class youths in groups of two or more, largely for 'kicks' [5][6]. The high recovery rate of stolen automobiles also suggests that most theft occurs for recreational and short-term use rather than for profit [7].

The social disorganization theory does not seem to explain the phenomenon of the auto theft in Taiwan, but it can apply to the motorcycle theft. Because personal income in American is much higher than that in Taiwan and the price of the automobile in Taiwan is much higher than that in US. The automobiles stolen in Taiwan are often for profit.

Routine activity theory, on the other hand, claims that crimes occur where there are attractive targets (opportunities), motivated offenders, and an absence of capable guardianship. Previous work – rational choice approach – has shown the impact of weak guardianship and ample opportunity [2][3]. In contrast with social disorganization theory, research on routine activity theory assumes that crime is engaged as a rational choice in which offenders attempt to maximize their gains and minimize their losses [8]. Routine activity theory also proposes that crime will occur where daily activities create the most numerous opportunities for the most profitable crime and the least chances of detection or arrest.

According to the previous empirical study of the auto theft in Taiwan, in most circumstance, routine activity theory can explain the reason why automobiles are stolen. In this research, we utilize this theory in establishing mining goals and choosing relevant features of classification and prediction. In addition, we hope to confirm this theory in the mining results.

2.2 Intelligence Analysis and Data Mining for Criminal Data

Law enforcement agencies around the world have been taking advantages of information technologies to investigate crimes. Among them, database technologies, management information systems, and expert systems have been used in data analysis. Many technologies use neural networks to solve problems by developing associations between information objects and being trained to solve problems by comparing known objects with unknown objects [9]. The Timeline Analysis System (TAS) utilizes visualization and time analysis to help analysts who visually examine large amounts of information by illustrating cause-and–effect relationships. This system graphically depicts relations found in the data, resulting in trends or patterns [10]. Expert systems that use rule-based information have also been developed to assist in knowledge-intensive active [11][12]. For instance, COPLINK has been developed at the University of Arizona's Artificial Intelligence Lab in collaboration with the

Tucson Police Department (TPD) and the Phoenix Police Department (PPD), and it is to develop intelligence and data mining technologies for capturing, accessing, analyzing, visualizing, and sharing law enforcement-related information in social and organizational contexts [13]. In Taiwan, Criminal Police Bureau has set up a knowledge base system for criminal cases in 2002, and it is a knowledge management system with intelligence queries and full-text mining for case narratives. These systems attempt to utilize all kinds of intelligence analysis and data mining tools to improve information retrieval and knowledge finding capabilities; these efforts aim to investigate tasks efficiently for law enforcement.

3 Methodology

3.1 Research Process

This research relies on the following steps to implement the whole data mining process:

- **Establishment of the Mining Goals.** We establish the mining goals and directions according to routine activity theory and the needs of practical investigation of the law enforcement.
- **Data Load and Data Transfer.** The data used in this research is a collection of 378 thousand records of auto thefts that cover a ten-year span from January 1991 to December 2001. They are collected and stored in a NEC database system, a dedicated system developed twenty years ago, unable to support all kinds of modern data mining tools. We have to export the original data to an open relational database system, where we export these data into text files, and then load to Sybase database management system. At the same time we transfer the data attributes.
- **Creation of Relational Database and Data Warehouse.** After the original data has been transferred into Sybase relational database and saved in table format, we rebuild the relations among tables. In addition, we create multiple dimensions for auto theft data to implement OLAP[3] analysis. The criteria used in the analysis are time, place, automotive type, automotive model, and so on.
- **Data Preparing and Preprocessing.** The following works include data filtering, attributes reduction, data cleaning, data integration, data transformation, and data reduction.
- **Data Mining Implementation.** This research uses various data mining techniques such as classification, association rule, prediction regression, generalization and summarization-based characterization to explore patterns of the auto thefts and discover knowledge to prevent related crimes. We make use of training data, test data and evaluation data to create and form best patterns or models.
- **Results Evaluation.** Finally, we have to evaluate the mining results upon domain knowledge of criminology.

---

[3] OLAP: On-Line Analysis and Processing.

3.2 Data Mining Techniques for Criminal Cases

We utilize classification, association rule, regression analysis, generalization and summarization to mine the stolen automobile data. The techniques used in this research are represented as follows:

- **Association Rule Mining.** The technique discovers interesting association or correlation relations among a large set of data items. A classical example is the market basket analysis, which runs against transactions database to find sets of items, or itemsets, that appear together in many transactions [14]. We use each label of each attribute as an item, and find association rules among items—for example, a item that represents a stolen automobile reported to the police within a week is frequently occurred with another item that represents a stolen automobile recovered, hence there is a association between the two items.
- **Classification.** The technique finds common properties among different automotive thefts and organizes them into predefined classes. We use it to decide which stolen automobiles could be recovered. However, the technique requires a predefined classification scheme. Classification also requires reasonably complete training and testing data because a high degree of missing data would limit prediction accuracy [15].
- **Prediction Regression.** The prediction of continuous values can be modeled by a statistical, called regression. The objective of regression analysis is to determine the best model that can relate output variables to input variables. More formally, regression analysis is the process of determining how a variable Y is related to one or more other variables X_1, X_2, X_3, ..., X_n [14]. We can apply this technique to find what independent variables (for example, make, model, and year for stolen automobile) can predict depend variable (for example, whether the case can be broken or not).
- **Data Generalization and Summarization-Based Characterization.** Data and objects often contain detailed information at primitive concept levels. It is useful if we summarize a large set of data and present it at a high conceptual [16]. For example, we can use some attribute-oriented induction approach or OLAP to summarize the top 10 models of automobile are frequently stolen in 2005, which can be very helpful for insurance and law enforcement managers.

4 Mining Results

The aim of this research is as follows: starting from case descriptions such as car type, car manufacturing year, case reporting date, etc. we try to find investigation clues to break the case or to recover the stolen automobile. With this purpose in mind, we present our mining results in this section.

4.1 Association Rule Analysis

With association rule analysis, when we set the minimum support 20 % and minimum confidence 90 %, we found a rule "car type='sedan'"——→"car category = 'small private car'" with support = 70.045% and confidence=97.376. This shows both attributes car type='sedans' and car category = 'small private automobile' are highly related to auto theft. We further analyze these cases and find that 72% of the stolen automobiles are sedans and 96% of the stolen automobiles are small private automobiles, leading to bias in association rule analysis. We will first exclude these two factors to search for other meaningful rules.

Association Between Reporting Date and Case Clearance. From previous empirical studies of the auto theft we learn that an auto theft had better been reported immediately on the day when it was stolen, since the case could be better cleared. Hence, we are going to discover the association between reporting date and case clearance to confirm this proposition.

As shown in Table 1, the association of same-day-reporting with case clearance has 48.796% support and 68.969% confidence. This is much higher than that of later-day-report followed by case clearance with support=18.827% and confidence=64.632%. This implies the earlier an auto theft could be reported, the more likely the case could be broken or the stolen automobile could be recovered.

Table 1. The association between reporting date and case clearance

Association Rule	Sup	Conf
Reported on the day when automobile was stolen → Case broken	**48.796**	**68.969**
Reported on the day when automobile was stolen → Case not broken	21.955	31.031
Reported some days after automobile was stolen → Case broken	**18.827**	**64.632**
Reported some days after automobile was stolen → Case not broken	10.422	35.632

Relation of Car Make and Loss Recovery. Because the proportion of any car make of the total stolen automobiles is not high, we may set minimum support at 7% and minimum confidence at 60%. As indicated in Table 2, this analysis will reflect which make of the lost cars could likely be recovered, but this also implies that the lost rate of four car makes is much higher than that of other makes. The four makes are native (manufactured or assembled in Taiwan), each of them having a large marketing share in Taiwan. Because those cars have a large demand of spare parts, they become the main targets of auto thieves.

Table 2. The association car make and loss recovery

Association Rule	Sup	Conf
Make='YULON MOTOR'⟶ lost automobile recovered	13.455	75.505
Make='CHINA MOTOR' ⟶ lost automobile recovered	11.467	74.453
Make='FORD MOTOR'⟶ lost automobile recovered	12.03	70.075
Make='SANYANG MOTOR' ⟶ lost automobile recovered	7.612	64.131

Association of Car Make and Lost Car Not Recovered. When we set minimum support = 0.1% and minimum confidence = 50%, we can find which make of automobiles could not be recovered if the car is lost (ref. Table 3). Furthermore, we can

Table 3. The association of car make and lost car not recovered

Association Rule	Sup	Conf
Make='SAAB' ⟶ lost automobile not recovered	0.152	56.973
Make= 'VOLVO' ⟶ lost automobile not recovered	0.364	56.399
Make= 'SUZUKI' ⟶ lost automobile not recovered	0.397	54.685
Make= 'TOYOTA' ⟶ lost automobile not recovered	1.433	51.966
Make= 'CITROËN' ⟶ lost automobile not recovered	0.134	50.099

find 'TOYOTA' automobiles, that enjoy a big market share, have a higher lost rate and a lower recovered rate. It implies that there is a large demand of their spar parts. The stolen 'TOYOTA' automobiles are often disassembled for sale.

Association of Car Production Year and Loss Recovery. Here we set minimum support = 7% and minimum confidence = 50%, and try to find in which year a car was manufactured that could be found when it is lost. From Table 4 we learn that the older the stolen car was, the easier it could be recovered. This also implies that the older the car is, the lower its value. Since the auto thieves could gain little from the stolen cars, they probably steal them only for short-term use.

Table 4. The association of the car manufacturing year and loss recovered

Association Rule	Sup	Conf
Manufacturing year = 1994-1993 ⟶lost automobile recovered	12.954	77.895
Manufacturing year = before1992 ⟶ lost automobile recovered	20.76	75.156
Manufacturing year = 1996-1995 ⟶ lost automobile recovered	12.839	69.421
Manufacturing year = 1998-1997 ⟶ lost automobile recovered	12.708	59.213
Manufacturing year = 2000-1999 ⟶ lost automobile recovered	8.359	52.948

4.2 Decision Trees Analysis

This research uses decision trees to predict whether a stolen automobile could be recovered. We use the stolen automobile data set of 2001 year as training data to implement decision trees, where we use two classes as left nodes of decision tree: one is the stolen automobiles recovered, the other is the stolen automobile not recovered.

We use ARNAVAC method to find which attributes are highly related to the case of loss recovery in order to implement decision tree. Furthermore we find "the manufacturing year of the automobile" is highly related to the lost automobile recovered. In addition, we also rely on domain knowledge to add two attributes that are "category of the stolen automobile" and "the theft reporting on the very day". The first and second attributes can affect the profitability of the lost car according to the inference principles of routine activity theory, and the third attribute can affect the investigative progress and efficiency in law enforcement. We use the above-mentioned three attributes and the two predefined classes — the lost car recovered and not — to construct the decision tree. The tree generated has 6 levels, 15 non-leaf nodes and 45 leaves, and the total classification error is 32.32%. In addition, we also implement a trans-formation of a decision rules, for example, if the manufacturing year of the automo-bile < 2 years and category of the stolen automobile = 'the private passenger car' and the theft reporting on the very day = true then classification = 'the lost car recovered'.

The interpretation of Table 5 is as follows: The vertical dimension indicates the predicted outcome of a stolen automobile whether it could be recovered; the horizon-tal dimension indicates the real outcome. Furthermore, Class 'No' represents that a lost car could not be found, and Class 'Yes' represents a successful recovery. From Table 5 we learnt that there are 657 lost cars that were predicted not to be recovered and they are actually not recovered. There are 255,235 lost automobiles found as predicted. On the other hand, there are 121,759 lost automobiles that are mistakenly predicted to be recovered, but in vain 444 lost automobiles are predicted not to be found, but actually recovered. In addition, undefined cases are zero.

Table 5. The count of each category of decision tree for stolen automobile recovered

Predicated / Real	No	Yes	Undefined
No	657	121759	0
Yes	444	255235	0

4.3 Prediction

This research uses 3 attributes ("the manufacturing year of the automobile", "category of the stolen automobile", and "the theft reporting on the very day") in previous sec-tion as independent variables and "the lost car recovered and not" as dependent vari-able to implement linear regression analysis. By this technique, we want to develop a regression equation to predict dependent variable from independent variables, and realize which independent attributes is significantly related to the dependent variables. We produce prediction rules in Table 6.

Table 6. Prediction result and rule table for stolen automobile recovered

Prediction Result	IF the prediction rule (see below) > 0.4894 THEN the stolen automobile recovered ELSE the stolen automobile not recovered
Prediction rule	0.4894 < (0.619283 +**0.0615684*** ("the manufacturing year of the automobile") -**0.190913*if** (category = the private passenger car) -**0.18414*if** (category = the general business bus) +**0.0764537*if** (category = the business passenger car) -**0.380972*if** (category =the special business large truck) -**0.160599*if** (category = the private bus) +**0.0658527*if** ("the theft reporting on the very day")

Table 7. The Parameter of Prediction Analysis for stolen automobile recovered

Attribute name	coef.	std dev.	F-Ratio	part sum of sq
"the manufacturing year of the automobile"	0.06157	0.000519	**1.41E+04**	0.03321
If (category = the private passenger car)	-0.1909	0.01721	123	0.002516
If (category = the general business bus)	-0.1841	0.01934	90.64	0.0004543
If (category = the business passenger car)	0.07645	0.01803	17.98	0.002858
If (category = the special business large truck)	-0.381	0.02068	339.3	0.0008677
If (category = the private bus)	-0.1606	0.01874	73.41	0.0001841
If (the theft reporting on the very day)	0.06585	0.001643	**1606**	0.004057

If the above-mentioned value of the regression equation is greater than 0.4894, we are allowed to say that a stolen automobile could be recovered; else it is predicted not to be recovered. Total prediction error is 32.32%, and the percentage of undefined prediction cases is 0.01%, P-Value is zero ($<10^{-7}$), showing that explanatory capability of the model of regression equation is sound.

In addition, we analyze F-ratio, and find that two attributes including "the manufacturing year of the automobile" and "the theft reporting on the very day" have a significant impact on dependent variable. This is represented in Table 7.

4.4 Data Generalization and Summarization-Based Characterization

We have implemented Generalization and Summarization-Based Characterization and conduct OLAP to find meaningful knowledge and investigation clues.

Rate of Stolen Automobile Recovered and Time Interval from Theft Reporting Date to the Day it was Recovered. We summarize the total rate of stolen automobiles recovered and the time interval from the date of auto theft reported to the day

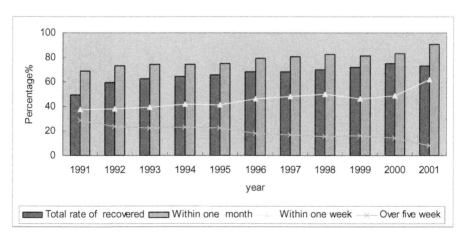

Fig. 1. Total Rate of stolen automobile recovered and time interval from theft reporting date to the day it was recovered

when it was recovered. The data are collected from 1991 to 2001 as shown in Fig. 1. Total recovery rate of stolen automobiles was 49.4% in 1991, it grew up to 73.30% in 2001. The highest was 74.91% in 2000. Furthermore, there was a growing trend year by year in terms of stolen car recovery. Similar tendency was found in the analysis in which a lost car was recovered in the first week and in the first month. For example, rate of cases cleared within a month was 68.68% in 1991, it grew up to 90.49% in 2001. In addition, rate of cases cleared within a week was 37.53% in 1991, it grew up to 61.72% in 2001. This shows the rate of stolen automobiles recovered was growing, and the needed time of a stolen automobile to be found was reduced.

Owners Whose Automobiles are Frequently Stolen. If an owner whose automobiles are frequently stolen, it might be a clue of crime. For example, when an auto rental company rents its car to a customer, the employee of the company could steal this automobile in order to cheat compensation from insurance companies.

We find an owner that has 126 automobiles stolen in the past ten years, an extreme case. In addition, there are 1268 cases in which each owner has more than 40 automobiles stolen. They occupy 0.34% of the total automobile thefts.

Analysis of the Make of the Stolen Automobiles. We analyze which make of automobiles are frequently stolen. This shows that the cars of YULON MOTOR, FORD LIO HO MOTOR, CHINA MOTOR and SANYANG MOTOR ranked the four most frequently stolen cars in the time span from 1991 to 2001, The case numbers of the automobile thefts from 1991 to 2001of the four auto companies as shown in Fig. 2.

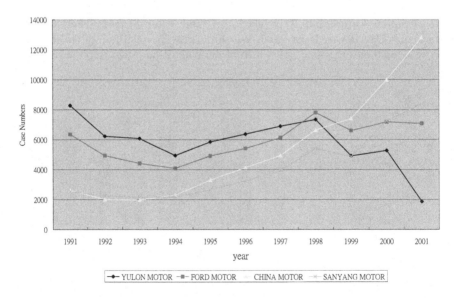

Fig. 2. An analysis of the makes of the automobiles stolen

5 Conclusion and Future Research Direction

In this study we use data mining technique including association rule, decision tree classification, prediction analysis, generalization and summarization-based characterization to mine the criminal data of auto thefts. It will assist law enforcement and its officers to find meaningful knowledge of auto thefts for assisting their investigation. The law enforcement can also adopted effective strategies to prevent auto thefts.

Our research results indicate which factors could be used to classify and predict whether an automobile theft is to be broken or not. In addition, we find these results confirm the previous empirical study of routine activity theory. An auto theft is linked to profit and risk, it helps us to determine the recovery possibility of the lost car. However, some important factors of routine activity theory cannot be examined because of the limitation of data resources. For example, we have not taken into account streetlamps and monitoring cameras deployed in the community. These data can help classify and predict the dependent variables more accurately, and produce more knowledge concerning auto thefts.

Our experience gained in this research project has other values because we are to use data mining techniques to build intelligent systems to mine other habitual crimes, for example, other kind of thefts, sexual abuses, frauds, arsons, gang offenses, drug trafficking, and cybercrime. Based on the above-mentioned results, we have suggested the law enforcement to consider data mining as a new means to investigate criminal cases, to set up a team of criminal data analysis and to launch a new program to crack down crimes

References

1. Coleman, C. and Moynihan, J., Understanding Crime Data, Milton Keynes: Open University Press (1996)
2. Barclay, P., Buckley, J., Brantingham, P. J., Brantingham, P. L., and Whinn-Yates, T., "Preventing Auto Theft in Suburban Vancouver Commuter Lots: Effects of a Bike Patrol." in Crime Prevention Studies, vol. 6, edited by Clarke, R., NY: Criminal Justice Press (1996) 133-62
3. Clarke, R.V., "Theoretical Background to Crime Prevention through Environmental Design (CPTED) and Situational Prevention," in Designing Out Crime: The Conference Papers, edited by Geason, S. and Wilson, P., Canberra: Australian Institute of Criminology (1989) 13-20
4. Sanders, W. B., Juvenile Delinquency, New York: Praeger (1976) 94
5. Chilton,R. J., "Middle Class Delinquency and Specific Offence Analysis." in Middle-Class Juvenile Delinquency, edited by Vaz, E. W., New York: Harper & Row (1967) 91-101
6. Schepses, E., "Boys Who Steal Cars." Federal Probation (1961) 56-62
7. Clarke, R. V. and Harris, P. M., "Auto Theft and Its Prevention," In Crime and Justice: A Review of Research, vol. 16, edited by Tonry, M., Chicago: University of Chicago Press (1992)
8. Massey, J. L., Krohn, M. D., and Bonati, L. M., "Property Crime and the Routine Activity of Individuals," Journal of Research in Crime and Delinquency, vol. 26 (1989) 378-400

9. Hauck, R. V. , and Chen, H., "Coplink: a case of intelligent analysis and knowledge management," In Proceeding of the 20th international conference on Information Systems (1999) 15-27
10. Pliant, L. "High-technology Solutions," The Police Chief, vol. 5, no. 38 (1996) 38-51
11. Bowen, J. E. "An Expert System for Police Investigators of Economic Crimes," Expert Systems with Applications, vol. 7, no. 2 (1994) 235-248
12. Brahan, J. W., Lam, K. P., Chan, H., and Leung, W. "AICAMS: Artificial Intelligence Crime Analysis and Management System," Knowledge-Based Systems, vol.11 (1998) 355-361
13. Atabakhsh, H., Schroeder, J. Chen, H., Chau, M., Xu, J., Zhang, J., and Bi, H., "COPLINK knowledge management for law enforcement: Text analysis, visualization and collaboration," National Conference on Digital Government, Los Angeles, CA (2001) 21–23
14. Kantardzic, M., Data Mining: Concepts, Models, Methods, and Algorithms, IEEE Press & John Wiley (2002)
15. Chen, H., Chung, W., Xu, J., Wang, G., and Chau, M., "Crime Data Mining: A General Framework and Some Examples," IEEE Computer Society (2004) 50-56
16. Han, J., and Kamber, M., Data Ming: Concepts and Techniques, Morgan Kaufmann Publishers (2001)

Country Corruption Analysis with Self Organizing Maps and Support Vector Machines

Johan Huysmans[1], David Martens[1], Bart Baesens[2,1],
Jan Vanthienen[1], and Tony Van Gestel[3,4]

[1] Department of Decision Sciences and Information Management,
Katholieke Universiteit Leuven, Naamsestraat 69, B-3000 Leuven, Belgium
[2] School of Management, University of Southampton, Southampton,
SO17 1BJ, United Kingdom
[3] Credit Risk Modelling, Dexia Group, Square Meeus 1, B-1000 Brussels, Belgium
[4] Department of Electrical Engineering, ESAT-SCD-SISTA,
Katholieke Universiteit Leuven, Kasteelpark Arenberg 10,
B-3001 Leuven (Heverlee), Belgium

Abstract. During recent years, the empirical research on corruption has grown considerably. Possible links between government corruption and terrorism have attracted an increasing interest in this research field. Most of the existing literature discusses the topic from a socio-economical perspective and only few studies tackle this research field from a data mining point of view. In this paper, we apply data mining techniques onto a cross-country database linking macro-economical variables to perceived levels of corruption. In the first part, self organizing maps are applied to study the interconnections between these variables. Afterwards, support vector machines are trained on part of the data and used to forecast corruption for other countries. Large deviations for specific countries between these models' predictions and the actual values can prove useful for further research. Finally, projection of the forecasts onto a self organizing map allows a detailed comparison between the different models' behavior.

1 Introduction

The amount of empirical research concerning corruption is impressive. An overview can be found in [1, 2]. Most of existing literature tries to find causal relations between some explanatory variable and the perceived level of corruption. For example, in [3] the influence of democracy on the perceived level of corruption is tested while other studies focus on the influence of religion [4], colonial heritage [4], abundance of natural resources [5] or the presence of women in parliament [6]. Other studies focus on the consequences of corruption: does corruption lead to a decrease of GDP, foreign investments or aid [7]? The main problem in all these empirical studies is to make the transition from 'highly correlated' to 'causes': many variables are highly correlated with the perceived level of corruption, but it is difficult to derive causal relations from it. For example, in [2] is reported that

H. Chen et al. (Eds.): WISI 2006, LNCS 3917, pp. 103–114, 2006.

GDP per head and corruption are reported to be highly positively correlated in most studies but that there is general agreement that there is no causality involved.

The general approach in the majority of these studies (e.g., [3]) is to regress a variable representing corruption on a number of independent variables for which the influence is tested with the possible inclusion of some control variables. In this paper, we apply a different technique to study corruption. We use self organizing maps (SOMs), also known as Kohonen maps, to gain deeper insight in the causes of corruption. This technique is derived from the data mining community and allows a clear and intuitive visualization of high-dimensional data. In the second part of the paper, we apply support vector machines (SVMs) to forecast changes in the perceived levels of corruption. Support vector machines have proven to be excellent classifiers in other application domains (e.g., credit scoring [8]) and are able to capture nonlinear relationships between the dependent and independent variables.

In the next section, a short introduction to the concept of SOMs is given. Afterwards, we describe the data that was used for this study. The next section discusses the application of SOMs on this data whereby special attention is paid to the visualization possibilities that these models offer. In the final section, we use least-squares support vector machines [9] to forecast changes in the perceived level of corruption. Input selection will be used to select the most significant variables. The main contribution of this paper is the projection of SVM predictions onto a SOM to gain more insight in the SVM model and the use of multi-year data sets to study evolutions in the perceived level of corruption.

2   Self Organizing Maps

SOMs were introduced in 1982 by Teuvo Kohonen [10] and have been used in a wide array of applications like the visualization of high-dimensional data [11], clustering of text documents [12], identification of fraudulent insurance claims [13] and many others. An extensive overview of successful applications can be found in [14] and [15]. A SOM is a feedforward neural network consisting of two layers. The neurons from the output layer are usually ordered in a low-dimensional grid. Each unit in the input layer is connected to all neurons in the output layer with weights attached to each of these connections. This is similar to a weight vector, with the dimensionality of the input space, being associated with each output neuron. When a training vector x is presented, the weight vector of each neuron c is compared with x. One commonly opts for the euclidian distance between both vectors as the distance measure. The neuron that lies closest to x is called the 'winner' or the Best Matching Unit (BMU). The weight vector of the BMU and its neighbors in the grid are adapted with the following learning rule:

$$w_c = w_c + \eta(t)\Lambda_{winner,c}(t)(x - w_c) \tag{1}$$

In this expression $\eta(t)$ represents the learning rate that decreases during training. $\Lambda_{winner,c}(t)$ is the so-called neighborhood function that decreases when the distance in the grid between neuron c and the winner unit becomes larger. Often a gaussian function centered around the winner unit is used as the neighborhood function with a decreasing radius during training. The decreasing learning rate and radius of the neighborhood function result in a stable map that does not change substantially after a certain amount of training.

From the learning rule, it can be seen that the neurons will move towards the input vector and that the magnitude of the update is determined by the neighborhood function. Because units that are close to each other in the grid will receive similar updates, the weights of these neurons will resemble each other and the neurons will be activated by similar input patterns. The winner units for similar input vectors are mostly close to each other and self organizing maps are therefore often called topology-preserving maps.

3   Description and Preprocessing of the Data

For this study, data from three different sources was combined. Demographic information, for example literacy and infant mortality rate, was retrieved from the CIA Factbook [16] together with macro-economical variables, like GDP per capita and sectorial GDP information.

Information concerning the corruption level in specific countries was derived from Transparency International [17] under the form of the Corruption Perceptions Index (CPI). This index ranks countries according to the degree to which corruption is perceived to exist among public officials and politicians. The CPI is created by interviewing business people and country analysts and gives a score between 0 (highly corrupt) and 10 (highly clean) to each country. In this study, data concerning the years 1996, 2000 and 2004 was used. In the index of 1996, 54 countries received a corruption score. We select only these countries and omit from the more elaborated 2000 and 2004 indices all other countries, resulting in a total of 162 observations: three observations from different years for each of the 54 countries[1]. We use ISO 3166 Codes, like BEL for Belgium or FRA for France, to refer to the individual countries whereby capitalization is used to indicate the year of the observation. Uppercase codes (e.g., BEL) indicate that the observation is from 2004, lowercase codes (e.g., bel) are used to refer to observations from the year 2000 and codes in proper case (only the first letter capitalized e.g., Bel) refer to 1996 observations.

Information about the democracy level in each country was obtained from Freedom House [18]. Each country is assigned a rating for political rights and a rating for civil liberties based on a scale of 1 to 7, with 1 representing the highest degree of freedom present and seven the lowest level of freedom. Similarly to the 'level of corruption', the 'level of democracy' in a country is a rather subjective

---

[1] Pakistan and Bangladesh received a CPI rating in 1996 and 2004, but not in 2000. These two countries are not removed from the data set.

Table 1. Variables included in the dataset

Corruption Perceptions Index (CPI)
Civil Liberties (CL)
Political Rights (PR)
Arable Land (%)
Age structure: 0-14 years
Age structure: 15-64 years
Age structure: 65 years or over
Population growth rate
Birth rate
Death rate
Net migration rate
Total Infant mortality rate (IMR)
Total Life expectancy at birth
Total fertility rate (children born/women)
GDP per capita
GDP agriculture
GDP industry
GDP services
Number of international organisations the country is member of
Literacy(Total Population %)

concept and therefore difficult to express in only two indices. We refer to [3] for some critiques on the inclusion of these indices.

An overview of all variables that were used in this study is given in Table 1.

4 SOM Analysis

4.1 Exploring the Data

We started by training a self-organizing map of 15 by 15 neurons: with this size it can be expected that each neuron will be the BMU for at most a few observations and this allows a clear visualization of the map. All available variables, including the CPI-scores, were used to create the map of Figure 1. We can see that European countries are likely to be projected on the upper right corner of this map, while the other corners are dominated by respectively African, South-American and Asian countries. A second point that draws the attention is the fact that for most countries the observations from the three years lie close to each other. The observations are either projected on the same neuron (e.g., Uganda (UGA), Denmark (DNK), Hong Kong (HKG)) or on adjacent neurons (e.g., Mexico (MEX), Australia (AUS)). The map also shows that for most of the countries for which the position changed over time, the capitalized 2004 observation lies closer to the upper right corner than the 1996 and 2000 observations. This is the case for Mexico (MEX), Brazil (BRA), Thailand (THA), Argentina (ARG), Chile (CHL) and Ecuador (ECU). It seems that these countries are in transition towards a "more European" model.

While the map of Figure 1 provides general indications about the degree of similarity between countries, it does not allow us to obtain detailed information about corruption. To overcome this limitation, component planes were used to gain deeper insight in the data. Component planes can be created for each input variable and

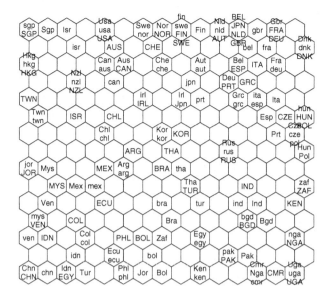

Fig. 1. Map of 15 by 15 neurons

show the weights that connect each neuron with the particular input variable. The component plane for the Corruption Perceptions Index is shown in Figure 2. In this Figure, light and dark shades indicate respectively 'non corrupt' and 'highly corrupt' countries. We can observe that the lower right corner contains the countries perceived to be most corrupt (e.g., Pakistan (PAK), Nigeria (NIG), Cameroon (CMR) and Bangladesh (BGD)). At the opposite side, it can easily be noted that the North-European countries are perceived to be among the least corrupt: they are all situated in the white-colored region at the top of the map. Remember that most European countries were also projected on the upper-half of the map indicating a modest amount of corruption and that several countries seemed to be in transition towards a more European- less corrupt- model.

Component planes for other variables are shown in Figure 3. The first component plane provides information about the literacy of the population. The dark spot indicates the countries where most of the population is illiterate. The second component plane shows Freedom House's index of Political Rights. The light colored spots indicate the regions on the map with the countries that score low on 'political freedom'. The resemblance between these two component planes and the component plane of the corruption index is remarkable. There is a significant correlation between 'corruption', 'literacy' and 'political freedom'. The third component plane (Figure 3(c)) shows the number of international organizations that each country is member of. This component plane can be used to test the hypothesis that corrupt countries are less likely to be member of international organizations because they are either not welcome or not willing to participate. We can see that this hypothesis can not be confirmed based on the

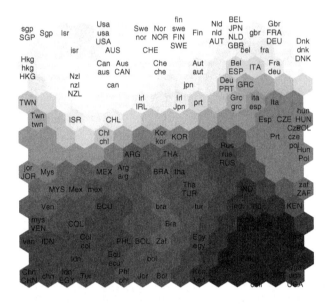

Fig. 2. Corruption Perceptions Index

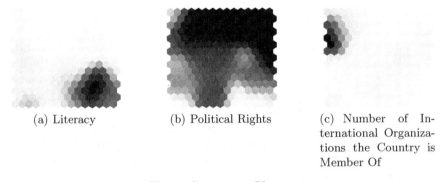

| (a) Literacy | (b) Political Rights | (c) Number of International Organizations the Country is Member Of |

Fig. 3. Component Planes

component plane. Countries in the corrupt region of the map do not differ from most European countries. Only some countries or regions close to the upper left corner (Hong Kong (HKG) and Taiwan (TWN)) seem to participate in fewer international organizations.

The same kind of analysis can be performed for each of the other input variables. Several of these component planes, like 'GDP per capita' or 'Total Life Expectancy', show a high degree of correlation with the CPI component plane. Others, like 'Birth Rate' or '% GDP in agricultural sector' are inversely correlated with the CPI component plane, indicating that in those countries corruption goes hand in hand with a young population and little industrialization.

4.2   Clustering of the SOM

In the preceding section, we have shown that SOMs are a suitable tool for the exploration of data sets. If the SOM grid itself consists of numerous neurons, analysis can be facilitated by clustering similar neurons into groups [19].

We performed the traditional k-means clustering algorithm on the trained map of 15 by 15 neurons. The result of this procedure, assuming 5 clusters are present in the data, is given in Figure 4. Several unsupervised labelling techniques have been proposed to identify those variables that characterise a certain cluster (e.g., [20–22]). We briefly discuss the method presented in [20].

After performing a clustering of the trained map, the unlabelled training examples are projected again onto the map and it is remembered which observations are assigned to each cluster. Consequently, for each cluster the so-called salient dimensions are sought. These are defined as the variables that have significantly different values for the observations belonging and not-belonging to that cluster. Finally, a human domain specialist can manually interpret the salient dimensions of each cluster and assign a descriptive label.[2]

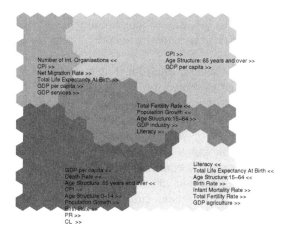

Fig. 4. Labelled Clusters

The above algorithm was executed on the clusters found by the k-means algorithm and the results are also shown in Figure 4. In each cluster we show the variables that were found to be salient. A $>>$ ($<<$) sign behind the variable

---

[2] We have made one important change to the algorithm described in [20]. The original algorithm calculates difference factors based on the following formula $\frac{\mu_{in}(k,v) - \mu_{out}(k,v)}{\mu_{out}(k,v)}$ and uses these difference factors to find the salient dimensions (=dimensions with large or small difference factors). This has the disadvantage that for $\mu_{out}(k,v)$ close to zero the difference factor becomes very large even if the difference between $\mu_{out}(k,v)$ and $\mu_{in}(k,v)$ is small. To avoid this problem we add 1 in both numerator and denominator when calculating the difference factors.

name indicates that countries within the cluster have on average significantly larger (smaller) values for this variable than countries outside the cluster. We can see that the analysis of the component planes can be largely automated by this procedure. For example, the procedure clearly indicates that countries from the cluster in the upper left corner seem to participate in few international organizations and score high on the CPI (low corruption). The cluster in the lower right corner on the other hand, is characterized by a low level of literacy, high fertility rate and a large percentage of GDP obtained from agriculture. A 'high level of corruption' is not preserved as a salient characteristic of this cluster because only the most salient features were included on this map and features like 'literacy' and 'agricultural GDP' were found to be more significant.

5 SVM Analysis

In this section several linear and nonlinear corruption forecasting models are evaluated. The models that are derived can be used for different goals. For countries without a CPI-score, the models can be adopted to obtain an estimate of the corruption in that country. For countries that have received a CPI-score, we can apply the models to investigate which countries have a CPI-score that is significantly different from the model predictions and study the reasons for these deviations.

In this part of the paper, the information that is available in the data of 1996 is used to make forecasts of the corruption level in 2000 and 2004. Thus, we use the 54 observations of 1996 for training a LS-SVM model and use this model to predict the corruption levels in 2000 and 2004. Additionally, the data sets of 2000 and 2004 are expanded by including those countries for which a 2000 or 2004 CPI value was available but a 1996 CPI value was not available. The result is a test data set consisting of 231 countries with 125 of them being observations from countries that are not present in the 1996 training data set. We will refer to these 125 observations as the 'new' (unseen) test data, while the other 106 observations are referred to as 'old' (unseen, but an observation for the same country is present in the training data).

First, a linear OLS regression model was constructed whereby input selection was performed on the variables of Table 1. Feature selection was performed with a backwards procedure, but instead of using the traditional t-statistics to decide which variable to remove, we use the leave-one-out crossvalidation error on the training data set. The complete feature selection procedure occurs as follows:

1. Build a linear model containing all available inputs and measure the leave-one-out error.
2. Remove each of the variables one at a time and measure the leave-one-out error of the resulting model.
3. Select the model with the smallest leave-one-out error and go back to the previous step until a model is obtained with only one variable left.

Afterwards, one selects from all models created in step 3 the model with the smallest overall leave-one-out error. This model is then used to create predictions for the 2000 and 2004 test observations.

If the above procedure is performed on the corruption data sets, the model with 5 variables is selected as the best performing model. An overview of the model (with corresponding t-statistics between brackets) is given in Equation 2:

$$CPI = 3.005 + 1.0666 * 10^{-4} \; GDP \text{ per capita} - 0.88722 \; CL - 0.015074 \; IMR$$
$$(2.4399) \qquad\qquad\qquad\qquad (-3.3354) \qquad (-1.5189)$$

$$+0.40462 \; PR + 0.052143 \; GDP \text{ services}$$
$$(1.9103) \qquad (2.0301)$$

$$(2)$$

Observe that the signs of the equation parameters correspond mostly to what one could expect based on common sense. Increases in 'GDP per capita' and 'GDP services' increase the CPI score (corresponding to a decrease in corruption) and vice versa for the 'Infant Mortality Rate'. The two variables approximating the democracy level in a country, Civil Liberties (CL) and Political Rights (PR), are also among the features selected by the backwards procedure. The negative sign for the CL-index indicates that an increase of the CL-index (less freedom) decreases the CPI-index (higher corruption). The positive sign of the PR-index seems counter-intuitive: an increase of the PR-index (less political rights) results in an increase of the CPI index (less corruption). This result might however be explained by research from Montinola and Jackman [23]. They found that the level of corruption is typically lower in dictatorships than in countries that have partially democratized, but once past a threshold, democratic practices inhibit corruption. If this non-linearity is indeed present, we should observe significant performance improvements when using a nonlinear LS-SVM model. This LS-SVM model is trained on the same five variables and suitable parameters for regularization and the RBF-kernel are selected by a gridsearch procedure as described in [9].

The constructed models are tested on the remaining data of 2000 and 2004. The results are shown in Table 2. It can be observed from the large R^2s that both models are able to explain most of the variance in the corruption index. The small values for the Mean Absolute Error (MAE) confirm this: on average the predictions differ only 0.86 and 0.78 units from the actual observed values for both models on the training data. The results on the test data are also shown in Table 2, where overall performance is indicated together with a breakdown by category. While the MAE is similar for 'old' and 'new' test data, there are huge differences in R^2. The main reason for this deviation is due to the fact that the observations from the 'new' test data have a smaller mean and variance of the CPI than observations from the 'old' test data, indicating that countries that were added to the CPI in recent years are on average more corrupt.

Table 2. Overview Model Performance

	Linear Model		LS-SVM Model	
	R^2	MAE	R^2	MAE
Training Data	0.81	0.86	0.84	0.78
Test Data	0.67	1.07	0.71	0.96
New	0.34	1.05	0.42	0.97
Old	0.73	1.09	0.75	0.98

6   Integration of SOM and SVM

From Table 2, one can observe that the LS-SVM model provides a better fore-casting accuracy than the corresponding linear model. However, the LS-SVM has a serious disadvantage: it is very difficult to understand the motivation behind this model's decisions due to its complexity. To relieve this opacity restriction and to gain more insight in the model's behavior we will project its forecasts and the forecasting errors onto a self organizing map (Figure 5).

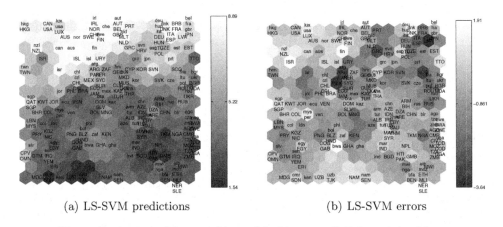

(a) LS-SVM predictions   (b) LS-SVM errors

Fig. 5. Projection of Support Vector Machine onto Self Organizing Map

To create Figure 5(a), a SOM is constructed from the 1996 training data, without use of the CPI, and on this trained map the observations from the test data are projected. Afterwards, each neuron of this map is assigned a color based on the average LS-SVM forecasts of the test observations projected onto that neuron. The neurons that were never the BMU are assigned the average color of the surrounding neurons. The same method was used to create Figure 5(b), but with the colors based on the forecasting errors instead of the actual forecasts. From Figure 5(a), it can be observed that observations projected on the upper half of the map are predicted to be among the least corrupt countries. From Figure 5(b), we learn that the model errors are evenly divided over the map. There are no regions where the LS-SVM model systematically over- or underestimates the perceived level of corruption. Both figures were also created for the linear model (not shown) and this allowed us to find out why this model was performing worse. The linear model's forecasts were very similar to the ones of the LS-SVM model, except for the lower right corner. In this region the linear model was systematically overestimating corruption, i.e. the actual corruption was less than predicted. Visual inspection also learned that both linear and LS-SVM model made similar forecasting errors for particular observations. For ARG (Argentina), GRC (Greece) and MEX (Mexico) the actual level of corruption is significantly higher than predicted by both models while the opposite is valid for bwa (Botswana) and fin (Finland). Further research is necessary to reveal the reasons for these deviations.

7   Conclusion

In this paper, a data mining approach for the analysis of corruption was presented. In the first part, the powerful visualization possibilities of self organizing maps were used to study the interconnections between various macro-economical variables and the perceived level of corruption The use of multi-year data sets allowed us to visualize the evolution of corruption over time for specific countries. In the second part, it was shown that forecasting models can be constructed that allow analysts to predict the level of corruption for countries where this information is missing. Finally, it was shown how self organizing maps can be used to study the behavior of supervised models. This allows us to open the 'black box' of some models and a more detailed comparison between the predictions made by different models.

References

1. Gerring, J., Thacker, S.: political institutions and corruption: The role of unitarism and parliamentarism. The British Journal of Political Science **34** (2004) 295–330
2. Lambsdorff, J.: Corruption in empirical research: a review. Transparency International Working paper (1999)
3. Bohara, A., Mitchell, N., Mittendorff, C.: Compound democracy and the control of corruption: A cross-country investigation. The Policy Studies Journal **32**(4) (2004) 481–499
4. Treisman, D.: The causes of corruption: a cross-national study. Journal of Public Economics **76**(3) (2000) 339–457
5. Leite, C., Weidmann, J.: Does mother nature corrupt? natural resources, corruption and economical growth. International Monetary Fund Working Paper 99/85 (1999)
6. Swamy, A., Knack, S., Lee, Y., Azfar, O.: Gender and corruption. Journal of Development Economics **64** (2001) 25–55
7. Alesina, A., Weder, B.: Do corrupt governments receive less foreign aid? National Bureau of Economic Research Working Paper 7108 (1999)

8. Baesens, B., Van Gestel, T., Viaene, S., Stepanova, M., Suykens, J., Vanthienen, J.: Benchmarking state of the art classification algorithms for credit scoring. Journal of the Operational Research Society **54**(6) (2003) 627–635
9. Suykens, J., Gestel, T.V., Brabanter, J.D., Moor, B.D., Vandewalle, J.: Least Squares Support Vector Machines. World Scientific, Singapore (2002)
10. Kohonen, T.: Self-organized formation of topologically correct feature maps. Biological Cybernetics **43** (1982) 59–69
11. Vesanto, J.: Som-based data visualization methods. Intelligent Data Analysis **3** (1999) 111–26
12. Honkela, T., Kaski, S., Lagus, K., Kohonen, T.: WEBSOM—self-organizing maps of document collections. In: Proceedings of WSOM'97, Workshop on Self-Organizing Maps, Espoo, Finland, June 4-6. Helsinki University of Technology, Neural Networks Research Centre, Espoo, Finland (1997) 310–315
13. Brockett, P., Xia, X., Derrig, R.: Using kohonen's self-organizing feature map to uncover automobile bodily injury claims fraud. International Journal of Risk and Insurance **65** (1998) 245–274
14. Kohonen, T.: Self-Organising Maps. Springer-Verlag (1995)
15. Deboeck, G., Kohonen, T.: Visual Explorations in Finance with selforganizing maps. Springer-Verlag (1998)
16. CIA: (http://www.cia.gov/cia/publications/factbook/)
17. Transparency International: (http://www.transparency.org/)
18. Freedom House: Freedom in the world country ratings (2005)
19. Vesanto, J., Alhoniemi, E.: Clustering of the self-organizing map. IEEE Transactions on Neural Networks **11**(3) (2000) 586–600
20. Azcarraga, A., Hsieh, M., Pan, S., Setiono, R.: Extracting salient dimensions for automatic som labeling. Transactions on Systems, Management and Cybernetics, Part C **35**(4) (2005) 595–600
21. Lagus, K., Kaski, S.: Keyword selection method for characterizing text document maps. In: Proceedings of ICANN99, Ninth International Conference on Artificial Neural Networks. IEE (1999) 371–376
22. Rauber, A., Merkl, D.: Automatic labeling of self-organizing maps: Making a treasure-map reveal its secrets. In: Proceedings of the third Pacific-Asia Conference on Knowledge Discovery and Data Mining (PAKDD'99). LNCS / LNAI 1574, Springer Verlag (1999) 228–237
23. Montinola, G., Jackman, R.: Sources of corruption: a cross-country study. British Journal of Political Science **32** (2002) 147–170

Temporal Representation in Spike Detection of Sparse Personal Identity Streams

Clifton Phua[1], Vincent Lee[1], Ross Gayler[2], and Kate Smith[1]

[1] Monash University, Clayton School of Information Technology, Melbourne
{clifton.phua, vincent.lee, kate.smith}@infotech.monash.edu.au
[2] Baycorp Advantage, Melbourne
r.gayler@mbox.com.au

Abstract. Identity crime has increased enormously over the recent years. Spike detection is important because it highlights sudden and sharp rises in intensity relative to the current identity attribute value (which can be indicative of abuse). This paper proposes the new spike analysis framework for monitoring sparse personal identity streams. For each identity example, it detects spikes in single attribute values and integrates multiple spikes from different attributes to produce a numeric suspicion score. Although only temporal representation is examined here, experimental results on synthetic and real credit applications reveal some conditions on which the framework will perform well.

1 Introduction

In security-related informatics, personal identity examples with sparse attributes arrive in streams. Sparse attributes usually consist of string occurrences and identifiers with an enormous number of possible values which can occur at widely spaced intervals (such as personal names and telephone numbers); in contrast with dense attributes which have a finite number of attribute values, and therefore occur more frequently (such as street numbers and postcodes). Each structured example is made up of a mixture of both sparse and dense attributes, and arrives rapidly and continuously into the data repository. To detect events of interest in streams, stream mining systems should be highly automated, scalable, and timely [6].

Some related work for analysing sparse attributes can be found in document and bio-surveillance streams. Kleinberg [10; 9] surveys threshold-, state-, and trend-based stream mining techniques used in topic detection and tracking. [16] surveys techniques for finding anomalies in time for disease outbreaks, and [7] use time series analysis techniques for a simulated bio-terrorism attack. Two significant stream processing systems are STREAM [1] which details the Continuous Query Language (CQL) and AURORA [2] which has been applied to financial services, highway toll billing, battalion and environmental monitoring.

This paper's main technical contributions are in the integration of spike detection and stream mining within a framework (Section 2.1): representation of time with respect to each attribute value (Section 2.2), use of EWMA (Exponentially Weighted Moving Average) in single attribute value spikes (Section 2.3), and integration of multiple attribute value spikes to score each example (Section 2.4). This paper

H. Chen et al. (Eds.): WISI 2006, LNCS 3917, pp. 115–126, 2006.

is novel within the credit application fraud detection context because it finds denser identity attribute values (which can be highly indicative of identity crime (Section 3.1) in a principled fashion. It describes the synthetic and real credit application data sets (Section 3.2), experimental design and evaluation measures (Section 3.3). Section 3.4 discusses the insights of using different temporal representations. Section 4 concludes and highlights likely future work.

2 Spike Analysis Framework

2.1 Overview

In Figure 1(a), the input data is extracted from the entire database and consists of examples sorted in descending arrival date and time order (a more recent example is placed above an older one); and these examples are either previously scored (exists within the window), the ones which has to be scored in arrival order (the data stream),

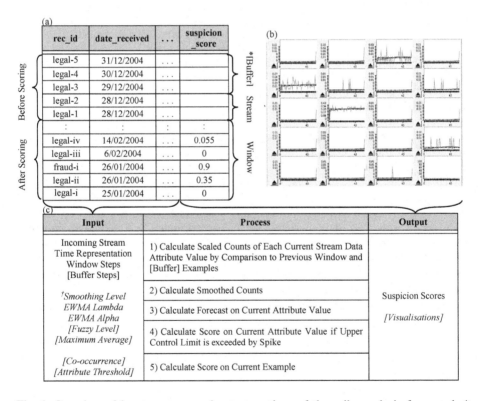

Fig. 1. Overview of input, process, and output sections of the spike analysis framework * square brackets indicate that the enclosed parameter is optional † *italic-typed parameters are not tested in this paper's experiments*

or the ones to be scored later (exists within the buffer). The buffer examples are always more recent than the stream examples, which are in turn, more recent than the window examples. For illustration, suppose the temporal representation is daily rate, window steps is one month and with no buffer, the two stream examples "legal-1" and "legal-2" are scored using prior examples which arrive between 29/11/2004 and 28/12/2004. The last column in Figure 1(a) contains the suspicion score output and the multiple time series plots in Figure 1(b) are the visual outputs for an example.

In Figure 1(c)'s "Input" column, the first four parameters determine how much input data to continuously extract using Structured Query Language (SQL) queries from the database to process an incoming stream; the next seven parameters can be used to fine-tune the processing capabilities of the spike detection system. For brevity, this paper presents only the results of varying the first four parameters (incoming stream, time representation, window and buffer steps) by holding the next seven parameters constant. Similarly for the "Output" column, this paper evaluates the suspicion scores without the assessment of visualisations. The "Process" column has five main calculation/algorithmic steps to generate a suspicion score for each example.

For concreteness, let Y represent a continuous data stream with an ordered set of $\{...y_{j-2}, y_{j-1}, y_j, y_{j+1}, y_{j+2}, ...\}$ discrete streams. Let y_j represent a discrete data stream with an ordered set of $\{d_{j,n}, d_{j,n+1}, d_{j,n+2}, ..., d_{j,n+p}\}$ examples to be processed online. Processing is carried out on p examples and from the viewpoint of the most recent stream y_j's oldest unscored example $d_{j,n}$ to the newest unscored example $d_{j,n+p}$. For simplicity, the subscript j is omitted to concentrate on processing one discrete stream and one example at a time. Let each d_n contain M number of attributes, where $d_n = \{a_{n,1}, a_{n,2}, ..., a_{n,M}\}$. Each current attribute value $a_{n,i}$ is compared to previous ones $a_{n-1,i}, a_{n-2,i}, ..., a_{n-W,i}$ in search of the same value ($a_{x,i} = a_{n,i}$) or approximate value ($a_{x,i} \approx a_{n,i}$), where W is the window size of extracted previous examples in the user-specified temporal representation. *Fuzzy level* is an optional parameter which utilises Levenshtein edit distance where at both extremes, 1 is an exact match and 0 is a complete mismatch. By default, *fuzzy level* is set to 1. W is needed to score p and has to be sufficiently large to maximise the detection capability of processing d_n.

In addition to comparing each $a_{n,i}$ to previous attribute values, $a_{n,i}$ can also be compared to subsequent ones $a_{n+1,i}, a_{n+2,i}, ..., a_{n+B,i}$, where B is the buffer size of extracted later examples in the user-specified temporal representation. B has the potential to reduce the number of false positives [8] and has to be small to minimise the wait-time delay of processing d_n. Therefore, the task is to examine the rate where past and future examples had the same or approximate attribute value as the present one as a function of relative time.

2.2 Temporal Representation

Temporal representation is the choice of the x-axis in the time series for $a_{n,i}$. $W = t * k$ and $B = 0.1t * k$ where W and B are split into user-defined number of steps t and into step size(s) k. Let $W_{user-defined-rate}$, $B_{user-defined-rate}$ represent the case where the constant k is user-defined; and $W_{stream-rate}$, $B_{stream-rate}$ where the constant k is automatically determined by the overall daily stream rate. k can also be automatically represented by finer-grained temporal measurements (such as seconds, minutes, and hours) or coarser-grained ones (such as days, weeks, months, and years). Let $W_{daily-rate}$ and $W_{weekly-rate}$ (each week starts on a Sunday) represent the case where the variable k is the number of examples in a specific day and week respectively. For clarity, this paper omits results from other useful temporal representations such as day-of-week, week-of-month, season, school holidays, and public holidays.

2.3 Spike Detection of Single Attribute Value

Sparsity. As a rule-of-thumb, our definition of sparsity in an attribute is: if more than 80% of its values are not missing, and there are more than 100 distinct values, and more than 50% of these distinct ones are unique (occur only once). In this spike

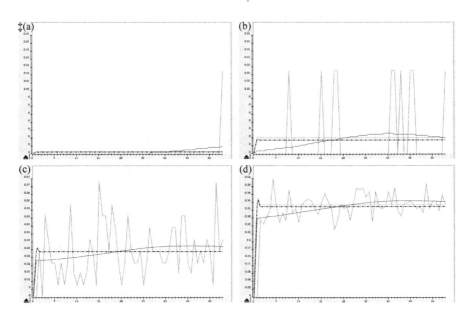

Fig. 2. Monitoring of $a_{n,i}$ in d_n with $W_{stream-rate} = t * k = 60 * 147 = 8820$ and $B_{stream-rate} = 0$: (a) Very sparse, (b) Sparse, (c) Dense, (d) Very dense ‡ y-axis is not able to display more than 2 decimal places

detection framework, assuming that $a_{n,i}$ is not a missing value, it is sparse if it occurs less than $0.01(W + B)$ times. For example in Figure 2, number of occurrences of "pan" in *last name* 2(a) - once in d_n, of "business systems" in *employer name* 2(b) - less than a hundred times, of "3" in *street number* 2(c) - a few hundred times, and of "vic" in *state* 2(d) - a few thousand times.

Maximum average is an optional parameter which is used to restrict dense attribute values where at both extremes, 1 includes and 0 excludes all attribute values. By default, *maximum average* is set to 1.

Scaling. It is needed to reduce variability of weekly and seasonal effects in raw counts, as well as to compare across different temporal representations. Rates, or the proportion of all attribute values in W and B having the specified attribute value $a_{n,i}$, are less sensitive to overall volume effects. For example in Figure 2, the orange (light solid) line signifies the scaled counts.

Smoothing. It is required to remove rare and chaotic effects in order to compare the current rate to the assumed constant background rate. Discrete Wavelet Transform (DWT) allows the decomposition of a time series into different resolutions using a mother wavelet. DWT has three main advantages over its other alternatives: efficiency, suitable for use with non-stationary data, and quantifies location in time and frequency [12]. For example in Figure 2, the red (dark solid) line is the background rate, and it is derived from applying the highest DWT *smoothing level* onto the scaled counts to get the least noisy curve.

Spike Detection. Linear forecasting on the smoothed time series is done by Exponentially Weighted Moving Average (EWMA) [15]. EWMA is a statistical quality control technique which specifies how much the current prediction is influenced by past observations. Given a measurement X_t at time step t, the definition of EWMA statistic Z_t is:

$$Z_t = \lambda X_t + (1 - \lambda)Z_{t-1} \text{ for } t = 1,2,...,n \tag{1}$$

where Z_0 is the desired process mean μ_0. n is the number of observations to be monitored including μ_0. $0 < \lambda \leq 1$ is the weighting factor where higher values give more weight to current observation, with $\lambda = 1$ referring to the Shewhart control chart.

The estimated variance of Z_t for a large t is approximately:

$$\sigma_{z_i}^2 = \left(\frac{\lambda}{2 - \lambda}\right)\sigma^2 \tag{2}$$

With the variance, the UCL applied from (2) is:

$$UCL = \mu_0 + \alpha\sigma_{z_i} \tag{3}$$

Advantages of using EWMA compared to many other time surveillance techniques include low implementation and computational complexity [16], and EWMA is a non-parametric monitoring algorithm as it makes no assumption about the distribution that X_t is drawn from [11]. For example, the dark dotted line is the average and the light dotted line is the UCL, and is obtained from setting $\lambda = 0.8$ and $\alpha = 0.0027$ (3σ).

If buffering is not implemented ($B = 0$), the score for each current attribute value $a_{n,i}$ is determined by how much the red line exceeds the light dotted line:

$$S(a_{n,i}) = \begin{cases} w_t(a_{n,i}) - UCL & \text{if } W_t(a_{n,i}) > UCL \\ 0 & \text{otherwise} \end{cases} \tag{4}$$

where $W_t(a_{n,i})$ is the actual smoothed count of the current time step t. For example in Figure 2 (b), the dark dotted line $W_t(a_{n,i})$ did not exceed the light dotted line UCL, therefore $S(a_{n,i}) = 0$.

If buffering is implemented ($B > 0$), the score for each $a_{n,i}$ is:

$$S(a_{n,i}) = \begin{cases} B_t(a_{n,i}) - UCL & \text{if } B_t(a_{n,i}) > W_t(a_{n,i}) > UCL \\ W_t(a_{n,i}) - UCL & \text{if } W_t(a_{n,i}) > B_t(a_{n,i}) > UCL \\ 2\sqrt{(W_t(a_{n,i}) - UCL)} & \text{if } W_t(a_{n,i}) > UCL > B_t(a_{n,i}) \\ 0 & \text{otherwise} \end{cases} \tag{5}$$

where $B_t(a_{n,i})$ is the averaged smoothed count of all time steps in the buffer.

2.4 Integration of Spikes from Multiple Attributes

The normalised score for each current example $d_n \in y_j$ is:

$$S(d_n) = \begin{cases} \dfrac{1}{\max\left[\sum\limits_{i=1}^{M} S(a_{x,i})\right]} \left[\sum\limits_{i=1}^{M} S(a_{n,i})\right] & \text{if } 1 > S(d_n) \\ 1 & \text{otherwise} \end{cases} \tag{6}$$

where $a_{x,i} \in d_x \in y_{j-1}$ and $0 \le S(d_n) \le 1$.

Co-occurrence is an optional parameter which allows for the searching of 2 or 3 combinations of attribute values. By default, *co-occurrence* is set to 1. *Attribute threshold* is another optional parameter which restricts the scoring of an example when the number of spiking attribute values exceeds it. By default, *attribute threshold* is set to number of attributes.

In summary, the basic idea involves monitoring attribute value frequency over time, in particular if any attribute value spikes. Spiking refers to any attribute value which rises sharply in intensity within a short and more recent time period relative to the current example. Based on the number and intensity of the attribute value spikes, each current example is then given a numeric suspicion score between 0 and 1 relative to other examples in the previous stream.

3 Application Domain

3.1 Identity Crime

Identity crime, consisting of identity fraud and theft, is about taking advantage of fictitious identities and/or real unsuspecting individuals' personal information to hide the perpetrators' real identities for their illegal goals. It features in a myriad of other crimes such as terrorism and financial crime [13]. It is well-known that identity crime is the fasting growing crime in the developed world and its monetary cost is often estimated to be in billions of dollars annually.

Credit bureaus collect millions of enquiries relating to credit applications annually. In Australia, there are currently around half a million enquiries made per month. Each enquiry contains many identity attributes and it is easy for criminals to tamper the attributes with seemingly valid values. [5] explains that the visible patterns of organised identity crime rings constantly change and it is difficult to detect with standard identity verification tools. However, these organised fraudsters exhibit detectable link and temporal patterns throughout the scams. In particular, they seem to target attacks on specific organisations at specific times for short durations.

3.2 Data Description

Synthetic Data Set. It has around 20 attributes such as primary key label, date received, personal names, addresses, phone numbers, personal and employer details; and has 52,750 applications (9% are fraudulent) which span the entire year 2004. This data set has been specifically created with the assumption that fraudsters will purposely use these fraudulent attribute values regularly, occasionally, seasonally, and/or once-off. Also, identity attribute values are reused within a very short period of time. It has very few missing attribute values. The justification, generation, and details of this synthetic data can be found in [14; 4]. Experiments on this data set can reveal if the spike analysis framework can perform well on sparse identity streams evaluated by weeks and imbalanced classes. On average in Table 1, each weekly

Table 1. Synthetic data streams for experiments

Stream number	Week	Total applications	Percentage fraudulent
1	10/03/2004 to 16/03/2004	990	13%
2	17/03/2004 to 23/03/2004	1070	14%
3	24/03/2004 to 30/03/2004	1032	11%
4	31/03/2004 to 06/04/2004	1117	16%

stream consists of slightly more than 1,000 applications to be scored in March and April 2004, and percentage fraudulent is higher than the average due to injected seasonal frauds.

Real. In comparison, the real data set has very similar number and type of attributes to the synthetic one except that some attributes have been hashed for privacy and confidentiality reasons. In contrast, the real one has 27,546 applications (50% are fraudulent) which start from July 2004 to July 2005 (13 months). The fraud percentage is very high because the legitimate applications have been randomly under-sampled by selecting 1 in a few hundred applications which has not been flagged as fraudulent. It has a significant amount of missing attribute values. Experiments on this data set offer a rare glimpse into the temporal behaviour of identity fraudsters. It also can determine if the spike analysis framework can perform well with sparse identity streams evaluated by weeks and missing attribute values. On average in Table 2, each weekly stream consists of around 600 applications to be scored in January 2005.

Table 2. Real data streams for experiments

Stream number	Week	Total applications	Percentage fraudulent
1	06/01/2005 to 12/01/2005	730	50%
2	13/01/2005 to 19/01/2005	698	50%
3	20/01/2005 to 26/01/2005	584	50%
4	27/01/2005 to 02/02/2005	392	50%

3.3 Experimental Design and Evaluation Measures

The first step is to simulate a streaming environment where incoming credit applications can be continuously scanned for significant spikes in its attribute values. Applications in the window and buffer are extracted to process the incoming application stream. An alarm is raised on an application if the suspicion score is ranked high amongst the applications before it. The second step is to select only sparse attributes to monitor. In both the synthetic and real data, only the sparsest attributes have been chosen for the experiments (the actual attributes used in experiments cannot be revealed).

In Table 3, $W_{user-defined-rate}$ ($t;k$) is used to determine the effects of the same W but different t and k. $W_{stream-rate}$ is used to examine the outcomes of the constant overall daily stream rate k (147 for synthetic and 70 for real data) but steadily increasing t. $W_{daily-rate}$ and $W_{weekly-rate}$ are used to study the results of the variable k but steadily increasing t. $B_{user-defined-rate}$ and $B_{stream-rate}$ are used to learn about the consequences of buffering $0.1t$ with a user-defined k.

Table 3. Different temporal representations for experiments

$W_{user\text{-}defined\text{-}rate}$	$W_{stream\text{-}rate}$	$W_{daily\text{-}rate}$	$W_{weekly\text{-}rate}$	$B_{user\text{-}defined\text{-}rate}$	$B_{stream\text{-}rate}$
20;500	10	10	7	2;500	1;500
40;250	20	20	14	4;250	2;250
50;200	30	30	21	5;200	3;200
80;125	40	40	28	8;125	4;125
100;100	50	50	35	10;100	5;100
200;50	60	60	42	20;50	6;50

Other parameters are held constant: *Smoothing level* = 5 (maximum), *EWMA lambda* = 0.8, *EWMA alpha* = 0.0027 (3σ), *Fuzzy level* = 1, *Maximum average* = 1, *Co-occurrence* = 1, and *Attribute threshold* = 20 (number of attributes).

The non-threshold-based, diverse measures of performance implemented in [3] are:

- **NTOP10** is an ordering metric which should be **maximised**. What is the percentage of positives in the top 10% of ranked examples?
- **AUC** (Area Under the ROC Curve) is another ordering metric which should be **maximised**. What is the performance under all possible thresholds?
- **RMS** (Root Mean Squared Error) is a probability metric which should be **minimised**. How much is the deviation of predictions from true class labels?

3.4 Results and Discussion

- **3(a) and 3(b) have the highest and most similar results but 3(b) uses a much smaller W.** In contrast, 3(c) performed poorly and 3(d) very poorly.
- **Stream 4 has the best and stream 3 has the worst NTOP10 and AUC**; except in 3(d) where Stream 1 has the best and stream 4 has the poorest NTOP10 and AUC.

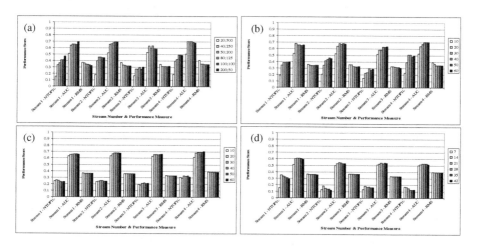

Fig. 3. Results on <u>**synthetic data with no buffer**</u> (a) user-defined rate, (b) stream rate, (c) daily rate, (d) weekly rate

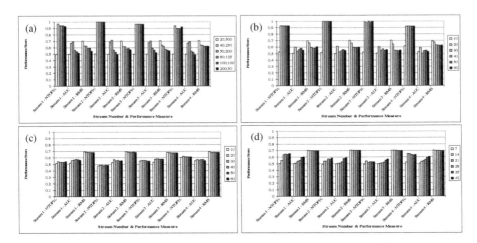

Fig. 4. Results on real data with no buffer (a) user-defined rate, (b) stream rate, (c) daily rate, (d) weekly rate

- **4(a) and 4(b) have the best results although 4(b) uses much smaller W. 4(a) is better than 4(b) in NTOP10 and AUC.** In contrast, both 4(c) and 4(d) perform significantly poorer in NTOP10.
- **Stream 2 has the best and stream 4 has the worst NTOP10 and AUC in 4(a) and 4(b).** Stream 4 has best and 2 have poorest NTOP10 and AUC in 4(c). Stream 1 and stream 4 has best; and stream 3 have poorest NTOP10 and AUC in 4(d).

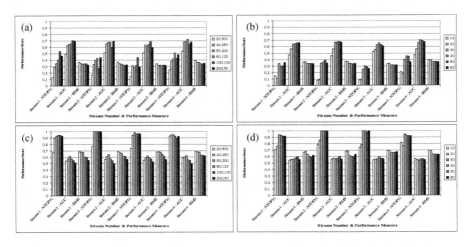

Fig. 5. Results on synthetic data with buffer (a) user-defined rate (b) stream rate, and on **real** data with buffer (c) user-defined rate (d) stream rate

- **5(a) has significantly better NTOP10s than 5(b), while AUC is basically similar. 5(c) is generally the same as 5(d), except *t*=20 of 5(d) is much lower than 5(c) for NTOP10 (Different from without buffer).**

- **Stream 4 has the best and stream 3 has the worst NTOP10 and AUC in 5(a) and 5(b). Stream 2 has the best and stream 4 has the poorest NTOP10 and AUC in 5(c) and 5(d) (Same as without buffer).**

Lessons learnt from experimenting with temporal representations are listed below:

- There is no optimal t, but the **optimal k** measured by AUC and RMS, is approximately the **overall daily stream rate** for all synthetic and real data streams.
- Overall, **as t gets larger, RMS decreases correspondingly**.
- The similar results of user-defined and stream rate windows show that **window size W does not have to be large**.
- Intuitively, user-defined and stream rate window steps produce much better in all 3 measures than daily and weekly window steps because the former two always process d_n on prior examples in a fixed step size k. On the other hand, **daily and weekly window steps can be overly sensitive** when processing d_n on few examples which have the same attribute values early in the start of day and week.
- In comparison with **synthetic data, NTOP10 for real data is significantly higher** (due to balanced binary classes), but **AUC for real data is lower** (most likely due to missing values in real data).
- **Buffers** do cause more irregular variations in results as t gets larger and k gets smaller, but on the whole, it **makes no overall improvement**. There are more significant differences between the results of synthetic data with buffer and without buffer (due to imbalanced classes).
- The **more sparse the attribute(s), the better the results**.
- On average, **fraudulent applications do exhibit more spiky behaviour than legitimate ones.** Measured by NTOP10 (top 10% of ranked examples), the spike detection framework results in about **two-fold increase in detection rate** for both synthetic data (>0.3) and real data (>0.9), compared to random selection of synthetic data (0.14) and real data (0.5) respectively.
- The **computation time is small** - about 1 minute for 1 attribute to score 1000 streaming applications on a normal workstation.

4   Conclusion

This paper has reported on a stream-in and score-out system for sparse personal identifiers. It has described the spike analysis framework and taken a step toward building a highly automated, scalable, and timely detection tool on credit application data. Using synthetic and real data, experiments with different temporal representations showed that window step size is best determined by the overall daily stream rate, window size does not have to be very large, buffers have not been proven to be useful yet, and the best detection rates are obtained with the sparsest attributes. Future extensions on this work will include testing out the other seven parameters on a few million real credit applications.

Acknowledgements

This research is financially supported by the Australian Research Council under Linkage Grant Number LP0454077. Ethics approval is granted by Monash SCERH under Project Number 2005/694ED. The real credit application data is provided by Baycorp Advantage. Special thanks to developers of FEBRL data set generator, Ironic Chart Plotter, and PERF evaluation software.

References

1. Arasu, A., Babcock, B., Babu, S., Datar, M., Ito, K., Nishizawa, I., Rosenstein, J. and Widom, J.: STREAM: The Stanford Stream Data Manager Demonstration description - short overview of system status and plans. Proceedings of SIGMOD03, 2003.
2. Balakrishnan, H., Balazinska, M., Carney, D., Çetintemel, U., Cherniack, M., Convey, C., Galvez, E., Salz, J., Stonebraker, M., Tatbul, N., Tibbetts, R., Zdonik, S.: Retrospective on Aurora. VLDB Journal, 13(**4**), 2004, pp370-383.
3. Caruana, R. and Niculescu-Mizil, A.: Data Mining in Metric Space: An Empirical Analysis of Supervised Learning Performance Criteria. Proceedings of SIGKDD04, 2004, pp69-78.
4. Christen, P.: Probabilistic Data Generation for Deduplication and Data Linkage. Proceedings of IDEAL05, 2005.
5. Cook, M.: Fraud and ID Theft – The Lowdown on Fraud Rings. In Collections and Credit Risk **10**, 2005.
6. Fawcett, T. and Provost, F.: Activity Monitoring: Noticing Interesting Changes in Behaviour. Proceedings of SIGKDD99, 1999, pp53-62.
7. Goldenberg, A., Shmueli, G. and Caruana, R.: Using Grocery Sales Data for the Detection of Bio-Terrorist Attacks. In Statistical Medicine, Submitted, 2002.
8. Keogh, E., Chu, S., Hart, D. and Pazzani, M.: Segmenting Time Series: A Survey and Novel Approach. In Last, M., Kandel, A. and Horst, B. (eds.): Data Mining in Time Series Databases, World Scientific, 2004.
9. Kleinberg, J.: Bursty and Hierarchical Structure in Streams. Proceedings of SIGKDD02, 2002, pp91-101.
10. Kleinberg, J.: Temporal Dynamics of On-Line Information Streams. In Garofalakis, M., . Gehrke, J. and Rastogi, R. (eds.): Data Stream Management: Processing High-Speed Data Streams, Springer, 2005.
11. Montgomery, D.: Introduction to Statistical Quality Control. John Wiley and Sons Inc, 4th edition.
12. Percival, D. and Walden, A.: Wavelet Methods for Time Series Analysis (WMTSA). Cambridge University Press, 2000.
13. Phua, C., Lee, V., Gayler, R. and Smith, K.: A Comprehensive Survey of Data Mining-based Fraud Detection Research. Artificial Intelligence Review, submitted.
14. Phua, C., Gayler, R., Lee, V. and Smith, K.: On the Approximate Communal Fraud Scoring of Credit Applications. Proceedings of Credit Scoring and Credit Control, 2005.
15. Roberts, S.: Control-Charts-Tests based on Geometric Moving Averages. In Technometrics, **1**, pp239-250.
16. Wong, W.: Data Mining for Early Disease Outbreak Detection. PhD Thesis, Carnegie Mellon University, 2004.

Mining Positive Associations of Urban Criminal Activities Using Hierarchical Crime Hot Spots

Peter Phillips and Ickjai Lee

School of Information Technology,
James Cook University, QLD 4811, Australia
{Peter.Phillips, Ickjai.Lee}@jcu.edu.au

Abstract. We present a framework for discovering positive associations in urban crime datasets using hierarchical clustering and an association test based on a hybrid minimum bounding circle and average bounding circle approach. We justify the virtue of our framework by comparing its computational speed and quality of associations using real crime datasets.

1 Introduction

Crime data analysis allows a greater understanding of the dynamics of unlawful activities, providing answers to where, why and when certain crimes are likely to happen. The majority of crime analysis is currently done by human criminologists or spatial statisticians. With recent technology improvements, spatial data collection has become much easier and as such the volume and complexity of crime data easily exceeds the capability of human analysts. This data deluge has led to research for finding better ways to achieve crime analysis. Data mining is the process of searching for deeply hidden information in data that can be turned into knowledge. Clustering and postclustering (reasoning about clusters) are two core techniques used in geographic data mining. Most research into crime analysis using data mining techniques has focused on answering the question of where and when certain crimes happen, mostly using clustering techniques [1–5]. Relatively little research has been done into finding reasons or causes for these crime hot spots (postclustering) in the criminal data mining community [6, 7]. In this paper, we propose a hybrid framework for reasoning about multi-level hot spots. We apply hierarchical clustering to detect multi-level hot spots and then apply a fast reasoning approach to identify positive associations. We analyze the framework's efficiency with time complexity and its effectiveness with experimental results using real urban crime data.

2 Reasoning About Crime Hot Spots

Several approaches have been made to identify data-oriented shapes of crime hot spots in the geographical data mining community [2–5]. These approaches identify base-map-free hot spots based on various clustering criteria. However, relatively little research has been conducted on postclustering and reasoning about crime hot spots for "why they are there and then?". Estivill-Castro and Murray [4] present a

H. Chen et al. (Eds.): WISI 2006, LNCS 3917, pp. 127–132, 2006.
© Springer-Verlag Berlin Heidelberg 2006

partitioning clustering algorithm using a k-medoid type optimization function. They show that clustering in respect to a given feature set (such as schools and parks) allows positive associations to be discovered. The downside to their approach is that the clustering algorithm only produces single-level clusters and uses k-partitioning clustering. It is known that criminal activities are inherently hierarchical and the number of clusters is unknown [2, 8]. Choosing the best value for k is not easy but laborious. Recently, Lee and Estivill-Castro [7] presented a framework for mining interesting associative patterns in complex crime datasets. They use clustering to identify hot spots, transform them into polygons, and then find possible associative relations with association-rule mining. Their framework considers layers of different spatial features and how they impact on each other. The performance of the framework is heavily dependent on the clustering technique and the boundary extraction technique used. For massive crime datasets, the computational burden of computing and extracting cluster boundaries limits the usability of this technique. In addition, it uses single-level clustering.

3   A Framework for Mining Urban Criminal Activities

Criminal activities are complex and often show hierarchical properties. To reveal such complex hierarchical spatial aggregations, multi-level (hierarchical) clustering can be used. Traditional cluster reasoning approaches discussed in the previous section are limited to single-level clustering and are not applicable to these hierarchical clustering results. In this section, we propose a framework for reasoning about multi-level criminal clustering structure.

3.1   Testing for an Association Between Two Clusters

Before we can detect associative relationships between multi-level clusters and discover positive associations, we need to determine how to test for an association between two clusters of points. Figure 1 shows two clusters C_1 (black) and C_2 (red) exhibiting an association. Note that, intersection is one popular way of measuring associations and topological relationships [9]. One approach to measure association is to use the Minimum Bounding Circle (MBC) of each cluster. The MBC of a cluster C_1 is the smallest circle that contains all points of C_1 as seen in Fig. 1(a). It can be calculated in $O(n)$ expected time by using a randomized linear programming algorithm [10]. The main disadvantage to using the MBC approach for complex datasets is that it is highly susceptible to noise points and can easily lead to false-positive associations. A similar approach using Minimum Bounding Rectangle (MBR) is shown in Fig. 1(b), however it also suffers from the same problems as the MBC. Both the MBC and MBR are computationally fast to calculate, but due to their susceptibility to noise points they are not ideally suited to discovering positive associations in complex crime data. To overcome the problem of noise points whilst staying computationally fast, the Average Bounding Circle (ABC) method can be used. The ABC of a cluster C_1 is the circle that represents the average Euclidean distance of points in C_1 to the mean point of C_1. As shown in Fig. 1(c) it is smaller in diameter than the MBC. Odd

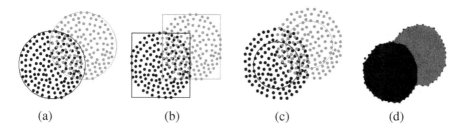

Fig. 1. Checking for an association between two clusters, C_1 (black) and C_2 (red): (a) MBC; (b) MBR; (c) ABC; (d) Region extraction

shaped clusters are not represented well by MBC, MBR or the ABC. However, our experiments with real crime data suggest that this is not a major problem when used in conjunction with a hierarchy of clusters. This is due to the fact that as we progress further down the hierarchy, the clusters become smaller and better represented by these tests, as shown by own experimental comparisons in Section 4. The approach taken by Lee and Williams [6] is to extract the cluster region (boundary) and then use RCC to determine the relationship between the two clusters. As shown in Fig. 1(d), the polygon of C_1 intersects the polygon of C_2 and thus an association exists.

Determining if two clusters show an association is efficient and simple when using either the MBC or ABC. Two circles, say B_1 and B_2, are disjoint (no association) if the distance between their centers is greater than the sum of their radii. The calculation for MBR is also computationally simple and efficient. Determining if two regions show an association with region extraction is more complex and computationally expensive compared with the tests for MBC, MBR and ABC (see [6] for details). We present experiments comparing these methods in Section 4.

3. 2 Hybrid Association Test

To allow our framework to be computationally efficient and robust to noise data, and to allow cluster pruning, we use a hybrid association test consisting of MBC and ABC. For clusters that have children (parent clusters), we use the MBC association test so that cluster pruning is always correct. For all other clusters (leaf clusters) we use the ABC test so that even if the parent showed a false-positive association due to noise data, the children clusters will reveal the true association. This can be thought of as a refining top-down approach: higher levels have a coarse association test (MBC) which is refined at lower levels (ABC). The computational speed increase that cluster pruning provides outweighs the decrease of false-positives at high levels of the cluster hierarchy in our experiments.

3.3 Association Measure for Two Datasets

We define an asymmetric association measure that gives an overall expression as to the extent that two datasets show an association with each other. Let D denote a given dataset and a set $C = \{C_1,...,C_k\}$ be a number of first-level clusters in hierarchical clustering. Here, C_i for $1 \leq i \leq k$ may have its subclusters $\{C_{i1},...,C_{ij}\}$ where $C_{im} \cap C_{in} = \emptyset$

for $1 \le m \ne n \le j$, and $C_i = \bigcup_{l=1}^{j} Cil$. The association measure of $Dataset_1$ to $Dataset_2$ is a sum of associated size of each cluster defined as follows:

$$\sum_{i=1}^{k} AssociatedSize(C_i) \,/\, \|Dataset_i\|, \tag{1}$$

where $AssociatedSize(C_i)$ is defined as $\|C_i\| - \sum_{l=1}^{j} \|C_i\|$ when C_i is a non-leaf cluster, otherwise it is $\|C_i\|$. In other words, if a cluster is a leaf cluster (that does not have its subclusters), then an associated size of this cluster is the size (the number of points) of this cluster. If a cluster is a non-leaf cluster (that has its subclusters), then an associated size of this cluster is propagated to and measured by its subclusters. For example, let us assume a dataset D has a first-level cluster C_1 ($\|C_1\| = 200$) which has two second-level clusters C_{11}($\|C_{11}\| = 100$), C_{12}($\|C_{12}\| = 100$). The cluster C_{12} has further split into two subclusters C_{121}($\|C_{121}\| = 50$), C_{122}($\|C_{122}\| = 40$). In the dataset D_1 with another dataset D_2 where C_1, C_{12} and C_{121} show positive associations, the association measure of D_1 to D_2 would be $C_{122} + (C_{12} - (C_{121} + C_{122})) + (C_1 - (C_{11} + C_{12}))$ over $\|D_1\|$ which is 50/200.

4   Comparison with Other Techniques

Here we present experiments conducted using real crime data collected from Brisbane, Australia. We justify the virtue of our framework by comparing its computational speed and quality of associations against the region extraction [6]. Both our framework and the region extraction use hierarchical Short-Long clustering [8] to discover crime hot spots, we limit the number of cluster levels to four. We performed experiments against five sets of crime data, varying in size from 2917 to 64249 points.

4.1   Efficiency Comparison

To compare the efficiency of all techniques, we measured the CPU time in milliseconds that each took to complete the association phase of processing. Experiments were performed on a Pentium 4 1.6Ghz with 512 MB RAM. All frameworks used the same clustering results, so the time taken for clustering is not compared, however the time taken for each framework to prepare information about clusters is included in the total reasoning time. That is, for the region extraction [6], the time taken to extract cluster polygons is included, and for our hybrid, MBC and MBR approaches, the time taken to compute the mean, average distance, MBC and MBR is included.

As can be seen from Fig. 2, our framework is computationally faster than that of the region extraction and both MBC and MBR with large datasets. The reason for this is that our hybrid framework is based on a simple reasoning test, whereas the region extraction uses a complex algorithm for extracting the boundary of each cluster and the other two techniques must calculate the MBC or MBR for each cluster. Run with different datasets, the time comparison could be slightly different, due to the fact that different datasets would result in different cluster hierarchy. The boundary extraction algorithm is dependent on the number of edges between points in a cluster, whereas our hybrid framework, MBC and MBR are all dependent on the number of clusters.

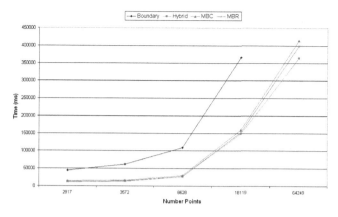

Fig. 2. Time comparison for reasoning about multi-level clustering

4.2 Effectiveness Comparison

To compare the effectiveness of the resulting associations we take the associations produced by the framework of the region extraction as a baseline [6].

Fig. 3 shows the average error of the associations for each test set produced by our hybrid framework, MBC and MBR compared to that of the region extraction. These results indicate that the associations produced by all three techniques are very close to the real associations present in the data, with MBR giving the closest results followed by our hybrid technique. The error between associations of the different approaches is dependent on the data - specifically the shape of clusters. Spherical shaped clusters will favor the hybrid and MBC approaches while squarer clusters will favor the MBR. Further experiments will need to be carried out to verify the result in massive datasets.

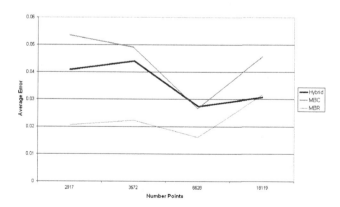

Fig. 3. Average error of reasoning about multi-level clustering

5 Concluding Remarks

We have presented a hybrid framework using MBC and ABC that allows autonomous exploratory analysis and knowledge discovery in massive crime datasets. It successfully discovers positive associations and is computationally fast. The framework presented here is part of a larger research project aimed at reasoning about crime hot spots using spatial data mining techniques within massive crime datasets. Further research into extending this framework is to allow full association-rule mining is needed. We also hope to research and compare a bottom-up approach to this framework and also a hybrid MBR and ABC approach to compare quality of associations versus computation time.

References

1. Hirschfield, A., Brown, P., Todd, P.: GIS and the Analysis of Spatially-Referenced Crime Data: Experiences in Merseyside. U. K. Journal of Geographical Information Systems 9(2) (1995) 191–210
2. Levine, N.: CrimeStat: A Spatial Statistics Program for the Analysis of Crime Incident Locations. In: Proc. of the 4th Int. Conf. on Geocomputation, Mary Washington College, Virginia (1999) GeoComputation CD-ROM: GC105.
3. Grubesic, T., Murray, A.: Detecting Hot Spots Using Cluster Analysis and GIS. In: The Fifth Annual Int. Crime Mapping Research Conf., Dallas, Texas (December 1-4, 2001)
4. Ratcliffe, J.: The Hotspot Matrix: A Framework for the Spatio-temporal Targeting of Crime Reduction. In: Police Practice and Research. Volume 5. (2004) 5–23
5. Craglia, M., Haining, R., Wiles, P.: A Comparative Evaluation of Approaches to Urban Crime Pattern Analysis. Urban Studies 37(4) (2000) 711–729
6. Lee, I., Williams, M.A.: Multi-level Clustering and Reasoning about Its Clusters Using Region Connection Calculus. In Proc. of the 7th Pacific-Asia Conf. on Knowledge Discovery and Data Mining. LNAI 2637, Seoul, Korea, Springer (2003) 283–294
7. Lee, I., Estivill-Castro, V.: Exploration of Massive Crime Datasets through Data Mining Techniques. (Journal of Geographical Systems) In press.
8. Lee, I.: Multi-Purpose Boundary-Based Clustering on Proximity Graphs for Geographical Data Mining. PhD thesis, The University of Newcastle (2002)
9. Cohn, A.G., Bennett, B., Gooday, J., Gotts, N.M.: Qualitative Spatial Representation and Reasoning with the Region Connection Calculus. GeoInformatica 1(3) (1997) 275–316
10. Gärtner, B.: Fast and robust smallest enclosing balls. In: ESA. (1999) 325–338

VCCM Mining: Mining Virtual Community Core Members Based on Gene Expression Programming[*]

Shaojie Qiao[1], Changjie Tang[1], Jing Peng[1],
Hongjian Fan[2], and Yong Xiang[1]

[1] School of Computer Science and Engineering, Sichuan University,
Chengdu 610065, China
{qiaoshaojie, tangchangjie}@cs.scu.edu.cn
[2] Department of Computer Science and Software Engineering,
the University of Melbourne, Australia
hfan@csse.unimelb.edu.au

Abstract. Intelligence operation against the terrorist network has been studied extensively with the aim to mine the clues and traces of terrorists. The contributions of this paper include: (1) introducing a new approach to classify terrorists based on Gene Expression Programming (GEP); (2) analyzing the characteristics of the terrorist organization, and proposing an algorithm called Create Virtual Community (CVC) based on tree-structure to create a virtual community; (3) proposing a formal definition of Virtual Community (VC) and the VCCM Mining algorithm to mine the core members of a virtual community. Experimental results demonstrate the effectiveness of VCCM Mining.

1 Introduction

Terrorist organization [1] is a complex adaptive system that emerged as an agent of change within the strategic system of nation states. It is an intricate network of individual small groups coupled by a common sense of purpose. So, how to distinguish the terrorists from the most likely suspects becomes a meaningful work.

Gene expression programming (GEP) [2, 3] is a new technique of evolutionary algorithm for data analysis. GEP combines the advantages of both GA and GP, while overcoming some of their individual limitations. If the attributes of classification samples are numeric, when applying GEP in the multi-dimension space classification, it will perform a global search in which genetic operators can select many attributes at a time. This paper makes the following contributions:

- Introduces a GEP-based classification algorithm to classify terrorists;
- Proposes a CVC algorithm to create a virtual community based on tree-structure;
- Presents an algorithm to mining the core members of a virtual community and experiments demonstrate that the searching cost can be reduced by this algorithm.

---

[*] This work was supported by National Science Foundation of China (60473071), Specialized Research Fund for Doctoral Program by the Ministry of Education (20020610007).

H. Chen et al. (Eds.): WISI 2006, LNCS 3917, pp. 133–138, 2006.

2 Related Work

Recently, there is a great deal of work about collecting terrorists' information and analyzing the system structure of the terrorist cell by computer [4, 5].

1. Searching the core of a terrorist group by computer. Jafar Adibi, a computer scientist at the University of Southern California, is developing ways to find hidden links between known terrorists and their as-yet-unknown confederates. He labels 20% of a terrorist group's members as "known" and challenges the program to find the rest.
2. Building a virtual al-Qaeda. Computer scientist Kathleen M. Carley heads a lab that tries to simulate terrorist organizations. The lab has built simulations of al-Qaeda by dumping newspaper articles into a computer database. A program then takes that information and looks for patterns and relationships between individuals.
3. Filtering data based on mathematical models. Mathematician Jonathan Farley of the Massachusetts Institute of Technology employs "order theory"—a branch of abstract mathematics that looks at the hierarchies within groups—to characterize the terrorist cells that intelligence agencies are trying to break up.

The differences between our work and these proposed methods lie in: comparing with related work one, this paper uses GEP to classify the terrorists, and treat classification as a means of data preprocessing; related work two builds a virtual al-Qaeda manually, but we uses computer to analyze and generate a virtual community.

3 Classification Algorithm Based on GEP

The preliminary concept is defined as follows.

Definition 1 (GEP Classifier). A GEP classifier $C = (M, T, F, Op, v)$, where M is the set of GEP chromosomes [3]; T is the terminal set, such as $\{1, 2, a, b\}$; F is the function set, such as $\{+, -, *, /, sqrt\}$; Op is the set of genetic operators [6], i.e., selection, crossover, mutation and transposition [3]; v is the fitness value.

There are five steps in solving this problem by GEP (see Sect. 5.1 for detail).

1. to choose the fitness function;
2. to choose the set of terminals T and the set of functions F;
3. to choose the chromosomal architecture;
4. to choose the kind of linking function;
5. to choose the set of genetic operators and their rates.

4 VCCM Mining

In the communication perspective, al-Qaeda is much like a virtual community. The terrorist network can be described as Fig. 1 (a). The members of a virtual community are separated into two groups: *heads* and *members*. As shown in Fig. 1 (b), the nodes of the first three levels are heads, others are members. The nodes have the following features: (1) the nodes of the same level do not have edges linking with each other; (2) the weight of the edge is used to record the communication frequencies.

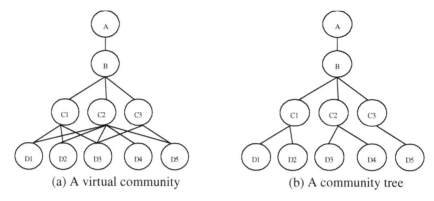

(a) A virtual community   (b) A community tree

Fig. 1.

Definition 2 (Community Tree). A community tree is a 5-turple $T = (N, E, S, t, r)$, where N is a set of nodes; E is a set of undirected edges (u, v, c), where $u, v \in N$, u is the parent of v and c is the weight maps each node $n \in N$ to a set of values which is used to record the communication frequencies; S is a set of labels (C_h, C_i), C_h is the height of node n, and C_i is the sequence number of n in level C_h; t is a distinguished node called "taproot" of the tree; r is the root of the tree.

4.1 Creating a Virtual Community

There are four major steps in Create Virtual Community (CVC) algorithm.

1. Initialize the node set of the first three levels, i.e., {A, B, {C1,C2,...,Ci}};
2. Traverse each node (start from the fourth level) to find the nodes in the upper level which link with it and record all the communication frequencies (note, one node may have many edges joined by the nodes in the upper level), and let it be weight[i], where $i \in N$; after that, compute each node's weights, let count = $\sum$ weight[i];
3. Sort the nodes of the same level by count in descending order using bubble-sort algorithm. In this way, one layer of nodes has been generated;
4. Repeat step 2-3 to create the following layer of nodes.

4.2 VCCM Mining

Definition 3 (Core Member of Community Tree). Let S[i] be the i-th set of leaf nodes which are siblings, and W be the weight sum of the nodes in S[i], $W=\sum_{j=1}^{k}$ weight[j], where k represents the node's number. S[i]' is a subset of S[i], S[i]'$\subseteq$S[i], where S[i]' = { n_{ij} | j =1,2,...,m, where j represents the j-th node}, $W'=\{\sum_{j\in M}$ weight[j]| $M\subseteq[1,k]\}$, $\eta=W'/W$, η is named *Factor*. If $\eta\geq\xi$ (ξ is a predefined threshold, where $\xi\in(0,1)$, and represents the significance of S[i]'), then n_{ij} is named Core Member of Community Tree and S[i]' is the set of Core Members.

VCCM Mining has two phrases: *pruning* and *searching core members*.

The *Pruning* Phrase:

i) Compare the weights of node m_{ij}, where i represents the level number and j represents the j-th node (start from the fourth level), find the maximum, and save it;

ii) Delete other branches of node m_{ij};

iii) Use the same method to trim other nodes' branches until the last one.

The *Searching Core Members* Phrase: Let T be a community tree, where r represents the root and let M be the set of known core members (the node in M is *leaf*, and we use M to find other core members). First sort r's children by weight in descending order, then create a stack S and push r's children into it (note that, each sub-community which treats r's child as its root at lest has one child in M), and sort these nodes by weight. Let W' be the weight sum of nodes in S, and W be the weight sum of nodes in T, calculate $\eta = W'/W$ and perform the following steps:

1) If $\eta \geq \xi$, go to step 3;
2) Otherwise, push the first node (r's child) which is not in S into it, recalculate η; if η is still less than ξ, then push another node into it until $\eta \geq \xi$, go to step 3;
3) For each node k in S, if k is not a *leaf* node, repeat step1-2; if k is a *leaf* node, put it into a new stack S' the nodes of which are core members;
4) Output the nodes in S'.

5   Experimental Evaluation

A model used to simulate the process for mining virtual community core members has been implemented in the developing platform of Microsoft Visual C++6.0. Experiments are conducted on a P4, 1.5 GHz PC with 256M RAM, running Microsoft Windows XP Professional. In order to validate the effectiveness of GEP-based classification algorithm, we use APS [7] to perform these experiments.

5.1   Experiment 1: Terrorist's Classification Problem

The data sets for classifying are synthetic data sets based on newspaper articles and other information about the terrorist organizations, and we named the terrorist database *Terrorist*. The training set contains 350 instances where the binary 1-bit encoding in which represents two possible output classes ("0" for false and "1" for true) and this database contains four testing sets: T1, T2, T3 and T4 which are discriminated by size shown in Table 1. Each instance is described by six attributes: *religion*, *origin*, *gender*, *is_educated*, *age* and *has_criminal_ records*.

The GEP function set includes {+, -, *, /, sqrt}, and the terminal set contains all the attribute names. In our experiments, the values of the parameters are: the head length is 8; the number of genes, chromosomes, and generations are 3, 100 and 100; crossover rate is 0.3; mutation rate is 0.044; and transposition rate is 0.1. Each experiment runs for ten times, and we use the average value to compare GEP approach with C4.5. Table 1 represents the test accuracy from these algorithms.

Table 1. Comparison of classification accuracy in terrorist's classification problem

Dataset	C4.5	GEP	Number of testing instances
T1	64.102	97.057	100
T2	64.062	96.628	200
T3	64.456	96.685	500
T4	62.678	96.571	1000

5.2 Experiment 2: Comparison of Efficiency Between GEP and GP

It is trivial to compare the CPU time between GEP with other traditional classification algorithms, i.e., C4.5, NaiveBayes and SMO [8], since GEP is definitely more time-consuming. But it is necessary to compare GEP with GP approach.

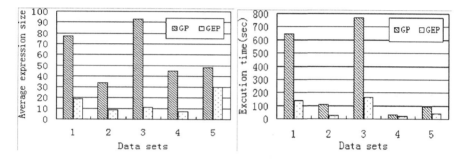

Fig. 2. Comparison of the average expression size and the execution time between GEP and GP

Figure 2 gives a comparison of the average expression size [2] generated by GEP and GP, and shows the comparison of the average execution time over ten different runs between GEP and GP on five benchmark data sets from UCI repository, i.e., *breast cancer*, *balance scale*, *waveform*, *zoo* and *iris*. It can be concluded that GEP tends to generate shorter expressions and costs less time compared with GP.

5.3 Experiment 3: Performance Evaluation of VCCM Mining

In Fig. 3 (a), X-axis represents the number of nodes generated by computer, and Y-axis is the *leaf* nodes (core members of a community tree), note that by using Normal Searching algorithm you have to search all *leaf* nodes.

Figure 3 (a) shows the cost for searching core members by VCCM Mining algorithm compared with Normal Searching algorithm. It is supposed that the time for searching each leaf node is equal, and experimental results demonstrate that the VCCM Mining algorithm can reduce the searching cost. Figure 3 (b) shows the changes of the searching cost with the number of nodes increasing. With the size of a community tree increasing, the VCCM Mining algorithm is still efficient.

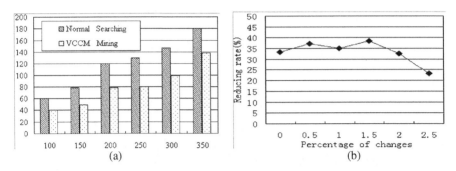

Fig. 3. Contrast of the cost of searching by VCCM Mining and Normal Searching algorithm

6   Conclusions and Future Work

In this paper, we analyze the characteristics of the terrorist organization and introduce a GEP-based classification approach. By using Community Tree, an algorithm is proposed to mining the VCCM. Experimental results show that VCCM Mining algorithm can reduce the cost for searching core members of a virtual community.

Our future work contains: extracting the important information about terrorists from Internet websites, because manual extracting is laborious and time-consuming; using the information to create the architecture of a terrorist group automatically; comparing the proposed algorithm with the traditional key network member identification methods such as network centralities and Carley's NETEST tool that combines multi-agent technology with hierarchical Bayesian inference models.

References

1. Larry K. Wentz and Lee W. Wagenhals: Effects Based Operations for Transnational Terrorist Organizations: Assessing Alternative Courses of Action to Mitigate Terrorist Threats. Proceedings of Command and Control Research and Technology Symposium, San Diego (2004)
2. Chi Zhou, Weimin Xiao, Peter C. Nelson, and Thomas M. Tirpak: Evolving Accurate and Compact Classification Rules with Gene Expression Programming. IEEE Transactions on Evolutionary Computation, Vol. 7, No. 6 (2003) 519–531
3. C. Ferreira: Gene Expression Programming: Mathematical Modeling by an Artificial Intelligence. Angra do Heroismo, Portugal (2002)
4. Matt Crenson: Math wizards offer help in fighting terrorism. http://www.azstarnet.com/dailystar/relatedarticles/42692.php (2004)
5. S. Qiao, C. Tang, Z. Yu, J. Wei, H. Li and L. Wu: Mining Virtual Community Structure Based on SVM. Computer Science, Vol. 32, No. 7 (2005) 208–212
6. J. Peng, C. Tang, J. Zhang and C. Yuan: Evolutionary Algorithm Based on Overlapped Gene Expression. ICNC 2005, Vol. 3612 of LNCS (2005) 194–204
7. C. Ferreira: Gene Expression Programming in Problem Solving. Soft Computing and Industry: Recent Applications, Springer-Verlag, Berlin Heidelberg (2002) 635–654
8. J. Platt: Sequential minimal optimization: A fast algorithm for training support vector machines. Advances in Kernel Methods-Support Vector learning, Cambridge, MA: MIT Press (1999) 185–208

Integration of a Cryptographic File System and Access Control

SeongKi Kim, WanJin Park, SeokKyoo Kim, SunIl Ahn, and SangYong Han

School of Computer Science and Engineering, Seoul National University,
56-1 Shinlim, Kwanak, Seoul, 151-742 Korea
ditoman@chollian.net
{wjpark25, anemone, siahn, syhan}@pplab.snu.ac.kr

Abstract. The importance of kernel-level security mechanisms such as a file system and access control has been increasingly emphasized as weaknesses in user-level applications. However, when using only access control, including role-based access control (RBAC), a system is vulnerable to a low-level or physical attack. In addition, when using only a cryptographic file system, a system also has a weakness that it is unable to protect itself. To overcome these vulnerabilities, we integrated a cryptographic file system into the access control, and developed a prototype.

1 Introduction

Since the development of the first computer system, security breaches have been a problem. In addition, with increasing numbers of systems being connected, these have been exposed to increased risk of such breaches. To avoid these risks, technologies such as firewalls, intrusion detection systems (IDS), and audit trails have become widespread. However, these technologies have their own limitations. For instance, a firewall cannot protect a system against an internal intruder. In addition, once an intruder gains access to the root privilege of a target system, there is no way to protect the system using only a firewall or IDS. An audit trail cannot prevent an intrusion, but can only help to trace the intruder by leaving messages. In addition, these features cannot protect themselves from being killed because they all operate on the application level. Application level security mechanisms can also collapse the entire security of a system, e.g. buffer-overflow attack. These problems have many researchers and vendors place a focus on kernel layers such as file systems and access controls as means of enhancing a security.

Among the access controls available, discretionary access control (DAC) [1] determines the legality of an access request using both the permissions provided by an owner and the identity of a user. Despite the widespread use of DAC, it has the disadvantage that objects can be accessed without limitations if the identity of a user is gained by an intruder because it classifies users only into completely trusted administrators and completely untrusted ordinary users. Mandatory access control (MAC) [2] classifies the security levels of users and objects, which are in turn used to determine whether access of the object is legal or not. Although MAC is widely used in government classified environments, it has the disadvantage that it is too coarse-grained

H. Chen et al. (Eds.): WISI 2006, LNCS 3917, pp. 139–151, 2006.

to realize the strict least privilege to achieve the separation of duty. To overcome these problems, role based access control (RBAC) [3] is emerging as an alternative. RBAC minimizes an intruder's possibility to gain limitless power by giving a user the least privilege required to carry out the user's own duty through a dense-grained privilege. Even if an intruder happens to gain a user's identity, the intruder can have only the least privilege. RBAC also supports high application flexibility by creating a role, changing its permissions, applying it to objects, and assigning it to users.

However, all of these access controls have the common weakness that they are vulnerable to both low-level and physical attacks. If an intruder finds ways to access the information under the level of the access control, then the intruder can access all of its information. In addition, if an intruder can remove the protected disk, physically attach it to another system without access control, and mount it, all of its information can be revealed. These low-level and physical problems can be avoided by using decryption and encryption when reading and writing information. In this case, even if an intruder accesses the information below the level of the access control or steals the disk, the information cannot be viewed because of the encryption. However, a cryptographic file system cannot protect itself because most of them are organized as dynamically loadable kernel modules or user-level applications without a protection mechanism. This protection problem can be remedied by controlling the unload and kill privilege of an access control. In other words, when a cryptographic file system is used with access control, these two mechanisms complement each other.

We designed a fast, simple, mandatory, policy-fixed access control model that includes some RBAC elements and DAC characteristics, and has no need to change an operating system because the overheads to support all of the RBAC features and policy flexibility are significant. In addition, to overcome the low-level and physical weaknesses of the access controls mentioned above, we also integrated a cryptographic file system into the access control. We then developed a prototype.

This paper is organized as follows. Section 2 describes various related works. Section 3 describes our model and implementation. Section 4 concludes.

2   Related Works

This section describes cryptographic file systems such as CFS [4], TCFS [5], and Cryptfs [6], as well as access controls such as RBAC [7].

2.1 Cryptographic File System (CFS) [4]

CFS is a cryptographic file system that was designed as a user-level NFS server by *Matt Blaze, AT & T Bell Lab* to support various ciphers. The cipher and key are specified when a directory is first created using the command *cmkdir*. CFS operates as in Fig. 1.

When a user accesses an attached directory, a general NFS client receives the request, and makes a request to a modified NFS server, which encrypts and decrypts contents using the key provided with *cattach*. When finished using the attached directory, the user should detach from it using the command *cdetach*.

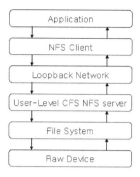

Fig. 1. Call path of CFS [8]

Although CFS is portable, it has serious overheads because the server is implemented as a user-level process. The NFS server needs to perform many context switches and data copies between a kernel and a user space, which significantly downgrades its performance. Besides its overhead, it has the inconvenience that a user who wants to use the encrypted directory has to input a key to attach a directory because there is no automatic key management mechanism.

2.2 Transparent Cryptographic File System (TCFS) [5]

TCFS is a cryptographic file system that was designed as a kernel-level NFS client by *Cattaneo and Persiano*. To encrypt a directory or a file, a user sets its key as one of the attributes within the client's NFS mount point. TCFS operates as shown in Fig. 2.

All of the calls to the NFS server pass through a modified TCFS NFS client, which encrypts and decrypts all of the contents to the NFS server, with a pre-established key as one of the directory or file attributes.

Although TCFS can transparently mount a file system within a file server and is faster than CFS because it is implemented in a kernel, it has the weaknesses that it saves keys in the client system and is implemented only on Linux kernel 2.2.17 or earlier.

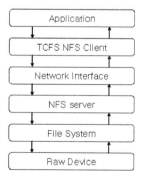

Fig. 2. Call path of TCFS [8]

2.3 Cryptfs [6]

Cryptfs is a stackable cryptographic file system that is part of the *FiST toolkit* [9] and exploits *vnode stacking* [10] to operate over various file systems. Cryptfs supports only one cipher, Blowfish [11], and implements a limited key management scheme. Fig. 3 shows the call path of Cryptfs.

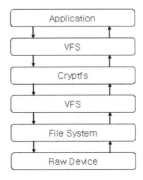

Fig. 3. Call path of Cryptfs [8]

When an application or a user makes a request to a file system, the request is translated into a vnode level call. The vnode level calls invoke its Cryptfs equivalents, which encrypt or decrypt the contents, and Cryptfs invokes an original file system call through the vnode level call.

Although Cryptfs is fast and secure because it is implemented on the kernel level and its keys are based on user and session IDs, it has the weakness that it can be unloaded by an intruder who gains root privilege because it is implemented as a dynamically loadable kernel module and does not control the unload system calls.

2.4 Role Based Access Control

RBAC supports mandatory control, dense-privileged control, and easier administration than either DAC or MAC. RBAC has elements such as users, roles, objects, sessions, and operations, as shown in Fig. 4.

A user represents a person who uses a system. A role has sets of both operations and objects determined by the security policy administrator, and is given to users. A session represents a connection to the system, with some of the roles activated during the session.

The cardinality between users and roles is many-to-many. In other words, a user can have many roles, and a role can be assigned to many users. The same principle also applies to the cardinality between roles and sessions, and between operations and objects. A session can have many activated roles, and inversely a role can be also activated during many sessions. More than one operation can be applied to more than one object. The permutation of operations and objects can be thought of as a parameter assigned to a role. A role can have many parameters and a parameter can be

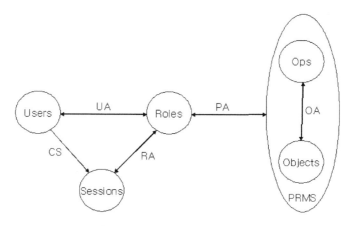

Fig. 4. Basic RBAC model [3, 12]

assigned to many roles. However, the cardinality between users and sessions is one-to-many. In other words, although a user can have many sessions, a session can only involve one user.

The basic RBAC model above is summarized as follows [3].

-USERS, ROLES, OPS, SESSIONS, and OBS represent respectively users, roles, operations, sessions, and objects.

-UA ⊆ USERS × ROLES, a many-to-many mapping user-to-role assignment relation.

-PA ⊆ PRMS × ROLES, a many-to-many mapping permission-to-role assignment relation.

-CS ⊆ SESSIONS, a one-to-many mapping user-to-session assignment relation.

-RA ⊆ ROLES × SESSIONS, a many-to-many mapping role-to-session assignment relation.

-OA ⊆ OPS × OBS, a many-to-many mapping operation-to-object assignment relation.

Besides this basic model, RBAC supports role inheritance to relieve the burden of the administrator. Role inheritance supports a role to be created by inheriting another role. In this case, the derived role has the same sets of operations to objects as those of the base role. Full RBAC also supports static and dynamic separation of duty to give a user the least privilege required to perform the user's own tasks through the facilities of role constraints. As examples of role constraints, a mutually exclusive role constraint guarantees that only one role is activated, a prerequisite role constraint guarantees that a prerequisite role is activated, and a cardinality role constraint guarantees that a limited number of roles are activated [3, 12].

3 Model and Implementation

This section describes our model and implementation of a cryptographic file system and access control.

3.1 Overall Architecture

The overall architecture is illustrated in Fig. 5.

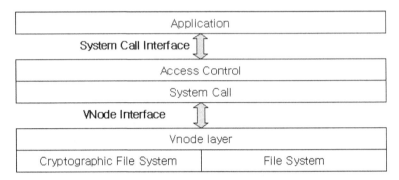

Fig. 5. Overall architecture

When a user accesses an object through an application, the access passes through our access control, which checks whether the access is legal or not. Then our cryptographic file system encrypts or decrypts its contents. Before or after encrypting or decrypting, our cryptographic file system calls the vnode layer that invokes the functions in the original file system.

In this architecture, the access control and cryptographic file system complement each other to protect precious resources. The access control protects the cryptographic file system from being controlled by unauthorized users. Our access control allows only authorized users to load and unload the cryptographic file system through the least privilege principle. The cryptographic file system protects the resources from a low-level detour or physical theft that can circumvent our access control. Even if an intruder detours our access control or steals the protected disk, the information cannot be read because of the encryption.

Using this model, we can apply the cryptographic file system to directories requiring protection, give CFS-loading/unloading privileges only to the CFS administrator, and resource-reading privileges only to specific users through the access control. When these policies are applied, the access control only allows specific users to read the directory, and an intruder cannot read its information or unload the cryptographic file system because of the lack of privileges through the access control. Even if an intruder can steal the disk and attach it to another system, or detour the access control, the information cannot be viewed because of the encryption through the cryptographic file system.

Two architectures can be chosen to implement this architecture. The first method is to create a kernel containing new functions. The second method is to add new functions to a kernel using a dynamically loadable kernel module. Most modern operating systems support a dynamically loadable kernel module. In addition, the first method is very difficult because most operating systems are not license-free. Therefore, we chose the second method, involving dynamic implementation. Besides kernel modules, we designed a server daemon and an administration tool for easy management.

We implemented our model as a prototype on a Sun Ultra 10 device, which has an UltraSparc-IIi 440-MHz CPU with 512 KB Cache, 256 MB RAM, 9-GB IDE hard drive, running the Solaris 2.8 operating system.

3.2 Cryptographic File System

We used vnode stacking [10] at the kernel level to enhance the speed and security. The architecture of our cryptographic file system is shown in Fig. 6.

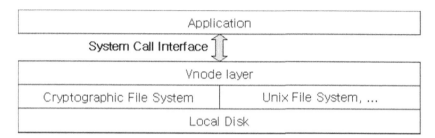

Fig. 6. Architecture of our cryptographic file system

An application or a user accesses a file through a *read()* system call, which calls the vnode layer, *vn_read()*, and thus invokes our cryptographic file system. This in turn invokes the Unix file system that reads and decrypts the contents. Our cryptographic file system has entry points such as *read()*, *getpage()*, *write()*, and *putpage()*, which were implemented as mentioned above.

As cryptographic algorithms, we chose 128-bit Blowfish [11] and SEED [13] because of their speed, compact size, and Korean standard when compared with DES [11]. We felt that 128-bit keys were secure enough not to be broken for several years when considering the current CPU capacity and the advancement. We designed the system so that its key information could be saved on the different disk from the protected disk with an encrypted status. When our cryptographic file system is first loaded by the CFS administrator, it can read the encrypted key information from the file mounted on this different disk, which is managed by the CFS administrator. If no removable disk is available on which to save the encrypted key information, the directory containing the key information should be at least protected by access control that allows only the CFS administrator to read it.

We chose a vnode stacking architecture in the kernel level because of its low overheads without context switches, its support of various file systems, and the relative security of the kernel memory. We chose the key-saving architecture under the assumption that the encrypted key information can be well protected by the access control if saved on the same disk, and by the CFS administrator if saved on a different disk. This assumption also removed the Cryptfs inconvenience of invoking a new shell to use session IDs as part of the key.

3.3 Access Control

We designed and implemented a fast, simple, mandatory, and application-flexible access control that has DAC characteristics, RBAC elements, and no kernel changes.

3.3.1 Model
Fig. 7 shows our access control model that was implemented to minimize overheads.

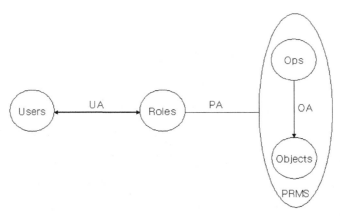

Fig. 7. Access control model

In comparison with the DAC model, our model is similar in that a user has permissions to objects, and different in that it does not maintain the access control list, extends from simple permissions to various permissions, has named roles, and is mandatory. Fig. 8 shows the extended permissions.

In comparison with the full RBAC model in Section 2.4, our model has a one-to-many relationship between OPS and OBS, a one-to-one relationship between ROLES and PRMS, and no sessions to both simplify implementation and make it fast. In this model, a set comprising an operation and objects represents the parameter for a role. A role can have only one parameter. However, the relationship between users and roles is still many-to-many. In other words, a role can be assigned to many users, and a user can have many roles.

The relationships can be summarized as follows.

-*UA* ⊆ *USERS* × *ROLES*, a many-to-many mapping user-to-role assignment relation.
-*PA*, a one-to-one mapping permission-to-role assignment relation.
-*OA* ⊆ *OBS*, a one-to-many mapping operation-to-object assignment relation.

Besides the relationships described above, we decided not to implement session, role hierarchy, or role constraint to make implementation easy and fast. We modified the standard RBAC model in order to minimize its overheads due to its complexity. A session and a role constraint weren't essential because we assumed that each user had

System calls	Contents
FORK	Create a process
EXEC	Execute a program
KILL	Terminate a process
SETUID	Change a user ID
CHMOD	Change a mode
CHOWN	Change an owner
READ	Read
WRITE	Write
LINK	Link
UNLINK	Unlink or Delete
RENAME	Change a name
MKDIR	Create a directory
RMDIR	Delete a directory
CHDIR	Change a directory
MOUNT	Mount a file system
UNMOUNT	Unmount a file system
MODLOAD	Load a kernel module
MODUNLOAD	Unload a kernel module
ROLE	Change an access policy

Fig. 8. Permissions checked in our model

the same set of roles during the constant period. From the viewpoint of security, our model is mandatory because only security policy administrators can set the policies. This model can support the least privilege through multiple-role assignments to a user. As an example of our model, if a role has a read operation, includes /a, and /b objects, and is assigned to root and test users, only root and test users can read /a, and /b files.

However, our model has the inconvenience that a role cannot be created by inheriting another roles, so that security policy administrators might have to create multiple roles to express a single role in the standard RBAC model, and maintain role lists for each task.

3.3.2 Implementation

Our implementation of the access control model is largely divided into five modules: a system call control module, an authentication module, a role management module, an audit module, and an access control module, as shown in Fig. 9.

The system call control module stores, hooks and restores old system calls. In addition, it provides new system calls to all of the other modules. The role management module adds and deletes roles, modifies their permissions, adds objects to them, and assigns them to users. The authentication module manages authentication information. The audit module records all user accesses. The access control module determines the legality of an access request.

In contrast to the double call architecture of SELinux [14] implementation, we adopted this direct call architecture without the separated security server in order to minimize the overheads that are caused by policy flexibility. Our implementation

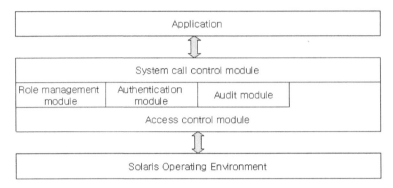

Fig. 9. Architecture of the access control model

consisted of 1 module, and had the fixed access control. Most of RBAC implementations have not concentrated on compactness and speed, but on policy flexibility to support various policies. As a representative example, the overheads of SELinux [15] were more than 5% in the Unixbench [16] case [15], 10% in the Lmbench [17] case [15], and 4% in the kernel compilation case [15]. Whenever a client wants to access an object, the client makes a request to an object manager, which in turn makes a request to the security server to determine the legality of the access. Although an object manager maintains the AVC [14] to minimize these overheads, this is not sufficient to cover all of these overheads.

3.3.2.1 System Call Control Module. The system call control module stores old system calls, registers new calls replacing old calls during initialization, calls all of the other modules during operation, and restores old calls during finalization.

When a kernel module is loaded into a Solaris kernel, the *_init()* entry point is called [18], and the system call control module stores old system calls and installs new ones. After these initial tasks, when an application makes a request to a system through system calls, new system calls are called.

The new system calls first call the privilege-checking function in the access control module with appropriate parameters. This function checks that the user has appropriate privileges. If so, this function simply calls an old system call. Otherwise, it returns an error.

In short, the system call control module calls functions in the other modules and, by hooking most of the system calls, prevents an unauthorized user from accessing objects by circumventing our implementation.

3.3.2.2 Authentication Module. The authentication module receives authentication information from a pluggable authentication module (PAM) [19] and maintains and manages authentication information for each process, using the information to determine the legality of an access request. This authentication information included process, user, and group IDs.

Authentication information is largely created in two cases: (i) when a user logs onto the system after inputting a user ID and password; and (ii) when a child process is created through a *fork()* system call. This authentication information is also changed in two cases: (i) when users change their own user ID using a *setuid()* system call; and (ii) when a user executes a new process by calling a *exec()* system call. Authentication information is destroyed when a process is exited or destroyed.

3.3.2.3 Role Management, Audit, and Access Control Modules. The role management module manages permissions for roles and applies permissions to objects, and manages user assignment to roles. This module is called when a property of a role is changed or access control module checks whether a user has permission to access an object or not.

The audit module maintains all of the access records, including both failed and succeeded logs, and sends them to the server daemon described so that it can write access records to files. When a user fails to access an object or succeeds in accessing an object, the corresponding structures are written in kernel memory, and the server daemons then reads them through the log system call added and writes them to log files. The server daemon should be always run to protect kernel memory, and thus we set policies so that only the server daemon can load our access control.

The access control module has a privilege-checking function. This function is called when a hooked system call is called and a privilege needs to be checked. The privilege-checking function first checks whether the object itself has a role that permits the user to access the object. If there is enough permission to process the request, the function returns a success. The hooked system call then calls the old system call. After checking its own privilege, this function checks whether there is inherited permission by iteratively checking the parent permission.

The process of checking permission can broadly be summarized by two procedures. First, the module searches role lists maintained by the role management module. Second, it checks whether the role includes permission to access the object and the object itself. If so, the function determines if the calling user is included in the specific role. If included, the function returns a success and access is granted.

3.4 Server Daemon and Administration Tool

For easy administration, we wanted to develop an administration tool on *Windows*. However, because implementations of our cryptographic file system and access control were on kernel modules that cannot directly communicate with an administration tool, we needed to develop an additional server daemon that communicates with such a tool. The server daemon receives a request from the administration tool and sends a request to the CFS or access control through a system call. Another role of the server daemon is to periodically call the audit module through a new system call to obtain succeeded and failed logs from kernel memory, and write them to files.

We also developed an administration tool on *Windows XP* with *Visual C++ version 6.0*. The administration tool receives inputs from users to mount a directory with Blowfish or SEED, unmount a directory, create a role, change its permissions, apply it to objects, and assign it to a user. In all of these cases, the administration tool sent an adequate message to the server daemon, which in turn made a request to our CFS or access control.

3.5 Kernel Module Protection

As we implemented all of our modules as dynamic kernel modules to avoid kernel changes, the implementation can be unloaded. However, unauthorized users should not be able to unload the modules. Thus, our modules protect themselves by hooking an unload system call and creating an unload role. Only users included in the role that has module-unloading privilege can unload the modules.

4 Conclusion

Security-enhancing mechanisms on the kernel level have become increasingly important as the number of security breaches have risen and the limitations of security mechanisms at the user level have been identified. These limitations can become serious threats to the system with the important data such as national and international data protected only by the user level mechanisms. Among many kernel level mechanisms, RBAC is widely used as one of the approaches to increasing security because of its mandatory control, application flexibility, and setting of the least privilege through a dense-privileged restriction. However, even powerful access controls such as RBAC have a weakness in that they are vulnerable to a low-level attack or physical theft. For example, if an intruder can find a way to circumvent the access control of a system, all of its information can be obtained. In addition, if the disk protected by access control is stolen by an intruder, all of its information can be revealed.

We designed a fast access control model that is simple to implement, is mandatory, policy-fixed, and application-flexible. The model has some RBAC elements and DAC characteristics, and there is no need to change operating system. We also integrated a CFS into the developed access control to complement each other, developed a prototype on the Solaris operating system 2.8.

Our associative modules give better system protection: (i) by minimizing the possibility of an intruder gaining full control through setting the least privilege in access control; (ii) by protecting against circumvention of the access control through hooking most of the system calls; and (iii) by making it impossible to steal and access the protected disk through the CFS encryption. As a research project, our model and implementation are also valuable, because, to the best of our knowledge, they represent the first integration of a cryptographic file system and access control.

References

1. National Computer Security Center, *A Guide to understanding Discretionary Access Control in Trusted Systems*, 30 December 1987.
2. M. Hitchens, V. Varadharajan, *Design and specification of role based access control policies*, In: IEE Proceedings Software, 147(4), 2000, pp. 117-129.

3. D.F. Ferraiolo, R. Sandhu, S. Gavrila, D.R. Kuhn, R. Chandramouli, *Proposed NIST standard for role-based access control*, ACM Transactions on Information and System Security, 4(3), 2001, pp. 224-274.
4. M. Blaze, *A cryptographic file system for UNIX*, In: First ACM Conference on Communication and Computing Security, Fairfax VA 1993, pp. 158-165.
5. G. Cattaneo, G. Persiano, *Design and Implementation of a transparent cryptographic file system for UNIX*, In: Proceedings of the FREENIX Track: 2001 USENIX Annual Technical Conference, pp. 199–212.
6. E. Zadok, I. Badulescu, A. Shender, *Cryptfs: A stackable vnode level encryption file system*, Technical Report CUCS-021-98, Computer Science Department, Columbia University, 1998.
7. D.F. Ferraiolo, J. Cugini, D.R. Kuhn, *Role-based access control: features and motivations*, In: Proceedings of The 11th Annual Computer Security Applications Conference, New Orleans, USA, December 1995, pp. 241-248.
8. C.P. Wright, J. Dave, E. Zadok, *Cryptographic file systems performance: What you don't know can hurt you*, In: Proceedings of the 2003 IEEE Security In Storage Workshop (SISW 2003), October 2003.
9. E. Zadok, J. Nieh, *FiST: A language for stackable file systems*, In: USENIX Annual Conference, June 2000.
10. J.S. Heidemann, G.J. Popek, *File system development with stackable layers*, Source ACM Transactions on Computer Systems (TOCS) Archive, 12(1), 1994, pp. 58-89.
11. B. Schneier, *Applied Cryptography*, Wiley & Sons, 2nd edition, 1995.
12. M. Koch, L.V. Mancini, F. Parisi-Presicce, *A graph-based formalism for RBAC*, ACM Transactions on Information and System Security (TISSEC) Archive, 5(3), 2002, pp. 332-365.
13. Telecommunication Technology Association, *128-bit Symmetric Block Cipher (SEED)*, September 1999.
14. R. Spencer, S. Smalley, P. Loscocco, M. Hibler, D. Andersen, J. Lepreau, *The Flask security architecture: system support for diverse security policies*, In: Proceedings of the 8th USENIX Security Symposium, Washington, DC, August 1999, pp. 123–139.
15. P. Loscocco, S. Smalley, *Integrating flexible support for security policies into the Linux operating system*, In: Proceedings of the FREENIX Track: 2001 USENIX Annual Technical Conference (FREENIX '01), June 2001.
16. D.C. Niemi, *Unixbench 4.1.0*, http://www.tux.org/pub /tux/niemi/unixbench.
17. J. Katcher, *PostMark*, http://www.netapp.com/tech library/3022.html.
18. J. Mauro, R. McDougall, *Solaris Internals Core Kernel Architecture*, 2001.
19. V. Samar, C. Lai, *Making login services independent of authentication technologies*, In: Proceedings of the SunSoft Developer's Conference, March 1996.

Applications of Homomorphic Functions to Software Obfuscation[*]

William Zhu[1], Clark Thomborson[1], and Fei-Yue Wang[2,3]

[1] Computer Science Department, The University of Auckland, Auckland, New Zealand
fzhu009@ec.auckland.ac.nz, cthombor@cs.auckland.ac.nz
[2] The Key Laboratory of Complex Systems and Intelligent Science,
Institute of Automation, The Chinese Academy of Sciences, Beijing 100080, China
[3] Systems and Industrial Engineering Department,
The University of Arizona, Tucson, AZ 85721, USA
feiyue@sie.arizona.edu

1 Introduction

As various computers are connected into a world wide network, software is a target of copyright pirates, attackers, or even terrorists, as a result, software protections become a more and more important issue for software users and developers. There are some technical measures for software protections, such as hardware-based protections and software-based techniques [1], etc. Software obfuscation [2] is one of these measures to protect software from unauthorized modification by making software more obscure so that it is hard for potential attackers to understand the obfuscated software. There are several algorithms of software obfuscation such as layout transformation, computation transformation, ordering transformation, and data transformation [2]. Variable transformation is a major method of data transformation to transform software into a new semantically equivalent one that is hard for attackers to understand the true meaning of variables in software.

Chow et al. applied residue number technique, an approach used in hardware design, high precision integer arithmetic, and cryptography, to software obfuscation by encoding variables in the original program to hide the true meaning of these variables [3], but part of the technique proposed there is incorrect. In order to compensate this drawback, in paper [4], we proposed homomorphic functions, developed an algorithm for division by several constants based on homomorphic functions, and applied them to variable transformation.

Data structures are important components of programme and they are key clues for people to understand codes. Obfuscating data structures of programme will make it very hard for an attacker to modify them. In this paper, we apply homomorphic functions to obfuscate arrays in software through array index change, array index and dimension change, array folding, and array flattening. As said in [2], by adding the data complexity in the program, these methods can make a program much more difficult to understand and reverse engineer. We are investigating the security of these applications.

---

[*] Research supported in part by the New Economy Research Fund of New Zealand.

H. Chen et al. (Eds.): WISI 2006, LNCS 3917, pp. 152–153, 2006.
© Springer-Verlag Berlin Heidelberg 2006

2 Application of Homomorphic Functions to Array's Change

We describe four methods to apply homomorphic functions to software obfuscation: index change, index and dimension change, array folding and array flattening.

1. Index change
For an array A[n], firstly, find an m such that m > n, and n and m are relatively prime, then change A[n] into B[n] and the element A[i] is turned into b[i*m mod n].

2. Index and dimension change
For an array A[n], firstly, find an m such that m > n, and n and m are relatively prime, then change A[n] into array B[m] and the element A[i] is turned into b[i*n mod m].

3. Array folding
For an array A[n], we assume n > 2. The array folding procedure is as follows.

  If n is a prime, let m = n+1; otherwise m = n.

  Extend A[n] into C[m] by C[i] = A[i] for $0 <= i < n$ and C[i] undefined for others.

  Factor m into m_1 and m_2. Replace C[m] with $B[m_1, m_2]$ through $B[i \bmod m_1, i \bmod m_2] = C[i]$ for $0 <= i < m$.

  Replace any A[i] with $B[i \bmod m_1, i \bmod m_2]$ in the unobfuscated program.

4. Array flattening
For a 2-dimensional array $A[n_1, n_2]$, the array flattening procedure is as follows.

  Find two relatively prime integers m_1 and m_2 such that $n_1 <= m_2$ and $n_2 <= m_2$. Let $m = m_1*m_2$.

  Turn the 2-dimension array $A[n_1, n_2]$ into another 2-dimension array $C[m_1, m_2]$ by C[i, j] = A[i, j] for $0 <= i < m_1$ and $0 <= j < m_2$, and C[i, j] undefined otherwise. Replace all A[i, j] with C[i, j].

  Find two relatively integers k_1 and k_2 such that $k_1*m_1 + k_2*m_2 = 1$.

  Turn the 2-dimension array $C[n_1, n_2]$ into a 1-dimension array B[m] and let B[i] = $C[i \bmod m_1, i \bmod m_2]$ for $0 <= i < m$.

  Replace any A[i, j] with $B[(i*k_1 + j*k_2) \bmod m]$ for $0 <= i < n_1$ and $0 <= j < n_2$.

3 Conclusion

We propose applications of homomorphic functions to obfuscate arrays in software.

References

1. W. Zhu, C. Thomborson, F.-Y. Wang, A survey of software watermarking, LNCS 3495, 2005, pp. 454-458.
2. C. Collberg, C. Thomborson, D. Low, A taxonomy of obfuscating transformations, Tech. Report, No.148, Dept. of Computer Sciences, Univ. of Auckland, 1997.
3. Chow, et al, Tamper resistant software encoding, US patent 6594761 (2003) 1-32.
4. W. Zhu, C. Thomborson, A provable scheme for homomorphic obfuscation in software security, in: The IASTED International Conference on Communication, Network and Information Security, CNIS'05, 2005, pp. 208-212.

Security Model for Informational Privacy

Sabah S. Al-Fedaghi

Computer Engineering Department,
Kuwait University
sabah@eng.kuniv.edu.kw

1 Introduction

Private/personal information is defined as any linguistic expression that has referent(s) of type natural person. Private information can be classified as: (1) atomic private information is an assertion that has a single human referent, and (2) compound private information is an assertion that has more than one human referent. If p is a piece of atomic private information of person v, then p is proprietary private information of v, and v is its *proprietor*. A *possessor* refers to any agent that knows, stores, or owns the information [2].

Private information ethics (PIE) hypothesizes that private information has intrinsic moral value such that while others may have a right to utilize private information for legitimate needs and purposes, this utilization should not be done in such a way that devalues private information as an object of respect [1]. The *significance* aspect of private information derives from its privacy value to a human being.

Consider the statement *John plans a terrorism attack*. Does this have privacy-significant value? The statement has an "attribution-based" value (e.g., John is afraid of consequences of uncovering his plan), but John does not have a claim for treating *John plans a terrorism attack* as private information that deserves respect. Such information is a type of identifying personal information that has no privacy value.

It is typically claimed that *privacy protects criminals*. This saying mixes privacy with secrecy. Privacy implies an intrinsic value of private information. Secrecy involves unconstrained control of information. Thieves desire controlling information about their involvement in the theft. The privacy-based significance involves non-retribution-based (non-fear of punishment) desire of the *proprietor* to control private information. The assertion that *privacy helps criminals* is wrong because privacy is a trait of an innocent person just as health is a trait of a healthy person. We would not apply "healthiness" to a sick person as we would not apply privacy to a criminal. Thus the argument that *John is innocent or criminal. To decide whether he is innocent or criminal, we deny his privacy rights* is similar to the argument: *John is healthy or sick. To decide whether he is healthy or sick, we deny his right to medicine.*

Consequently, privacy comes at the second decisional level after determining the type of person under consideration. For ordinary citizens, all privacy laws and ethics apply. If he/she is a criminal, then security is the dominant concern. Mixing privacy and security arises out of the failure in sorting out ordinary persons from criminals. However, the most important aspect of respecting private information is securing it. The rest of this paper introduces a model for private information security.

H. Chen et al. (Eds.): WISI 2006, LNCS 3917, pp. 154–155, 2006.
© Springer-Verlag Berlin Heidelberg 2006

2 Basic Model

We can distinguish two types of information security: (1) Private Information Security (PIS), and (2) Non-private information security. In this paper, we concentrate on the special security aspects that pertain only to private information.

The basic PIS model of 'information sharing' includes five actors who may participate in the sharing process: proprietors, possessors, sharers, casters, and attackers. The casters are individuals who handle private (e.g., communicate) information and are thus involved in the sharing of information. Casters are responsible for "moving" the private information. It is assumed that the first four actors are legal participants in information sharing. PIS aims at excluding attackers from this process in order to protect the private sharing of information (e.g., identities of individuals who share non-private information), and the sharing of private information (e.g., identities of proprietors when they share private information).

Private Sharing of Information: The actors in this type of sharing are limited to individuals (i.e., persons); however 'information' in this type of sharing entails two kinds of information:

(a) Non-private information— for example, if John and Robert share sensitive information (e.g., pornographic), then they want to preserve the privacy of this sharing. This sharing is called 'private communication' in the context of the classical communication model.

(b) Private information— for example, if John and Robert share compound private information, then they want to preserve the privacy of this sharing as in (a) and also the privacy of their compound private information.

Non-private Sharing of Information: The actors in this type of sharing are limited to non-individuals (i.e., companies, government agencies, etc.); however, 'information' in this type of sharing entails two types of information:

(a) Private information— for example, if two hospitals share private information of their patients, the 'privacy' aspect is not of the hospitals, rather, it is the privacy of the patients. Our definition of privacy is applied only to human beings. For example, *Sinai Hospital in NY is very expensive* is not private information because the assertion does not include a referent of type person.

(b) Non-private information— for example, two companies share their technical information. The security here is not directly a privacy-related issue.

References

[1] S. Al-Fedaghi, Crossing Privacy, Information, and Ethics. *17th International Conference Information Resources Management Association* (IRMA 2006), Washington, DC, USA, May 21-24, 2006.

[2] S. Al-Fedaghi, How to Calculate the Information Privacy. *Proceedings of the Third Annual Conference on Privacy, Security and Trust*, St. Andrews, New Brunswick, Canada, October 12-14, 2005. http://www.lib.unb.ca/Texts/PST/2005/pdf/fedaghi.pdf

A Viable System for Tracing Illegal Users of Video

Hyunho Kang[1], Brian Kurkoski[2], Youngran Park[3],
Sanguk Shin[3], Kazuhiko Yamaguchi[2], and Kingo Kobayashi[2]

[1] Graduate School of Information Systems,
University of Electro-Communications,
1-5-1, Chofugaoka, Chofu-shi, Tokyo 182-8585, Japan
kang@ice.uec.ac.jp
[2] Dept. of Inf. and Communications Eng.,
University of Electro-Communications,
1-5-1, Chofugaoka, Chofu-shi, Tokyo 182-8585, Japan
{kang, kurkoski, yama, kingo}@ice.uec.ac.jp
[3] Department of Information Security, Pukyong National University,
599-1 Daeyeon-3Dong,
Nam-Gu, Busan 608-737, Republic of Korea
Podosongei@hanmail.net, shinsu@pknu.ac.kr

Typical uses of watermarks include copyright protection and disabling unauthorized access to content. Especially, copyright protection watermarks embed some information in the data to identify the copyright holder or content provider, while receiver-identifying watermarking, commonly referred to as fingerprinting, embeds information to identify the receiver of that copy of the content. Thus, if an unauthorized copy of the content is recovered, extracting the fingerprint will show who the initial receiver was [1][2]. In this paper we generalize our previous work [3] of a video fingerprinting system to identify the source of illegal copies. This includes a logo embedding technique, generalization of the distribution system and detailed investigation of the robustness against collusion attacks.

In our method, ECC is integrated into the watermarking system proposed in [4]. ECC based on convolutional codes are easy to implement and fast to encode and decode, so we use this type of code to correct errors in the logo which are introduced by attacks, compression and fingerprinting. The resulting system is evaluated under our fingerprinting channel with collusion attacks and MPEG compression. In our experiment, a 3-level temporal wavelet transform was performed on 112 frames of video, resulting in 8 types of frames (LLL, LLH, LHL, LHH, HLL, HLH, HHL, HHH

Table 1. Symbols used in our system with examples

	# of sub-tree	Depth of sub-tree	Order of sub-tree	# of video frame	# of max user	Wavelet level	Buyer area	# of total user
symbol	M	d	r	f	$N=r^d$	$l=\left\lfloor log_2 \dfrac{f}{N} \right\rfloor$	$(L)^{l-1}H$	$M \times N$
example	1,000	3	2	112	8	3	LLH	8,000
	100,000	5	4	172,800	1,024	7	$LLLLLLH$	1.024×10^8

H. Chen et al. (Eds.): WISI 2006, LNCS 3917, pp. 156–158, 2006.
© Springer-Verlag Berlin Heidelberg 2006

where L and H stand for low and high frequency respectively). In the experiment, the 14 sequential frames from the LLH (low-low-high) frames were selected because it was found to have the minimum errors. The channel equivalent to the fingerprinting system was found to be a random error channel therefore we have reliable decoding using ordinary error correcting codes. This fact will give us better visibility for the extracted logo. Table 1 shows the generalized decision method of embedding areas in video content.

A powerful attack against digital fingerprinting is the collusion attack. The results of our experiment show that the algorithm has some built-in resilience to collusion attacks, since the algorithm uses a long, uniformly distributed random number as fingerprinting information.

A powerful collusion attack is the maximum-minimum collusion attack proposed by Stone [5]. The attacked video is created by taking the average of the maximum and minimum values across the components of the fingerprinted video. The new zero correlation attack [6] is a modification method from Stone's collusion attack. This attack selects a fingerprinted video from a number of available fingerprinted videos. In this attack, some fingerprinting information is destroyed. However, we know that $user_1$, $user_3$, $user_4$ and $user_7$ were colluding (see Fig. 1).

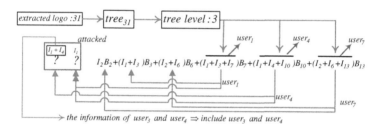

Fig. 1. Tracing illegal users under zero correlation attack

We also considered the averaging collusion attack of Cox, et al. [7] and the negative correlation collusion attack which drives the correlation coefficients to a negative value [5], and obtained similar good results. We have presented an approach for tracing illegal users in content distribution networks using video fingerprinting implementation. The video embedding method is robust to various attacks because of the use of the temporal wavelet transform. We improved the robustness of the tree number logo by using ECC, which permits support of a large number of users.

References

1. Judge, P., Ammar, M.: Security Issues and Solutions in Multicast Content Distribution. IEEE Network, Vol.17. (2003) 30-36
2. Furht, B., Kirovski, B.: Multimedia Security Handbook, CRC Press, (2005)

3. Kang, H.H., Kurkoski, B., Park, Y.R., Lee, H.J., Shin, S.U., Yamaguchi, K., Kobayashi, K.: Video Fingerprinting System using Wavelet and Error Correcting Code. WISA'05, Lecture Notes in Computer Science, Vol. 3786. Springer-Verlag, (2005) to appear
4. Kang, H.H., Park, Y.R., Park, J.H.: Blind Watermarking based on the Spatial Domain. Conference on Korea Multimedia Society, Vol. 5, No.1, (2002)
5. Stone, H.: Analysis of Attacks on Image Watermarks with Randomized Coefficients. NEC Technical Report. (1996)
6. Wahadaniah, V., Guan, Y.L., Chua, H.C.: A New Collusion Attack and Its Performance Evaluation. IWDW'02, Lecture Notes in Computer Science, Vol. 2613. Springer-Verlag, (2003) 64-80
7. Cox, I.J., Kilian, J., Leighton, T., Shanmoon, T.: Secure Spread Spectrum Watermarking for Multimedia. IEEE Trans. On Image Processing, Vol. 6, No. 12, (1997) 1673-1687

Privacy and Security Enhanced Offline Oblivious Transfer for Massive Data Distribution

Ickjai Lee and Hossein Ghodosi

School of Information Technology,
James Cook University, QLD 4811, Australia
{jai, hossein}@cs.jcu.edu.au

Abstract. Unauthorized accesses to digital contents are serious threats to international security and informatics. We propose an offline oblivious data distribution framework that preserves the sender's security and the receiver's privacy using tamper-proof smart cards. This framework provides persistent content protections from digital piracy and promises private content consumption.

1 Introduction

In many E-Business scenarios, online content distribution is a major source of services, and protecting valuable digital assets from unauthorized users is a main concern to content holders. Controlling and restricting the use of digital resources has become an important issue in these network-rich and data-rich environments. Privacy and security enhanced content distribution has become an important issue. Cybercrimes leading misuses of digital contents are great concerns to content holders and are major sources threatening E-business. Digital Rights Management (DRM) is one popular approach for secure content distributions. In this paper, we utilize Oblivious Transfer (OT) protocol [1] concepts to advantage DRM. We propose an offline oblivious data distribution framework that unconditionally preserves the sender's security and the receiver's privacy using a tamper-proof device called smart card. This framework provides persistent content protections from unauthorized accesses and promises unconditionally secure offline digital content distributions.

2 Smart Card Based Oblivious Content Transfer

We employ the privacy-preserving characteristics of OT in digital distributions to advantage and utilize physical means in order to overcome the weaknesses of OT as suggested by [2]. A smart card (micro-controller based card, chip card) is a portable and tamper-resistant computer [3]. Due to its portability and ease of use, it has been so popular and has been used in broad range of applications. In addition, its built-in computational power and security make it reliable in E-Commerce [3]. Our motivation to security and privacy preserving content distributions is to transfer all rights/licenses to the consumer in such a way that a user can choose only a portion of these rights/licenses depending on his/her payment. Usage rules can be programmed

H. Chen et al. (Eds.): WISI 2006, LNCS 3917, pp. 159–160, 2006.

and manufactured in a smart card according to the payment. As the consumer uses digital contents, then the usage rules in the smart card are updated according to the usage.

2.1 Framework and Implementation

First of all, the content owner needs to encrypt digital media to protect their assets. He passes all usage rules and necessary information for licenses to the smart card manufacturer (SC manufacturer) where usage rules are properly masked in smart cards. Note that, smart cards are self-protective and self-updating. Accesses to usage rules masked in smart cards are confined to functions available to the customer. Thus, the content owner can design these functions in such a way that he can protect his digital assets accordingly. In addition, smart cards update usage statistics in their mobile databases for every single content use in order to prevent excessive use. Thus, the consumer is not able to view more than he has purchased. Once smart cards are received, the content owner passes protected digital assets along with smart cards to the content distributor that is typically an offline retailer. Consumers purchase these contents from shops in a similar way they purchase newspapers and lotteries. These contents now can be played back on their smart card enabled viewers such as computers connected with a smart card reader or a viewer equipped with a smart card reader. In this framework, consumers do not have to contact the clearinghouse (or the SC manufacturer in our framework) online to obtain licenses. Thus, there will be no chance of being eavesdropped and revealing his privacy. In this way, we can enhance the content owner's security and unconditionally preserves the consumer's privacy.

3 Concluding Remarks

Various cybercrimes are major threats to content holders. Existing DRM systems put more emphasis on the sender's security, but relatively neglect the consumer's privacy. We put a step forward to open a relevant issue in the design and implementation of such systems in a way that not only the secrecy of the content owner needs to be maintained, but also the privacy of the customer is of paramount importance.

References

1. Rabin, M.: How to Exchange Secrets by Oblivious Transfer. Technical Report TR-81, Aiken Computation Laboratory (1981)
2. Naor, M., Pinkas, B.: Oblivious Transfer and Polynomial Evaluation. In: Proceedings of the Thirty-First Annual ACM Symposium on Theory of Computing, Atlanta, Georgia (1999) 245–254
3. Chen, Z.: Java Card Technology for Smart Cards: Architecture and Programmer's Guide. Addison-Wesley, USA (2000)

The Effectiveness of Artificial Rhythms and Cues in Keystroke Dynamics Based User Authentication

Pilsung Kang, Sunghoon Park, Sungzoon Cho,
Seong-seob Hwang, and Hyoung-joo Lee

Department of Industrial Engineering, Seoul National University,
San 56-1, Shillim-dong, Kwanak-gu, 151-744, Seoul, Korea
{xfeel99, shpark82, zoon, hss9414, impatton}@snu.ac.kr

In keystroke dynamics based user authentication, an access system utilizes not only a valid user's password, but also his/her typing patterns. Although high performances in terms of FAR(False Acceptance Rate) and FRR(False Rejection Rate) have been reported, most researches used a large number of valid users' typing patterns in order to implement complex algorithms in building a classifier[1]. However, collecting sufficient typing patterns to construct a complex classifier is practically impossible. When only a handful of typing patterns are available, the only way to compensate the lack of quantity is to improve quality. To improve the quality of typing patterns, using artificial rhythms and cues were proposed[2]. In this paper, we aim at verifying the effectiveness of artificial rhythms and cues by testing hypotheses.

We tested the hypotheses in terms of uniqueness, consistency, and discriminability. Uniqueness is how different one's typing patterns are from others'. Consistency is how similar one's typing patterns are to each other. Discriminability is how well one's typing patterns can be separated from others'. We assumed that using artificial rhythms increases uniqueness, and using cues increases consistency. Consequently, high discriminability can be achieved. As shown in Table 1 and Table 2, six strategies were used to implement artificial rhythms and cues, and four hypotheses were established. 25 users were involved in our experiment. Each user enrolled 30 typing patterns. The same number of pauses and the speed of cues were fixed for all users. 24 typing patterns of each user trying to access were collected, and 24 impostors' typing patterns were collected by giving away one's password to the others and let them try to access with the given password. Potential imposters knew the number of pauses and strategies, but they did not know whether a valid user used cues or not.

Experimental results are shown in Table 3. Strategies using artificial rhythms (2,4,5) clearly increased uniqueness compared to strategy 1(Top left). However, one of them(5) did not increase discriminability compared to strategy 1(Top right). When a user typed a password in a slow tempo without cues(5), it was more difficult to type the password consistently than other artificial rhythms. As a result, users lost consistency significantly and this cancelled out uniqueness gain so that discriminability did not improve in strategy 5. To handle this problem, adopting cues when typing a password was proposed and test results support that using cues improved consistency(Bottom left). In addition, improved consistency led a user to improved discriminability(Bottom right). To sum up, using artificial rhythms improved uniqueness and using cues improved consistency, both of which resulted in high discriminability. So, high quality of typing patterns can be achieved by adopting artificial rhythms and cues, even though only a small number of data is available.

H. Chen et al. (Eds.): WISI 2006, LNCS 3917, pp. 161–162, 2006.

Table 1. Strategies and employed artificial rhythms and cues for each strategy

Strategy Number	Strategy Name	Artificial Rhythm	User of Cues
1	Natural Rhythm	Nothing	No
2	Pause without Cue	Pause	No
3	Pause with Cue	Pause	Yes
4	Musical Rhythm	Musical Rhythm	No
5	Slow Tempo without Cue	Slow Tempo	No
6	Slow Tempo with Cue	Slow Tempo	Yes

Table 2. Hypotheses to verify the effectiveness of artificial rhythms and cues

Hypothesis	Description
H^{AU}	Artificial rhythms increase uniqueness
H^{AD}	Artificial rhythms increase discriminability
H^{CC}	Cues increase consistency
H^{CD}	Cues increase discriminability

Table 3. t-values and p-values for each hypothesis

Hypothesis	t-value	p-value	Hypothesis	t-value	p-value
H_{21}^{AU}	14.86	6.62×10^{-14}	H_{21}^{AD}	2.58	0.0082
H_{41}^{AU}	9.43	7.56×10^{-10}	H_{41}^{AD}	2.49	0.0101
H_{51}^{AU}	7.22	9.16×10^{-8}	H_{51}^{AD}	-0.58	0.7170
Hypothesis	t-value	p-value	Hypothesis	t-value	p-value
H_{32}^{CC}	1.55	0.0650	H_{32}^{CD}	2.34	0.0141
H_{65}^{CC}	3.26	0.0017	H_{65}^{CD}	2.83	0.0046

In conclusion, when enough typing patterns are not available, the quality of data becomes as important as the quantity of data. Using artificial rhythms and cues were suggested to improve the quality of typing patterns. We made typing strategies and established hypotheses to test the effectiveness of artificial rhythms and cues. The experimental results showed that using artificial rhythms and cues improved the quality of typing patterns.

Acknowledgement. This work was supported by grant No. R01-2005-103900-0 from the Basic Research Program of the Korea Science and Engineering Foundation.

References

1. Peacock, A., Ke, X., Wilkerson, M.: Typing Patterns: A Key to User Identification. IEEE Security & Privacy **2(5)** (2004) 40-47
2. Cho, S., Hwang, S.: Artificial Rhythms and Cues for Keystroke Dynamics based Authentication. To appear in IAPR International Conference on Biometrics. Honokong. (2006)

Cascade Damage Estimation Model for Internet Attacks

Taek Lee[1], Hoh Peter In[1,*], Eul-Gyu Im[2], and Heejo Lee[1]

[1] Department of Computer Science and Engineering,
Korea University, Seoul, 136-713, Republic of Korea
{comtaek, hoh_in, heejo}@korea.ac.kr
[2] College of Information and Communications,
Hanyang University, Seoul, 133-791, Republic of Korea
imeg@hanyang.ac.kr

1 Introduction

Risk analysis and damage estimation are inevitable studies to gain essential data for making a better decision in security investment. The most reasonable metrics to measure the damage of a security accident are *recovery cost* and *business opportunity cost*[1,2,3,4]. In the case of a worm accident, the costs mean just the direct damage caused by infected systems. However, collaterally cascading damage is also serious damage which can impact on other innocent systems having depended on the infected systems for the purpose of processing their business or demanding some service.

2 Our Proposed Damage Estimation Model

Cascade Damage Estimation Model(CDEM) is represented by a graph-based, so called Dependency Tree Diagram(DTD), algorithm to be able to identify dependence relation between systems and calculate the potential cascading damage caused by the business-dependent relation with an infected system. Given a domain, the algorithm(table 2) quantitatively estimates the degree of loss and its likelihood by a graphic and probabilistic approach.

Table 1. The definition of DTD

DTD=<*N,E*> *N* is a set of nodes, *N*={$n_1,n_2,n_3,\ldots$} *E* is a set of edges, *E*={$e_{i,j}$ | i≠j ∧ n_i,n_j∈ *N*} n_i=<*FP,OC,CD*>, $e_{i,j}$=<*BD,CP*>	*FP* : business failure probability *OC* : business opportunity cost *CD* : calculated cascade damage *BD* : business performance degrading rate *CP* : dependency connection probability

---

* Corresponding author.

H. Chen et al. (Eds.): WISI 2006, LNCS 3917, pp. 163–164, 2006.
© Springer-Verlag Berlin Heidelberg 2006

Table 2. Cascade Damage Estimation Algorithm

```
Cascading Damage Estimation Algorithm ()
{
Total_CD = 0
make_DTD_structure()
D = {"nodes damaged directly by a worm"}
X = N − D
for each x in X
{
x.FP = 1
Y = {"all parent nodes of node x"}
for each y in Y
{
  if (y.FP is not defined) { y.FP ← find_cp(y) }
  Likelihood ← y.FP × e_{y,x}.CP
  if (AND-case) x.FP ← x.FP × Likelihood
  elseif (OR-case) x.FP ← x.FP × (1-Likelihood )
  Loss ← e_{y,x}.BD × x.OC
  x.CD ← x.CD + Loss × Likelihood
}
if (OR-case) x.FP = 1 - x.FP
Total_CD ← Total_CD + x.CD
}
}
```

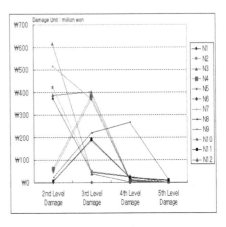

Fig. 1. Cascade damage in each level

3   Evaluation and Application of CDEM

The proposed algorithm was tested by random experiment simulation approach in order to check its validation in terms of calculating damage probability in each node. As the result, we could guarantee the consistency of our estimation algorithm. CDEM can be utilized not only in estimating cascade damage(figure 1) but also in identifying critical systems and hence analyzing Return On Security Investment(ROSI). The prioritization information of the cascade damages triggered by each causal node can be a good evidence to look for weak points on the infrastructure consisting of system nodes, in other words, the best promising points to be defended and invested in the perspective of cascade damage prevention.

References

[1] Incident Cost Analysis and Modeling Report I, II, Committee on Institutional Cooperation, 2000
[2] "Information Security Incident Survey and Damage Calculation Model", Japan Network Security Association, March 31, 2004
[3] Nicholas Weaver, Vern Paxson, "A Worst-Case Worm", May 5, 2004
[4] Thomas Dubendorfer, Arno Wagner, Bernhard Plattner, "An Economic Damage Model for Large-Scale Internet Attacks", WET ICE'04

A New Secure Key Exchange Protocol Between STB and Smart Card in DTV Broadcasting

Eun-Jun Yoon and Kee-Young Yoo[**]

Department of Computer Engineering, Kyungpook National University,
Daegu 702-701, South Korea
ejyoon@infosec.knu.ac.kr, yook@knu.ac.kr

Introduction: The Smart Card Security Users Group (SCSUG) consortium developed the security specifications using the new international security standard ISO/IEC 15408, which is known as the Common Criteria. ISO 10202 standards have been established for the security of financial transaction systems that use integrated circuit cards (IC cards or smart cards). The smart card originates from the IC memory card which has been in the industry for about 10 years. The main characteristics of a smart card are its small size and low-power consumption. The merits of a smart card regarding password authentication are its simplicity and its efficiency in terms of the log-in and authentication processes. Secure communication between set-top box (STB) and smart card is directly related with the benefit of service providers and the legal rights of users, while key exchange is the essential part of secure communication. In 2004, Jiang et al. [1] proposed a key exchange protocol for STB and smart card based on Schnorr's digital signature protocol and one-way hash function. The current paper, however, demonstrates that Jiang et al.'s protocol is vulnerable to an impersonation attack and does not provide perfect forward secrecy. Furthermore, we present a new secure key exchange protocol based on one-way hash function and Diffie-Hellman key exchange algorithm in order to isolate such problems.

Review of Jiang et al.'s Protocol: Jiang et al.'s protocol consists of five phases: registration, login, mutual authentication, key agreement, and CW transmission phase. For a more detailed discussion on Jiang et al.'s protocol, please refer to [1].

Cryptanalysis of Jiang et al.'s Protocol: (1) Jiang et al.'s protocol is vulnerable to an impersonation attack, where an attacker can easily impersonate other legal users (or the STB) to get a useful information. Suppose that E has eavesdropped a valid message $(X, T, Y, r, ID_c, M, e, d)$ from an open network. Then, E can easily compute the common session key $SK = h(r, e, ID_c, ID_s)$ by using the values r, e, ID_c and ID_s. In the CW transmission phase, E chooses a modified CW', computes forged $CW_e = E_{SK}(CW')$, and sends it to the STB. It is easy to check whether the STB will decrypt this forged message CW_e, as $CW' = E_{SK}^{-1}(CW_e)$. As a result, the STB will accept the attacker's CW', making Jiang et al.' protocol insecure. (2) Jiang et al.'s protocol does not provide perfect forward secrecy. Suppose an attacker E obtains the identity ID_s from the com-

---

[**] Corresponding author: Kee-Young Yoo (yook@knu.ac.kr). This research was supported by the ITRC support program.

H. Chen et al. (Eds.): WISI 2006, LNCS 3917, pp. 165–166, 2006.

promised STB and intercepts transmitted values $(X, T, Y, r, ID_c, M, e, d)$, then E can easily compute the common session key $SK = h(r, e, ID_c, ID_s)$ the values r, e, ID_c and ID_s.

Proposed Key Exchange Protocol: The proposed protocol also consists of five phases: registration, login, mutual authentication, key agreement, and CW transmission phase. In the registration phase, when a user applies to subscribe the charge program with his smart card identity ID_c and password PW for registration. SMS computes $R = h(ID_c \oplus x_s) \oplus PW$ and stores $R, g, ID_s, h(\cdot), E(\cdot)$ as well as MPK and other account information in the smart card and issues it to the user. In the login phase, when a user wants to receive the subscribed program, he or she must attach his smart card to his STB and input his ID_c and PW. The smart card generates a random number a in Z_q^* and computes $A = g^a \bmod p$. All of this work can be pre-computed in the idle time of last running period. Then the smart card computes $X = R \oplus h(PW)$ and $Y = h(X, A, ID_c, ID_s)$ and sends login request message $\{ID_c, Y, A\}$ to the STB for login. In the mutual authentication phase, upon receiving the login request, STB and smart card need do the following steps to realize mutual authentication: (1) STB first checks the validity of ID_c. If it is invalid, STB rejects this request. (2) STB computes $h(ID_c \oplus x_s)$ and checks $Y = h(h(ID_c \oplus x_s), A, ID_c, ID_s)$ true or not. If true, STB receives the login request and takes the next step; otherwise, rejects this login request. (3) STB generates a random number b in Z_q^* and computes $B = g^b \bmod p$. (4) STB computes $K = A^b = g^{ab} \bmod p$ and $M = h(K, A, ID_c, ID_s)$. Then, STB sends $\{B, M\}$ to smart card for identifying. (5) Smart card computes $K = B^a = g^{ab} \bmod p$ and $M' = h(K, A, ID_c, ID_s)$, and checks $M' = M$ true or not, if true, accepts the STB's identity and take the next step, otherwise denies this communication. (6) Smart card computes $D = h(K, B, ID_c, ID_s)$ and sends it to STB. (7) STB checks $D = h(K, B, ID_c, ID_s)$ true or not. If it is true, STB accepts the smart card; otherwise STB rejects the smart card. In the key agreement phase, if the mutual authentication is passed successfully for both STB and smart card, then they use the following equation to compute a common session key $SK = h(K, ID_c, ID_s)$, which includes both the random number chosen by STB and smart card. Finally, in the CW transmission phase, after decrypting out CW, smart card use SK to encrypt it as $CW_e = E_{SK}(CW)$ and sends CW_e back to STB for descrambling the program. STB can decrypt the CW as $CW = E_{SK}^{-1}(CW_e)$.

Security Analysis: For each communication, there needs mutual authentication and key exchange to reach a dynamic session key for which both entities provide key seed information (i.e., a and b), which can resist replay attack and impersonated attack as well as avoid perfect forward security problem. Moreover, at each time, the session key SK is different, which can increase the difficulty to attack the encryption algorithm with known plain-text attack.

References

1. Jiang, T., Hou, Y., Zheng, S.: Secure Communication between Set-top Box and Smart Card in DTV Broadcasting. IEEE Trans. on Consumer Electronics. Vol. 50. (August 2004) 882-886

The Effectiveness of Artificial Rhythms and Cues in Keystroke Dynamics Based User Authentication

Pilsung Kang, Sunghoon Park, Sungzoon Cho,
Seong-seob Hwang, and Hyoung-joo Lee

Department of Industrial Engineering, Seoul National University,
San 56-1, Shillim-dong, Kwanak-gu, 151-744, Seoul, Korea
{xfeel99, shpark82, zoon, hss9414, impatton}@snu.ac.kr

In keystroke dynamics based user authentication, an access system utilizes not only a valid user's password, but also his/her typing patterns. Although high performances in terms of FAR(False Acceptance Rate) and FRR(False Rejection Rate) have been reported, most researches used a large number of valid users' typing patterns in order to implement complex algorithms in building a classifier[1]. However, collecting sufficient typing patterns to construct a complex classifier is practically impossible. When only a handful of typing patterns are available, the only way to compensate the lack of quantity is to improve quality. To improve the quality of typing patterns, using artificial rhythms and cues were proposed[2]. In this paper, we aim at verifying the effectiveness of artificial rhythms and cues by testing hypotheses.

We tested the hypotheses in terms of uniqueness, consistency, and discriminability. Uniqueness is how different one's typing patterns are from others'. Consistency is how similar one's typing patterns are to each other. Discriminability is how well one's typing patterns can be separated from others'. We assumed that using artificial rhythms increases uniqueness, and using cues increases consistency. Consequently, high discriminability can be achieved. As shown in Table 1 and Table 2, six strategies were used to implement artificial rhythms and cues, and four hypotheses were established. 25 users were involved in our experiment. Each user enrolled 30 typing patterns. The same number of pauses and the speed of cues were fixed for all users. 24 typing patterns of each user trying to access were collected, and 24 impostors' typing patterns were collected by giving away one's password to the others and let them try to access with the given password. Potential imposters knew the number of pauses and strategies, but they did not know whether a valid user used cues or not.

Experimental results are shown in Table 3. Strategies using artificial rhythms (2,4,5) clearly increased uniqueness compared to strategy 1(Top left). However, one of them(5) did not increase discriminability compared to strategy 1(Top right). When a user typed a password in a slow tempo without cues(5), it was more difficult to type the password consistently than other artificial rhythms. As a result, users lost consistency significantly and this cancelled out uniqueness gain so that discriminability did not improve in strategy 5. To handle this problem, adopting cues when typing a password was proposed and test results support that using cues improved consistency(Bottom left). In addition, improved consistency led a user to improved discriminability(Bottom right). To sum up, using artificial rhythms improved uniqueness and using cues improved consistency, both of which resulted in high discriminability. So, high quality of typing patterns can be achieved by adopting artificial rhythms and cues, even though only a small number of data is available.

H. Chen et al. (Eds.): WISI 2006, LNCS 3917, pp. 161–162, 2006.
© Springer-Verlag Berlin Heidelberg 2006

Table 1. Strategies and employed artificial rhythms and cues for each strategy

Strategy Number	Strategy Name	Artificial Rhythm	User of Cues
1	Natural Rhythm	Nothing	No
2	Pause without Cue	Pause	No
3	Pause with Cue	Pause	Yes
4	Musical Rhythm	Musical Rhythm	No
5	Slow Tempo without Cue	Slow Tempo	No
6	Slow Tempo with Cue	Slow Tempo	Yes

Table 2. Hypotheses to verify the effectiveness of artificial rhythms and cues

Hypothesis	Description
H^{AU}	Artificial rhythms increase uniqueness
H^{AD}	Artificial rhythms increase discriminability
H^{CC}	Cues increase consistency
H^{CD}	Cues increase discriminability

Table 3. t-values and p-values for each hypothesis

Hypothesis	t-value	p-value	Hypothesis	t-value	p-value
H_{21}^{AU}	14.86	6.62×10^{-14}	H_{21}^{AD}	2.58	0.0082
H_{41}^{AU}	9.43	7.56×10^{-10}	H_{41}^{AD}	2.49	0.0101
H_{51}^{AU}	7.22	9.16×10^{-8}	H_{51}^{AD}	-0.58	0.7170
Hypothesis	t-value	p-value	Hypothesis	t-value	p-value
H_{32}^{CC}	1.55	0.0650	H_{32}^{CD}	2.34	0.0141
H_{65}^{CC}	3.26	0.0017	H_{65}^{CD}	2.83	0.0046

In conclusion, when enough typing patterns are not available, the quality of data becomes as important as the quantity of data. Using artificial rhythms and cues were suggested to improve the quality of typing patterns. We made typing strategies and established hypotheses to test the effectiveness of artificial rhythms and cues. The experimental results showed that using artificial rhythms and cues improved the quality of typing patterns.

Acknowledgement. This work was supported by grant No. R01-2005-103900-0 from the Basic Research Program of the Korea Science and Engineering Foundation.

References

1. Peacock, A., Ke, X., Wilkerson, M.: Typing Patterns: A Key to User Identification. IEEE Security & Privacy **2(5)** (2004) 40-47
2. Cho, S., Hwang, S.: Artificial Rhythms and Cues for Keystroke Dynamics based Authentication. To appear in IAPR International Conference on Biometrics. Honokong. (2006)

Hidden Markov Model Based Intrusion Detection

Zhi-Yong Liu and Hong Qiao

Key Lab of Complex Systems and Intelligence Science, Chinese Academy of Sciences,
Beijing, P.R. China
{zhiyong.liu, hong.qiao}@ia.ac.cn

Background

Network security is an important issue for Intelligence and Security Informatics (ISI) [1-3]. As a complementary measure for traditional network security tools such as firewalls, the intrusion detection system (IDS) is becoming increasingly important and widely-used [4]. Generally speaking, the IDS works by building a model based on the normal data patterns and treating the operations that deviated significantly from the model as malicious. In its early stage of development, the IDS takes certain statistics (e.g., mean and variance) of the audit data to discriminate between the normal usage and attacks. Such systems are easy to construct; however, they suffer from a poor generalization ability to detect unknown or new attacks. Recently other models such as the finite Markov mode [5] and support vector machines [6] have been introduced into IDS, providing finer-grained characterization of normal users' behavior. In this report we investigate the potential application of the Hidden Markov Model (HMM) for intrusion detection.

HMM for Intrusion Detection

Compared with the finite Markov model, the HMM introduces for each state additionally an output or emission. What can be observed is the emissions not the states as for the Markov model. Thus, the HMM relaxes the strict assumption made by the Markov model that the current observation depends only on the previous one. To apply HMM to IDS, the following three technical problems must be solved: 1) how to define the states and select the number of the state? 2) how to train and estimate the model parameters? and 3) how to discriminate between the normal and attack based on the trained model?

Below we briefly describe these three problems and some preliminary ideas to tackle them. Roughly speaking, the model states can be taken as what the users are currently doing. For instance, the login/logout operation can be taken as the initial/final state for an account intrusion detection system. In a specific application case, one may select the states by hand, based mainly on the system architecture and function. For example, for a typical e-banking website, after the user logged in, she/he may choose to browse the account information or directly transfer the money to another account. Such operations can be taken as the model states. The parameter estimation problem is one of the standard problems associated with the HMM [7]. In the literature, the Baum-Welch algorithm (EM algorithm) is commonly adopted for solving this problem. Though the Baum-Welch algorithm can only reach a local

H. Chen et al. (Eds.): WISI 2006, LNCS 3917, pp. 169–170, 2006.

optimum, in practice we may alleviate this problem by selecting proper initialization, thanks to the physical meaning of these system parameters. How to construct a proper classifier based on the trained HMM is crucial to the IDS. Generally speaking, we can classify a new audit data sequence into normal or attack according to its log-likelihood value given a proper threshold value. However, in practice we may need to pay more attention to some special operations, such as accessing the root or transferring money. One approach is to modify the conventional log-likelihood value by introducing a weight for each model state or operation.

We have preliminarily tested the HMM model on the KDD cup 1999 intrusion detection data set [8] and obtained early promising results. Our long-term objective is to build an on-line HMM based e-banking intrusion detection system, which, as the project proceeds, may use a hybrid approach integrating HMM with other models such as the support vector machine (SVM) and boosting approaches for performance gains.

Acknowledgement. This work is partially supported by the National Science Foundation of China (Grants: 60505003,60573078 and 60334020).

References

1. Chen, H., Wang, F.Y.: Arti⁻cial intelligence for homeland security. IEEE Intelligent Systems 20 (2005), pp.12-16.
2. Yao, Y.Y., Wang, F.Y., Wang, J., Zeng, D.: Rule + exception strategies for security information analysis. IEEE Intelligent Systems 20 (2005), pp. 52-57.
3. Chen, H., Wang, F.Y., Zeng, D.: Intelligence and security informatics for homeland security: Information, communication and transportation. IEEE Trans. Intelligent Transportation Systems 5 (2004), pp. 329-341.
4. Axelsson, S.: Intrusion detection systems: A survey and taxonomy. Technical Report 99-15, Depart. of Computer Engineering, Chalmers University (2000).
5. Jha, S., Maxion, R.A.: Markov chains, classi⁻ers, and intrusion detection. Proceedings of the 14th IEEE Workshop on Computer Security Foundations (2001).
6. Mukkamala, S., Janoski, G., Sung, A.: Intrusion detection using neural networks and support vector machines. proceedings of the 2002 International Joint Conference on Neural Networks (IJCNN) 2 (2002), pp. 1702-1707.
7. Bilmes, J.: A gentle tutorial on the em algorithm and its application to parameter estimation for gaussian mixture and hidden markov models. Technical Report, University of UC. Berkeley, ICSI-TR-97-021 (1997).
8. Lee, W., Stolfo, S.J.: A framework for constructing features and models for intrusion detection systems. ACM Transactions on Information and System Security (2000), pp. 227-261.

One-Class Strategies for Security Information Detection

Qing Tao, Gao-wei Wu, and Jue Wang

Institute of Automation, Chinese Academy of Sciences,
P.O. Box 2728, Beijing, 100080, P.R. China
{qing.tao, gaowei.wu, jue.wang}@mail.ia.ac.cn

Detecting security-related information is a critical component of ISI research, which involves studying a wide range of technical and systems challenges related to the acquisition, collection, storage, retrieval, synthesis, and analysis of security-related information.

Outlier or anomaly detection is a well-known problem in statistics which can be naturally described as Density Level Detection problems and outliers are intuitively understood as events with small probability. Unfortunately, these algorithms cannot be directly used for general security-related information detection problems since the imposed assumptions on the densities are often tailored to specific applications. Instead, the well-known Statistical Learning Theory (SLT) provides distribution-free conditions and guarantees for good performance of generalization for learning algorithms. In statistical machine learning, outlier or anomaly detection can be equivalently described as one-class problems.

We advocate that SLT-based data description and analysis techniques can be reformulated as a general framework to accomplish various kinds of data-mining tasks for ISI applications. In particular, this article focuses on a common security information detection task: how to employ and further develop one-class learning algorithms as an efficient data analysis framework and related automated learning and detecting mechanisms to describe and identify large-scale abnormal situations or behaviors.

It is important to note that a typical feature of security-related applications is that only unlabeled samples are available (i.e., too few negative examples exist). On the other hand, there exist two competing fundamental problems called information preservation and dimension reduction. Therefore, one has to make some a-priori assumptions on practical anomalies in order to distinguish between normal and anomalous future observations. All these determine our philosophy in employing and developing learning algorithms to solve security-related information detecting. First, one-class learning, which can deal with the extremely unbalanced detection problems even without negative samples, can be directly applied. Second, we can restrict information preservation by making some a-priori assumptions on the loss function and dimension reduction by specifying the hypothesis space.

One of the most common ways to define anomalies is by saying that anomalies are not concentrated. Until now, almost all the one-class learning algorithms are based on this kind of viewpoint, especially a classification framework (called DLD-SVM) for anomaly detection established by I. Steinwart et al. It turns out that their empirical classification risk can serve as an empirical performance measure for the anomaly detection problem. Furthermore, by the above interpretation, a well-known heuristic

H. Chen et al. (Eds.): WISI 2006, LNCS 3917, pp. 171–172, 2006.

of artificially sampling "labeled" samples is strongly justified, provided that the sampling plan is well chosen. However, the obvious disadvantage of DLD-SVM is that we need to specify a distribution to produce artificial negative samples. This may prevent ISI researchers from efficiently using for security detection in domains where the density of negative samples is unknown.

Different viewpoints about outliers will lead to different algorithms. We argue that the centralized viewpoint can apply to all kinds of security-related information detections. In security-related domains, some abnormal situations may be characterized as a function estimation problem. Under the assumption that the outliers are as few as possible, we find out that this function estimation viewpoint leads to a new one-class learning algorithm, which implements a desired slab region for detecting outliers in its simplest case. In application, it is reported that the learning algorithms under the function estimation viewpoint can effectively detect the abnormal behaviors in the stock markets.

Generally speaking, almost all the available one-class learning algorithms can be formulated as linear or quadratic optimization problems in their simplest cases. Until now, there exists a huge body of literatures and well-known methods on solving these problems which require enormous matrix storages and intensive operations. Fortunately, the structure of the one-class optimization problem permits a class of specially tailored algorithms to be constructed to achieve fast convergence and small memory requirement even for large-scale problems. Moreover, several fast one-class algorithms, in particular, the geometric methods can be further developed to have the performance of on-line learning. As a result, the SLT-based fast algorithms can be directly applied to accomplish the large-scale security-related detection in real time.

We are currently applying and evaluating the above-mentioned SLT-based techniques in ISI applications. We expect that the specific characteristics and requirements of ISI applications may lead to unique domain-specific problem formulations and constraints. These challenges will not only inspire new machine learning algorithms but also encourage the use and adaptation of SLT and its algorithms to solve practical security-related problems.

Acknowledgments. The work of Q. Tao was supported by the Excellent Youth Science and Technology Foundation of Anhui Province of China (04042069). This work was supported in part by the National Basic Research Program (2004CB318103) and NNSF Grants (60575001, 60573078 and 60334020) of China.

References

1. Hsinchun Chen and Fei-Yue Wang, "Artificial Intelligence for Homeland Security", IEEE Intelligent Systems, Vol. 20, Issue 5, 2005, pp. 12-16.
2. Y. Y. Yao, Fei-Yue Wang , J. Wang, D. Zeng "Rule + Exception Strategies for Security Information Analysis" , IEEE Intelligent Systems, Vol. 20, Issue 5, 2005, pp. 52-57.
3. H. Chen, F.-Y. Wang, and D. Zeng, "Intelligence and Security informatics for Homeland Security: Information , Communication and Transportation", IEEE Trans. Intelligent Transportation Systems, Vol. 5, No. 4, 2004, pp. 329-341.

Design of an Emergency Prediction and Prevention Platform for Societal Security Decision Support Using Neural Networks

Zeng-Guang Hou and Min Tan

Key Laboratory of Complex Systems and Intelligence Science,
The Chinese Academy of Sciences,
P.O. Box 2728, Beijing 100080, P.R. China
{zengguang.hou, min.tan}@ia.ac.cn

1 Background

Disasters, either naturally-occurring or man-made, frequently occur. For example, the recent chemical plant explosion on Nov. 13, 2005 at the Jilin Petrochemical Company caused a major environmental catastrophe in the water system of Songhua River. The explosion produced about 100 tonne of toxic chemicals, including benzene, spilled into the Songhua River and created an 80 km slick. The river contamination forced the shutdown of water supply in Harbin, a city located downstream with 3.8 million residents. The water pollution also brought problems to cities in China and Russia further downstream. Shortly afterwards, on Dec. 17, 2005, the City Central Hospital in Liaoyuan, Jilin Province, caught fire and left 39 people dead. In 2005, several serious coal mine disasters happened in China, which caused great losses in both life and economic assets. The lack of work safety and poor management has led to the high frequency of such coal mine accidents in recent years in China. In addition to the above disasters, there are other emergencies such as the Severe Acute Respiratory Syndrome (SARS), mad-cow disease and bird flu that caused world-wide attention and resulted in huge economic losses. Societal security has been a very important topic for civilians, governments, officials, and researchers as well.

In this paper, we will summarize our ongoing research aimed at building a platform for the prediction and prevention of societal security-related events. Emergencies demand immediate actions to reduce losses and damages, and to help those in need how to act during and after the disastrous events. The objective of this paper is to give an outline for building various disaster models, providing comprehensive analysis and decision support.

2 Decision-Support Platform for Prediction and Prevention of Emergent Events

The first step to build the platform is to model various disastrous events using the neural network method. An automatic data-searching and collecting system is constructed and different data bases are built using the collected data which are updated regularly. This can be done using the data provided by government reports, and

H. Chen et al. (Eds.): WISI 2006, LNCS 3917, pp. 173–174, 2006.

various media such as the newspapers and internet which can be accomplished using the available commercial Web search engines.

For different type of events, we need to consider different input data. For example, to build a water surveillance and altering model, we have to collect such data as flows of branches, nearby chemical and manufacturing plants, and information about cities and villages close to the water. To build coal mine disaster alerting models, we need to get a large amount of the geological and hydrographic data, methane and other gases, dusts, equipments and activity of miners, and so on.

Since this platform is basically a model- and data-based decision support system, the models that we built include various optimization-based formulations; that is, the system considers some optimization criteria, e.g. to minimize the loss criteria and to maximize the benefit criteria.

We use the neural network methods to process the data acquired. It is well-known that neural networks can be used to model various problems with high accuracy. If needed, the principal components analysis is used to analyze the data so as to reduce the complexity and dimensionality of the problems.

The system will finally provide decision support services on how to act in case of emergencies. It will give reminders and alerting services to users for accident prevention purposes. The platform is designed for analyzing and managing various societal emergencies before, while, and after they come into being.

Acknowledgments. This research was supported in part by the National Natural Science Foundation of China (Grants 60205004, 60334020, 50475179 and 60573078), and the National Basic Research Program (973) of China (Grant 2002CB312200).

References

1. Konar, A.: Computational Intelligence: Principles, Techniques and Applications. Berlin Heidelberg: Pringer-Verlag (2005).
2. Kantor, P.B., et al.: Intelligence and Security Informatics, Lecture Notes in Computer Science. New York: Springer-Verlag (2005).
3. Chen, H. and Wang, F.Y.: Artificial Intelligence for Homeland Security. IEEE Intelligent Systems (2005), pp. 12-16.
4. Yao, Y.Y., Wang, F.Y., Wang, J., Zeng, D: Rule + Exception Strategies for Security Information Analysis. IEEE Intelligent Systems (2005), pp. 52-57.
5. Chen, H., Wang, F.Y., and Zeng, D: Intelligence and Security informatics for Homeland Security: Information, Communication and Transportation. IEEE Trans. Intelligent Transportation Systems (2004), pp. 329-341.

A Novel Identity Authentication Technique Without Trustworthy Third-Party Based on Fingerprint Verification

Liang Li, Jie Tian, and Xin Yang

Institute of Automation, Chinese Academy of Sciences, Graduate School of the Chinese Academy of Science, P.O. Box 2728, Beijing 100080, China
tian@doctor.com

1 Introduction

Computer networks have evolved from close local networks to open interconnected networks and the operations from data communication to online transaction. As such, identity authentication is indispensable in today's computing platform. Current identity authentication techniques primarily focus on Public Key Infrastructure (PKI) or Identity Based Encryption (IBE). However, these techniques authenticate users' identity relying on tokens or keys and one or many trustworthy third-party(s) that require databases running online, with multiple points of vulnerability and low efficiency.

A novel identity authentication technique without a trustworthy third-party based on fingerprint verification is proposed in this paper. We argue that this proposed approach is inherently more reliable than traditional authentication methods because of the incorporation of fingerprint-based biometric characteristics.

2 Major Research Issues

Our method is comprised of (a) the fingerprint feature coding technique, (b) the fingerprint cipher template matching technique, and (c) the fingerprint certificate technique. The fingerprint feature coding technique extracts features from fingerprint images to a digital representation. The key challenge of developing this technique is how to bridge the gap between the fuzziness of fingerprint biometric and the exactitude of cryptography. The Fourier-Mellin transformation (FMT) and discretization are applied to fingerprint images to form feature code. The FMT feature code is invariant in translation, rotation, and scaling. Experimental results have proved its power as to pattern representation. The fingerprint cipher template matching technique matches two cipher templates on terminal unit. In practical applications, fingerprint feature is ensured reliable protection in communication for its privacy and secrecy. An asymmetric encryption method protects feature templates reliably provided the availability of a trustworthy third-party. We propose a new method in which fingerprint templates are locked with a pre-defined random key to form a phase-phase product stored in a USB token. A cipher template can be unlocked by another cipher template in case two templates are from the same finger. Fingerprint certificates record personal information and fingerprint cipher templates of legitimate users, which contain the digital signature of authority as well.

H. Chen et al. (Eds.): WISI 2006, LNCS 3917, pp. 175–176, 2006.

These certificates can then be downloaded and accessed by other users. The cipher template of live-scan fingerprints can be matched against the one stored in certificate for identity authentication. This combination of cipher template matching and fingerprint certificate implements identity authentication without a trustworthy third-party.

The roles in this proposed system can be abstracted as the authority TA, user A and user B. TA is central to the entire system which produces and preserves the master key, computes the private key for user, and delivers the USB token. In the initialization stage of system operation, TA sets up a secure communication region and computes the master key and public parameters on a hyper-singular elliptic curve. The underlying mathematical theory is based on the bilinear Diffie-Hellman problem. In the registration stage, users show their legitimate documents to authority. Then TA sets the harden key of the USB token and stores the cipher template of the live-scan fingerprint into token. The public parameters and cryptography functions are stored in the token as well. The USB token has the function of plagiary-resistant, cryptography computation, and fingerprint verification. TA delivers the token to users face to face and produces the fingerprint certificates. In the case of secret communication between user A and user B, the message receiver must authenticate the identity of the message sender. Assuming that A sends message M to B, A computes the communication key K with a bilinear map and the ID of B and then encrypts M and the fingerprint cipher template with K. A sends the encrypted message and the cipher template to B together with the hash of the plain text. After B receives the cipher text, B matches the received cipher template with A's fingerprint certificate. This completes the first round of authentication. B then computes the communication key with B's private key and the ID of A, completing the second round of authentication.

In summary, the proposed approach uses both fingerprints and certificates to authenticate identity in a rigorous manner, combining fingerprint verification with asymmetric encryption thus avoiding the need of third-party participation.

Acknowledgement. This research has been supported by the National Natural Science Foundation of China (Grants 60573078 and 60334020).

References

1. Hsinchun Chen and Fei-Yue Wang, Artificial Intelligence for Homeland Security, IEEE Intelligent Systems, Vol. 20, Issue 5, 2005, pp.12-16.
2. Y. Y. Yao, Fei-Yue Wang, J. Wang,, D. Zeng, Rule + Exception Strategies for Security Information Analysis" , IEEE Intelligent Systems, Vol. 20, Issue 5, 2005, pp. 52-57.
3. H. Chen, F.-Y. Wang, and D. Zeng, Intelligence and Security informatics for Homeland Security: Information, Communication and Transportation, IEEE Trans. Intelligent Transportation Systems, Vol. 5, No. 4, 2004, pp. 329-341.
4. Amit Sahai,Brent Waters, Fuzzy Identity-BasedEncryption, In Advances in Cryptology-Eurocrypt'05. LNCS 3494, pp. 457-473, Springer, 2005.
5. Umut Uludag, Sharath Pankanti, Salil Prabhakar,Anil K.Jain, Biometric Cryptosystems: Issues and Challenges, Proceedings of the IEEE, Special. Issue on Enabling Security Technologies for Digital Rights Management, Vol. 92, No. 6, June. 2004.

Cyberspace Community Analysis and Simulation Using Complex Dynamic Social Networks

Baihua Xiao, Huiguang He, Yaodong Li, and Chunheng Wang

Institute of Automation, Chinese Academy of Sciences,
P.O. Box 2728, Beijing 100080, China
{baihua.xiao, huiguang.he,yaodong.li,
chunheng.wang}@ia.ac.cn

Background

Social network analysis (SNA) is the study of social relations among a set of actors. It is an emerging discipline that maps and measures the relationships between people, groups, organizations, computers or other information processing entities. SNA has been widely applied into many areas [1-3].

In this paper, we present SNAC (Social Network Analysis in Cyberspace), a prototype system for extracting, analyzing, visualizing and simulating the relations between users and user groups in Internet communities. Communications among the members of such Internet communities are analyzed to reveal social relationship structures. Link analysis [7] and content similarities are combined in this analysis.

Overview of SNAC

In SNAC, the text generated by Internet communities is extracted automatically using probabilistic information retrieval techniques. Interaction patterns within and between groups are modeled by group density, cohesion measures, and topological characteristics in terms of level of centralization and degree of hierarchy. A browser-based visualization interface allows users to query the database and explore the structure relationships between the group members and the groups. Below we summarize the major components of SNAC.

1. *Web Page Analyzer*

   The Web Page Analyzer parses the content of postings made by and communications between members of Internet communities. It also extracts the text and hyper links for further processing. The non-text parts such as multimedia contents are filtered out.

2. *Linkage Analyzer*

   The Linkage Analyzer scans the text and hyperlinks of each posting or communication. It extracts information concerning the author, topic, content, time and so on. In addition, it collections information on (a) the identification (ID) of the current message or posting, and (b) the IDs of the previous postings to which the current posting responds.

H. Chen et al. (Eds.): WISI 2006, LNCS 3917, pp. 177–178, 2006.

3. *Feature Extractor and Hierarchical classifier*

Singular Value Decomposition (SVD), Semi-Discrete Decomposition (SDD) [4] and Independent Component Analysis (ICA) [5] are popular matrix decomposition techniques used in SNA. In our system, we begin with the posting dataset containing m postings, each of them with n attributes. Principal Component Analysis (PCA) is then used to decompose the original feature space to its subspaces which we call eigen postings. Each person's postings are projected onto the eigen posting subspaces. The resulted vector can be used to calculate the distances that measure the similarities among these group members' behaviors. Finally, SDD is used to create an unsupervised hierarchical classification tree. This feature extraction and hierarchical clustering technique enhances the link and social network analysis by incorporating content analysis.

4. *Social Network Visualization*

A browser-based visualization prototype displays the dynamic relationships identified in the previous step. Graphical representation reveals a macroscopic view of the group as well as substructures that would otherwise remain undetected. Each node of the network is described by a geometrical solid model and the networks are rendered by OpenGL techniques in real time.

5. *Social Network Simulation*

We choose to use a multi-agent based simulation model in SNAC. When the simulation runs, the status of agents, agent groupings, and relationships between agents, are sent to the Network Visualizer, in which the attributes of the network will be visualized through a Web-based browser.

Acknowledgments. This research has been supported in part by the National Natural Science Foundation of China (Grants 60573078 and 60334020).

References

1. H. Chen and F.-Y. Wang, "Artificial Intelligence for Homeland Security", IEEE Intelligent Systems, Vol. 20, Issue 5, 2005, pp. 12-16.
2. Y. Y. Yao, F.-Y. Wang, J. Wang, D. Zeng "Rule + Exception Strategies for Security Information Analysis" , IEEE Intelligent Systems, Vol. 20, Issue 5, 2005, pp. 52-57.
3. H. Chen, F.-Y. Wang, and D. Zeng, "Intelligence and Security informatics for Homeland Security: Information, Communication and Transportation", IEEE Trans. Intelligent Transportation Systems, Vol. 5, No. 4, 2004, pp. 329-341.
4. G. Kolda and D.P. O'Leary. "A semi-discrete matrix decomposition for latent semantic indexing in information retrieval," ACM Transactions on Information Systems, Vol. 16, 1998, pp. 322-346.
5. A. HyvÄarinen and E. Oja. "Independent component analysis: Algorithms and applications," Neural Networks, 13(4-5), 2000, pp. 411-430.
6. C. Joslyn, "Link Analysis of Social Meta-Networks," the 2002 Conference on Computational Analysis of Social and Organizations Systems (2002).

Analysis of Infectious Disease Data Based on Evolutionary Computation

Dong-bin Zhao and Jian-qiang Yi

Institute of Automation, Chinese Academy of Sciences
{dongbin.zhao, jianqiang.yi}@ia.ac.cn

1 Project Background

An international cooperative research project on intelligence and security informatics (ISI) was initialized in 2005 with funding support by the Chinese Academy of Sciences. This abstract summarizes an ongoing study on ISI data analysis using evolutionary computation methods, conducted by the Chinese team of this international project.

Infectious diseases outbreaks, no matter by nature or terrorism, are critical threats to public health and national security. Analyzing infectious disease data will provide valuable information to prevent, detect, respond to, and manage infectious diseases. A critical challenge facing infectious disease data analysis is the clustering of disease cases or related observations in the spatial and temporal context, also known as spatial-temporal hotspot analysis [1]. Lots of researchers have invested their efforts on such an analysis. As an example of recent attempts, a risk-adjusted support vector clustering approach was successfully developed to cluster dead bird sightings as early warning of West Nile Virus outbreaks [2].

Evolutionary computation has become a major branch of computational intelligence in the past twenty years. Evolutionary computation algorithms are inspired and abstracted from natural evolution of species and have been applied to solve all kinds of optimization, modeling, and control problems. Examples of evolutionary computation algorithms include genetic algorithms, the recently proposed particle swarm optimization algorithm, the ant colony optimization algorithm, and the artificial immune algorithm.

Our research is aimed at developing data analysis approaches based on evolutionary computational algorithms and applying these approaches in the domain of infectious disease informatics.

2 Major Research Issues

Our research is currently focused on spatial-temporal hotspot analysis. Given the center and radius of candidate clusters, a clustering function can be formulated. This function can be optimized using evolutionary computation approaches to (near) optimally decide the center and area of infectious disease hotspots. Take the genetic algorithm as an example. The center and radius can be encoded as

H. Chen et al. (Eds.): WISI 2006, LNCS 3917, pp. 179–180, 2006.

an individual and the number of the infectious disease cases divided by the radius can be adopted as the fitness measure. Through a genetic learning process, an optimal or sub-optimal solution could be found, representing the infectious disease hotspots. Other kinds of evolutionary computation methods can also be applied to solve such optimization problems. We are currently experimenting with a selected set of such methods to perform spatial-temporal hotspot analysis. These methods are being evaluated based on their run-time performance, scalability, accuracy, flexibility, and extensibility in the context of ISI data analysis. One particular challenge is to identify multiple hotspots from the data at the same time. Possible solutions include (a) incorporating multiple cluster centers/radii into one fitness function, and (b) using immune algorithms with intrinsic multiple-modal considerations.

We are currently collecting data on Severe Acute Respiratory Syndrome (SARS) and avian influenza outbreaks. Such datasets will be used to test the proposed algorithms. For evaluation purposes, we will carry out a comparative study using both simulated and real-world datasets to compare our approach with existing ones (e.g., scan statistic-based approaches and the risk-adjusted support vector clustering method).

Acknowledgement. This work is supported by the National Science Foundation of China Grants 60573078 and 60334020.

References

1. Chen, H.C., Wang, F.Y., Zeng, D.: Intelligence and Security Informatics for Homeland Security Information, Communication, and Transportation. IEEE Transactions on Intelligent Transportation Systems 5(4) (2004) 329-341
2. Chen, H.C., Wang, F.Y.: Artificial Intelligence for Homeland Security. IEEE Intelligent Systems 20(5) (2005) 12-16

Rule+Exception Learning-Based Class Specification and Labeling in Intelligence and Security Analysis

Jue Wang[1], Fei-Yue Wang[1], and Daniel D. Zeng[2]

[1] Chinese Academy of Sciences, Beijing 100080, China
{jue.wang, feiyue.wang}@ia.ac.cn
[2] University of Arizona, Tucson, Arizona 85721, USA
zeng@eller.arizona.edu

One of the key tasks in intelligence and security informatics (ISI) is to find anomalies and exceptions from typically voluminous datasets and observations [1-4]. For example, in the context of societal security, finding "exceptions" may involve discovering irregular behaviors in a community where it is assumed that most people behave normally.

There are two major approaches for addressing this anomaly and exception detection problem: (a) establishing a model for irregular behaviors and then identifying irregular behaviors based on this model, and (b) establishing a model for regular behaviors and treating irregular behaviors as exceptions to regular behaviors. In many situations, the first approach can be difficult to apply and implement due to potentially significant diversity and wide variation in irregular behaviors, whereas the second approach might be effective and practical. In addition, for many ISI applications, one cannot rely entirely on the automated systems to determine irregularities. An effective ISI system is expected to liberate human agents from tedious and routine efforts while directing their attention to few special and potentially abnormal cases.

In our ongoing "Rule + Exception" Learning Project, we are developing a new approach for identifying irregular behaviors. First, in our approach it is assumed that irregular behaviors are not absolute and thus can not be represented by simple statistics on occurrences, as by most of the current methods. In other words, different irregular behavior models should be developed for different purposes and needs in a context-sensitive manner. Second, not every irregular behavior is harmful or significant, suggesting the needs for further investigation or evaluation of identified irregular behaviors. Finally, irregular behaviors should be explainable, at least relative to the regular behaviors. Such explanations can provide valuable information to human agents analyzing behaviors or data in specific ISI application contexts.

Our technical approach is based on the consideration that "rules" are the model of regular behaviors with respective to a particular problem, while "exceptions" are irregular behaviors in relative to those "rules." The key issues to be solved here are: (a) how to establish the required model from available data sets, and (b) based on the model, how to specify exceptions effectively. Our initial effort has been focused on developing models and algorithms for "rules + exceptions" learning based on reduct theory and one-class method for class construction and classification of data sets with initial labels in certain special domains. The proposed approach can also be easily

H. Chen et al. (Eds.): WISI 2006, LNCS 3917, pp. 181–182, 2006.
© Springer-Verlag Berlin Heidelberg 2006

extended to analyze datasets without labels. Computational experiments are under way to evaluate this approach.

Acknowledgments. This research was supported in part by the National Natural Science Foundation of China through Grants #60573078 and #60334020 and the National Basic Research Program through Grant #2004CB318103.

References

1. Chen, H. and Wang, F.Y.: Artificial Intelligence for Homeland Security. IEEE Intelligent Systems (2005), pp. 12-16.
2. Chen, H., Wang, F.Y., and Zeng, D: Intelligence and Security informatics for Homeland Security: Information, Communication and Transportation. IEEE Trans. Intelligent Transportation Systems (2004), pp. 329-341.
3. Kantor, p. Muresan, G. Roberts, F. Zeng, D., Wang, F.Y., Chen, H. and Merkle, R.C.: Intelligence and Security Informatics. Proceedings IEEE Conference on Intelligence and Security informatics, Atlanta, GA,USA, May 2005.
4. Yao, Y.Y., Wang, F.Y., Wang, J., Zeng, D: Rule + Exception Strategies for Security Information Analysis. IEEE Intelligent Systems (2005), pp. 52-57.

A Computational Framework for Decision Analysis and Support in ISI: Artificial Societies, Computational Experiments, and Parallel Systems

Fei-Yue Wang

Chinese Academy of Sciences, Beijing 100080, China
University of Arizona, Tucson, Arizona 82521, USA
feiyue.wang@ia.ac.cn

In response to the September 11, 2001 terrorist attacks, many governments and citizens across the world have been mobilized at an unprecedented scale to contribute to national/international and societal security. The scientific and engineering research communities are no exception and have been called upon to play an important role in this effort. With such background, Intelligence and Security Informatics (ISI) has emerged since 2003 as a fast growing multidisciplinary field of study aimed at developing advanced information technologies, systems, algorithms, and databases for national- and homeland security-related applications, through an integrated technological, organizational, and policy-based approach [1-3].

Observation, analysis, and classification of human behaviors under various situations are among key issues in ISI research. Although huge amounts of historical data sets and vast sources of new intelligence information are available, studies of human behaviors and their social impacts still remain extremely difficult mainly due to the following two facts: 1) problems can not be reduced to simple cases and must be integrated as a whole, and 2) situations or events are not repeatable or re-constructible so that experiments are virtually impossible in many cases. While traditional approaches are not effective for addressing those problems, new concepts and methods developed in complex systems could provide a potential solution [4-8]. This consideration is the motivation for establishing a computational framework for ISI decision analysis and support based on a newly developed computational theory of complex systems using artificial societies, computational experiments, and parallel systems [9]. Specifically, our approach consists of three components:

1) *Modeling and Specification of ISI Problems Using Artificial Societies*
We consider computers as social labs by creating artificial human and societal relationships in artificial societies using autonomous agent programming. This is a natural extension of computer simulations in the sense that we no longer take the accuracy to real systems as our only criterion for model construction. Instead, we consider "model" as an alternative to the reality and "equivalent" to a real system. Based on this concept, various artificial systems can be constructed for testing and validating in ISI research and development. This is not only useful for fast prototype studies, but also fundamental to computational experiments and parallel systems for analysis and implementation of actual ISI strategies and methods.

H. Chen et al. (Eds.): WISI 2006, LNCS 3917, pp. 183 – 184, 2006.
© Springer-Verlag Berlin Heidelberg 2006

2)   *Analysis and Evaluation of ISI Methods using Computational Experiments*
Computational experiments are natural applications of artificial systems. For many problems in ISI, it is very difficult and sometimes impossible to study concerned objects through active and controlled experiments in reality. Computational experiments through computers and artificial systems provide an alternative and complement to actual physical experiments. Various techniques in experiment design and statistical analysis can be applied here directly.

3)   *Implementation and Execution of ISI Systems Based Parallel Systems*
The basic idea is to run "simulations" side by side with actual operations. A parallel system consists of a real system and an artificial system that can be linked in different modes of operations: 1) off-line for teaching and learning, 2) off/on-line for testing and evaluation, and 3) on-line for management and control in real ISI applications. Various concepts and methods developed in adaptive control can be used in operations of parallel systems.

Acknowledgments. This research was supported in part by the National Natural Science Foundation of China (60573078 and 60334020) and the National Basic Research Program (2004CB318103).

References

1. Chen, H. and Wang, F.Y.: Artificial Intelligence for Homeland Security. IEEE Intelligent Systems (2005), pp. 12-16.
2. Chen, H., Wang, F.Y., and Zeng, D: Intelligence and Security informatics for Homeland Security: Information, Communication and Transportation. IEEE Trans. Intelligent Transportation Systems (2004), pp. 329-341.
3. Kantor, p. Muresan, G. Roberts, F. Zeng, D., Wang, F.Y., Chen, H. and Merkle, R.C.: Intelligence and Security Informatics. Proceedings IEEE Conference on Intelligence and Security informatics, Atlanta, GA,USA, May 2005.
4. Fei-Yue Wang and Steve Lansing: From Artificial Life to Artificial Societies – The State of the Art of Complex Social Systems and Beyond, Journal of Complex Systems and Complexity Science (2004), Vol. 1, No. 1, pp. 33-41.
5. Fei-Yue Wang: Computational Experiments for Behavior Analysis and Decision Evaluation of Complex Systems, Journal of Systems Simulation (2004), Vol. 16, No.5, pp. 893-897.
6. Fei-Yue Wang: Parallel Systems for Management and Control of Complex Systems, Journal of Control and Decision (2004), Vol.19, No.5, pp. 485-490.
7. Fei-Yue Wang and J. Wang: Issues and Applications of Intelligence and Security Informatics, China Basic Sciences (2005), Vol.7, No.3, pp. 24-29.
8. Fei-Yue Wang: Social Computing and Dynamic Analysis of Digital and Networked Societal States, Science and Technology Review (2005).
9. Fei-Yue Wang: On a Computational Theory for Complex Systems, China Basic Science (2004), Vol. 6, No.5, pp. 3-10.

Author Index

Lecture Notes in Computer Science

For information about Vols. 1–3828

please contact your bookseller or Springer

Vol. 3878: A. Gelbukh (Ed.), Computational Linguistics and Intelligent Text Processing. XVII, 589 pages. 2006.

Vol. 3877: M. Detyniecki, J.M. Jose, A. Nürnberger, C. J. '. van Rijsbergen (Eds.), Adaptive Multimedia Retrieval: User, Context, and Feedback. XI, 279 pages. 2006.

Vol. 3876: S. Halevi, T. Rabin (Eds.), Theory of Cryptography. XI, 617 pages. 2006.

Vol. 3875: S. Ur, E. Bin, Y. Wolfsthal (Eds.), Hardware and Software, Verification and Testing. X, 265 pages. 2006.

Vol. 3874: R. Missaoui, J. Schmidt (Eds.), Formal Concept Analysis. X, 309 pages. 2006. (Sublibrary LNAI).

Vol. 3873: L. Maicher, J. Park (Eds.), Charting the Topic Maps Research and Applications Landscape. VIII, 281 pages. 2006. (Sublibrary LNAI).

Vol. 3872: H. Bunke, A. L. Spitz (Eds.), Document Analysis Systems VII. XIII, 630 pages. 2006.

Vol. 3870: S. Spaccapietra, P. Atzeni, W.W. Chu, T. Catarci, K.P. Sycara (Eds.), Journal on Data Semantics V. XIII, 237 pages. 2006.

Vol. 3869: S. Renals, S. Bengio (Eds.), Machine Learning for Multimodal Interaction. XIII, 490 pages. 2006.

Vol. 3868: K. Römer, H. Karl, F. Mattern (Eds.), Wireless Sensor Networks. XI, 342 pages. 2006.

Vol. 3866: T. Dimitrakos, F. Martinelli, P.Y.A. Ryan, S. Schneider (Eds.), Formal Aspects in Security and Trust. X, 259 pages. 2006.

Vol. 3865: W. Shen, K.-M. Chao, Z. Lin, J.-P.A. Barthès, A. James (Eds.), Computer Supported Cooperative Work in Design II. XII, 659 pages. 2006.

Vol. 3863: M. Kohlhase (Ed.), Mathematical Knowledge Management. XI, 405 pages. 2006. (Sublibrary LNAI).

Vol. 3862: R.H. Bordini, M. Dastani, J. Dix, A.E.F. Seghrouchni (Eds.), Programming Multi-Agent Systems. XIV, 267 pages. 2006. (Sublibrary LNAI).

Vol. 3861: J. Dix, S.J. Hegner (Eds.), Foundations of Information and Knowledge Systems. X, 331 pages. 2006.

Vol. 3860: D. Pointcheval (Ed.), Topics in Cryptology – CT-RSA 2006. XI, 365 pages. 2006.

Vol. 3858: A. Valdes, D. Zamboni (Eds.), Recent Advances in Intrusion Detection. X, 351 pages. 2006.

Vol. 3857: M.P.C. Fossorier, H. Imai, S. Lin, A. Poli (Eds.), Applied Algebra, Algebraic Algorithms and Error-Correcting Codes. XI, 350 pages. 2006.

Vol. 3855: E. A. Emerson, K.S. Namjoshi (Eds.), Verification, Model Checking, and Abstract Interpretation. XI, 443 pages. 2005.

Vol. 3854: I. Stavrakakis, M. Smirnov (Eds.), Autonomic Communication. XIII, 303 pages. 2006.

Vol. 3853: A.J. Ijspeert, T. Masuzawa, S. Kusumoto (Eds.), Biologically Inspired Approaches to Advanced Information Technology. XIV, 388 pages. 2006.

Vol. 3852: P.J. Narayanan, S.K. Nayar, H.-Y. Shum (Eds.), Computer Vision – ACCV 2006, Part II. XXXI, 977 pages. 2006.

Vol. 3851: P.J. Narayanan, S.K. Nayar, H.-Y. Shum (Eds.), Computer Vision – ACCV 2006, Part I. XXXI, 973 pages. 2006.

Vol. 3850: R. Freund, G. Păun, G. Rozenberg, A. Salomaa (Eds.), Membrane Computing. IX, 371 pages. 2006.

Vol. 3849: I. Bloch, A. Petrosino, A.G.B. Tettamanzi (Eds.), Fuzzy Logic and Applications. XIV, 438 pages. 2006. (Sublibrary LNAI).

Vol. 3848: J.-F. Boulicaut, L. De Raedt, H. Mannila (Eds.), Constraint-Based Mining and Inductive Databases. X, 401 pages. 2006. (Sublibrary LNAI).

Vol. 3847: K.P. Jantke, A. Lunzer, N. Spyratos, Y. Tanaka (Eds.), Federation over the Web. X, 215 pages. 2006. (Sublibrary LNAI).

Vol. 3846: H. J. van den Herik, Y. Björnsson, N.S. Netanyahu (Eds.), Computers and Games. XIV, 333 pages. 2006.

Vol. 3845: J. Farré, I. Litovsky, S. Schmitz (Eds.), Implementation and Application of Automata. XIII, 360 pages. 2006.

Vol. 3844: J.-M. Bruel (Ed.), Satellite Events at the MoDELS 2005 Conference. XIII, 360 pages. 2006.

Vol. 3843: P. Healy, N.S. Nikolov (Eds.), Graph Drawing. XVII, 536 pages. 2006.

Vol. 3842: H.T. Shen, J. Li, M. Li, J. Ni, W. Wang (Eds.), Advanced Web and Network Technologies, and Applications. XXVII, 1057 pages. 2006.

Vol. 3841: X. Zhou, J. Li, H.T. Shen, M. Kitsuregawa, Y. Zhang (Eds.), Frontiers of WWW Research and Development - APWeb 2006. XXIV, 1223 pages. 2006.

Vol. 3840: M. Li, B. Boehm, L.J. Osterweil (Eds.), Unifying the Software Process Spectrum. XVI, 522 pages. 2006.

Vol. 3839: J.-C. Filliâtre, C. Paulin-Mohring, B. Werner (Eds.), Types for Proofs and Programs. VIII, 275 pages. 2006.

Vol. 3838: A. Middeldorp, V. van Oostrom, F. van Raamsdonk, R. de Vrijer (Eds.), Processes, Terms and Cycles: Steps on the Road to Infinity. XVIII, 639 pages. 2005.

Vol. 3837: K. Cho, P. Jacquet (Eds.), Technologies for Advanced Heterogeneous Networks. IX, 307 pages. 2005.

Vol. 3836: J.-M. Pierson (Ed.), Data Management in Grids. X, 143 pages. 2006.

Vol. 3835: G. Sutcliffe, A. Voronkov (Eds.), Logic for Programming, Artificial Intelligence, and Reasoning. XIV, 744 pages. 2005. (Sublibrary LNAI).

Vol. 3834: D.G. Feitelson, E. Frachtenberg, L. Rudolph, U. Schwiegelshohn (Eds.), Job Scheduling Strategies for Parallel Processing. VIII, 283 pages. 2005.

Vol. 3833: K.-J. Li, C. Vangenot (Eds.), Web and Wireless Geographical Information Systems. XI, 309 pages. 2005.

Vol. 3832: D. Zhang, A.K. Jain (Eds.), Advances in Biometrics. XX, 796 pages. 2005.

Vol. 3831: J. Wiedermann, G. Tel, J. Pokorný, M. Bieliková, J. Štuller (Eds.), SOFSEM 2006: Theory and Practice of Computer Science. XV, 576 pages. 2006.

Vol. 3830: D. Weyns, H. V.D. Parunak, F. Michel (Eds.), Environments for Multi-Agent Systems II. VIII, 291 pages. 2006. (Sublibrary LNAI).

Vol. 3829: P. Pettersson, W. Yi (Eds.), Formal Modeling and Analysis of Timed Systems. IX, 305 pages. 2005.